17/7/08 d

Lines

Wh   ind
writ   ok
Tim   of
inte   ely
new
In   of
cont   ng,
from   ese
calli   the
pres
Se   ind
betw   of
line   or
diss   ace
of a   as
affec   ief
expl   on
betw   be
diffe   ine
beca   of
post
D   cal
stud   nd
man   ces
us o   at
the

Tim _____ is Professor of Social Anthropology at the University of Aberdeen. His previous publications include *The Perception of the Environment* (2000) which explores the relations between perception, creativity and skill. He is currently working on the interface between anthropology, archaeology, art and architecture.

Lines

A brief history

Tim Ingold

 Routledge
Taylor & Francis Group

LONDON AND NEW YORK

First published 2007
by Routledge
2 Park Square, Milton Park, Abingdon, Oxon OX14 4RN

Simultaneously published in the USA and Canada
by Routledge
270 Madison Ave, New York, NY 10016

Reprinted 2008

Routledge is an imprint of the Taylor & Francis Group, an informa business

© 2007 Tim Ingold

Typeset in Goudy by
RefineCatch Limited, Bungay, Suffolk
Printed and bound in Great Britain by
Antony Rowe Ltd, Chippenham, Wiltshire

British Library Cataloguing in Publication Data
A catalogue record for this book is available from the British Library

Library of Congress Cataloging in Publication Data
Ingold, Tim, 1948–
Lines : a brief history / Tim Ingold.
p. cm.
Includes bibliographical references and index.
1. Signs and symbols—History.   2. Writing—History.   3. Drawing—
History.   I. Title.
GN452.5.I54 2007
302.2′223—dc22
2006036700

ISBN 10: 0–415–42426–7 (hbk)
ISBN 10: 0–415–42427–5 (pbk)
ISBN 10: 0–203–96115–3 (ebk)

ISBN 13: 978–0–415–42426–4 (hbk)
ISBN 13: 978–0–415–42427–1 (pbk)
ISBN 13: 978–0–203–96115–5 (ebk)

Contents

Figures

Acknowledgements

This book was conceived in July 2000, when I received an invitation from Fionna Ashmore, then Director of the Society of Antiquaries of Scotland, to deliver the Rhind Lectures for 2003. These lectures, delivered annually on a subject pertaining to history, archaeology or anthropology, have been given since 1876. They commemorate Alexander Henry Rhind of Sibster (1833–63), a noted Scottish antiquary, born in Wick, who is remembered above all for his pioneering work on the Ancient Egyptian tombs of Thebes. I felt very privileged to have been invited to deliver the lectures and, thinking that the three years' notice would give me ample time to prepare, I eagerly accepted. I had been looking for an excuse to set aside some time to work on a topic by which I had long been fascinated but which I knew little about, namely the comparative history of the relation between speech, song, writing and musical notation. For my title I chose 'Lines from the past: towards an anthropological archaeology of inscriptive practices'.

Of course the time I thought I would have to prepare the lectures never materialized. It never does. The years from 2000 to 2003 were hectic. I had arrived at the University of Aberdeen only the year before, charged with establishing a new programme of teaching and research in anthropology, and this had absorbed the greater part of my energies. Indeed the programme had got off to a very good start, and by 2003 we already had our own Department of Anthropology, a nucleus of highly committed staff, and a growing cohort of research students. The first students from the University with honours degrees in Anthropology would be graduating in the summer of that year. With all this going on time flew by, until it suddenly dawned on me, around March 2003, that I had little more than a month left to prepare the lectures. Putting everything else on hold, and without much of an idea of how my topic would develop, I set to work on my theme of language, music and notation.

It was slow going at first, but somehow – and much to my surprise – the subject 'took off' in a way that I had never anticipated, so that what I had initially set out to accomplish turned out to be but a launch pad for a much broader and more ambitious inquiry into human line-making in all its forms. It was as though, almost by accident, I had struck intellectual gold. From then on, I am not sure whether it was I who was writing the lectures or the

lectures that were writing me. They just seemed to tumble out. Still scribbling on the train down to Edinburgh, with the series due to begin that
evening, I had all but the final lecture written – and for that I had to impro-
vise once the script ran out. Fortunately, I don't think anyone noticed. Thus
the lectures were duly delivered, at the Royal Museum of Scotland, over
three days, 2–4 May 2003. To be able to set out my ideas 'in the raw', to an
appreciative audience, over six 50-minute lectures all crammed into one long
weekend, was a unique opportunity and an unforgettable experience. It was
like the kind of conference you can only dream about, when you are the only
speaker, when everyone has come to listen to you and no one else, and when
you can have all the time you could possibly wish for to set out your ideas.
For this opportunity, and for the hospitality extended to me and my family,
I would like to express my appreciation to Fionna Ashmore, to the then
President of the Society of Antiquaries of Scotland, Lisbeth Thoms, and to
the Society itself.

Once the lectures were over, thoughts turned to publication. Realizing that
it would take decades of work to do justice to the subject, and that this was
probably beyond my competence anyway, I initially resolved to write up the
lectures more or less as they were, in a rough-and-ready form, without even
attempting to refine them further. I knew there were gaps to fill, and that I
needed to reorder some of the material, but otherwise that would be that. But
once again, the usual pressures of academic life took over. First I was going to
do the work over the summer of 2003, then it was put off to the following
summer, and then to the summer following that, but there was always
something more urgent to do. And all the while, my ideas were moving on.

I had opportunities to present what eventually became Chapter 1 of this
book to the Laurence seminar on 'Sensory Perceptions' in the Faculty of
Classics, Cambridge University, in May 2003 and some time later to the
Anthropology Seminar at the London School of Economics. An early
draft of Chapter 2 was presented at the Institute of Social and Cultural
Anthropology at the University of Oxford, and subsequently, in May 2005,
as an invited lecture at the Department of Archaeology, University of Porto,
Portugal, for which I have particularly to thank my host Vitor Jorge. Chapter
3 acquired its current form and title through having been presented as part
of a seminar series in the School of Anthropological Studies at Queen's
University, Belfast, and was later presented to the conference 'Culture,
Nature, Semiotics: Locations IV', in Tallinn and Tartu, Estonia (September
2004) and the Fifth International Space Syntax Symposium, Delft University
of Technology (June 2005). Although the material of the remaining three
chapters (4–6) has not otherwise been presented, I should note that Chapter 5
actually began life as a Munro Lecture presented at the University of
Edinburgh way back in 1995. Although almost everything about it has
changed since then, I think this is where my interest in the theme of 'writing
technology', the subject of the lecture, first began to bear fruit.

My ideas over the past few years have also been influenced by my involvement in a major project of research funded by the (then) Arts and Humanities Research Board (AHRB) for the three years 2002–05, with the hopelessly cumbersome title 'Learning is understanding in practice: exploring the interrelations between perception, creativity and skill'. Indeed in many ways this book is one outcome of the project, and I wish to acknowledge my gratitude to the AHRB for its support. The project was carried out in collaboration between the Department of Anthropology at the University of Aberdeen and the School of Fine Art at Dundee University, and involved an ethnographic study of the knowledge practices of fine art, conducted among students at Dundee, complemented by an Aberdeen-based study of the applicability of practical, studio-based approaches in fine art to teaching and learning in anthropology. As a context for this latter study, I designed and taught a course called 'The 4 As: Anthropology, Archaeology, Art and Architecture', which I first presented to advanced undergraduate students in the spring semester of 2004, and have repeated in the subsequent two years. Not only did the students taking the course hear a lot about lines, they also contributed a great many ideas of their own from which I have directly benefited, and I am grateful to them all.

I am indebted, moreover, to Murdo Macdonald, who co-directed the project with me, to Wendy Gunn, who carried out most of the work and whose ideas have – over the years – profoundly shaped my own, and to Ray Lucas, whose AHRB-funded doctoral research was an integral part of the project. Ray's research, a wide-ranging and cross-disciplinary study of inscriptive practices and notations as tools of thought, meshed extremely closely with my own interests in line-making, and it has been a privilege to work with him. Two other outcomes of the project should be mentioned, both of which have influenced the present book. The first was the exhibition 'Fieldnotes and Sketchbooks', designed by Wendy Gunn and displayed at Aberdeen Art Gallery from April to June 2005. The exhibition explored notational and descriptive uses of the line across the disciplines of art, architecture and anthropology. The second was the conference of the Association of Social Anthropologists on 'Creativity and Cultural Improvisation', which my colleague Elizabeth Hallam and I convened at the University of Aberdeen in April 2005. It was a pleasure working with Liz, and many of her ideas, along with ideas arising from the conference itself, have found their way into this book.

People draw lines, of course, not only by gesturing with their hands but also by walking around. This is a theme of Chapter 3 of the present book, which to some extent embodies the results of a project entitled 'Culture from the ground: walking, movement and placemaking', funded by an award from the Economic and Social Research Council (ESRC) (February 2004 to April 2006), in which we explored how walking binds time and place in people's experience, relationships and life-histories. I am indebted to the ESRC for its support, and to Jo Lee, who carried out the ethnographic research for the project and has been a constant source of ideas and support.

However, I have more reason than that to be grateful to the ESRC, for in 2005 the Council awarded me a three-year Professorial Fellowship for a programme of work entitled 'Explorations in the Comparative Anthropology of the Line'.

In the longer term, the extended period of research leave that this affords will give me the possibility to develop further some of the ideas that are only adumbrated in this book. In the immediate term, however, I have to confess that without this leave I would never have been able to finish the book at all. Having already put it off by two years, my plan had been to complete the book in the summer of 2005, before my Fellowship started. Ironically, however, it was the ESRC itself that scuppered that plan, by requiring me – along with numerous colleagues up and down the land – to devote the only time we might have had for research to collecting data and filling up forms for its postgraduate training recognition exercise. Indeed between the massively bureaucratized and time-consuming operations of funding research on the one hand, and of having it assessed on the other, only the smallest chinks remain to actually carry it out, and one must be grateful for any opportunity for these chinks to be opened up. Even as I write, having put all else aside for the past month to finish the book, I am being chased for my now delayed draft of our Department's entry for the next Research Assessment Exercise!

I do not, however, wish to end on a note of complaint. I would rather like to acknowledge, and indeed to celebrate, the support I have been lucky enough to have had from so many people. Ideas, information, suggestions for reading and so on have literally poured in from all quarters. Too many individuals have helped for me to be able to list them all, so rather than naming names I shall simply say a big thank-you to everyone. You know who you are. An especially big thank-you goes to all my colleagues at the Department of Anthropology at Aberdeen University, who are the finest set of colleagues that anyone could wish for, to my students from whom I have learned so much, and to all the members of my family who have kept me alive. One, in particular, played a rather crucial role in bringing me into the world in the first place. Now 101 years of age, he will be the first to read this book, and it is his line that I am carrying on with it. He, too, knows who he is, and I dedicate the book to him.

Tim Ingold
Aberdeen
September 2006

Figure credits

1.5 From *The Notation of Medieval Music* by Carl Parrish.
© 1957 by W. W. Norton & Company Inc. Used by
permission of W. W. Norton & Company Inc.
1.6 From *The Oxford Book of Carols*. © Oxford University Press
1928. Reproduced by permission.

1.8   Reproduced by permission of Kawori Iguchi.
1.9   bpk/Antikensammlung, Staatliche Museen zu Berlin. Photo: Johannes Laurentius. Reproduced by permission.
1.10 Reproduced by permission of Sugi Ichikazu.
2.2   Reproduced by permission of Richard Long.
2.4   Photo: Ian Alexander. Reproduced by permission.
2.5   By permission of Historic Collections, King's College, University of Aberdeen.
2.7   By permission of Historic Collections, King's College, University of Aberdeen.
2.10 Photo: Jörg Hauser. Reproduced by permission of Jörg Hauser and Brigitta Hauser-Schäublin.
2.11 Reproduced by permission of the Bodleian Library, University of Oxford, shelfmark 247236 d.13.
2.12 Reproduced by permission of University of Cambridge Museum of Archaeology and Anthropology E 1907.342 (Z 6067).
2.16 Photo: Barbara and Dennis Tedlock, reproduced with their permission.
2.17 By permission of Oxford University Press.
3.2   Reproduced by permission of Ordnance Survey on behalf of HMSO. © Crown Copyright 2006. Ordnance Survey Licence Number 100014649.
3.3   Reproduced by permission of Sonderjyllands Statsamt from the *Grænseatlas* of 1920.
3.4   Charles Goodwin, 'Professional Vision', American Anthropologist, Vol. 96, No. 3: 606–633. © 1994, American Anthropological Association. Used by permission. All rights reserved.
3.9   By permission of Oxford University Press.
4.2   By permission of Editions Gaud.
4.3   By permission of Cambridge University Press.
5.1   © The Estate of E. H. Shephard, reproduced with permission of Curtis Brown Limited, London.
5.5   By permission of Historic Collections, King's College, University of Aberdeen.
5.10 MS Cosin V.III.1, f.22v. Reproduced by permission of Durham University Library.
5.11 Reproduced by permission of Rosemary Sassoon.
6.3   Reproduced by permission of Wendy Gunn.
6.5   Reproduced by permission of Marion Boyars Publishers
6.6   © Studio Daniel Libeskind. Reproduced by permission.

Every effort has been made to trace and contact copyright holders. The publishers would be pleased to hear from any copyright holder not acknowledged here, so that this acknowledgements page can be amended at the earliest opportunity.

Introduction

What do walking, weaving, observing, singing, storytelling, drawing and writing have in common? The answer is that they all proceed along lines of one kind or another. In this book I aim to lay the foundations for what might be called a comparative anthropology of the line. So far as I know, nothing quite like this has been attempted before. Indeed when I have broached the idea to friends and colleagues, their initial response has usually been one of blank incredulity. Did they mishear me: was I talking about lions? 'No', I would answer, 'I mean lines, not lions.' Their bafflement was understandable. The line? This is hardly the kind of thing that has served traditionally as the focus of our attention. We have anthropological studies of visual art, of music and dance, of speech and writing, of craft and material culture, but not of the production and significance of lines. Yet it takes only a moment's reflection to recognize that lines are everywhere. As walking, talking and gesticulating creatures, human beings generate lines wherever they go. It is not just that line-making is as ubiquitous as the use of the voice, hands and feet – respectively in speaking, gesturing and moving around – but rather that it subsumes all these aspects of everyday human activity and, in so doing, brings them together into a single field of inquiry. This is the field that I seek to delineate.

It was not, however, with such grandiose preoccupations that I first set out along this path. On the contrary, I had been perplexed by a particular problem that, on the face of it, has nothing to do with lines at all. It was the problem of how we have come to distinguish between speech and song. The fact is that this distinction, at least in the form in which we recognize it nowadays, is relatively recent in the history of the Western world. For much of this history, music was understood as a verbal art. That is, the musical essence of song lay in the sonority of its words. Yet we have somehow arrived today at a notion of music as 'song without words', stripped of its verbal component. And complementing that, we have also arrived at a notion of language as a system of words and meanings that is given quite independently of its actual voicing in the sounds of speech. Music has become wordless; language has been silenced. How can this have come about? The search for an answer led me from mouth to hand, from vocal declamations to manual gestures, and to the relation between these gestures and the marks they leave on surfaces of various kinds. Could it be that the silencing of language had something to do with changes in the way writing itself is understood: as an art of verbal composition rather than manual inscription? My inquiry into line-making had begun.

I soon discovered, however, that it was not enough to focus only on the lines themselves, or on the hands that produced them. I had also to consider the relation between lines and the surfaces on which they are drawn. Somewhat daunted by the sheer profusion of different kinds of line, I resolved to draw up a provisional taxonomy. Though even this left many loose ends, two kinds of line did seem to stand out from the rest, and I called them threads and traces. Yet on closer inspection, threads and traces appeared to be not so much categorically different as transforms of one another. Threads have a way of turning into traces, and vice versa. Moreover, whenever threads turn into traces, surfaces are formed, and whenever traces turn into threads, they are dissolved. Following through these transformations took me from the written word, whence I had commenced my inquiry, into the twists and turns of the labyrinth, and into the crafts of embroidery and weaving. And it was through the weaving of textiles that I eventually returned, by this roundabout route, to the written text. Yet whether encountered as a woven thread or as a written trace, the line is still perceived as one of movement and growth. How come, then, that so many of the lines we come up against today seem so static? Why does the very mention of the word 'line' or 'linearity', for many contemporary thinkers, conjure up an image of the alleged narrow-mindedness and sterility, as well as the single-track logic, of modern analytic thought?

Anthropologists have a habit of insisting that there is something essentially linear about the way people in modern Western societies comprehend the passage of history, generations and time. So convinced are they of this, that any attempt to find linearity in the lives of non-Western people is liable to be dismissed as mildly ethnocentric at best, and at worst as amounting to collusion in the project of colonial occupation whereby the West has ruled its lines over the rest of the world. Alterity, we are told, is non-linear. The other side of this coin, however, is to assume that life is lived authentically on the spot, in places rather than along paths. Yet how could there be places, I wondered, if people did not come and go? Life on the spot surely cannot yield an experience of place, of being some*where*. To be a place, every somewhere must lie on one or several paths of movement to and from places elsewhere. Life is lived, I reasoned, along paths, not just in places, and paths are lines of a sort. It is along paths, too, that people grow into a knowledge of the world around them, and describe this world in the stories they tell. Colonialism, then, is not the imposition of linearity upon a non-linear world, but the imposition of one kind of line on another. It proceeds first by converting the paths along which life is lived into boundaries in which it is contained, and then by joining up these now enclosed communities, each confined to one spot, into vertically integrated assemblies. Living *along* is one thing; joining *up* is quite another.

Thus from the line of movement and growth I was led to its obverse, the dotted line – the line that is not a line – a succession of instants in which nothing moves or grows. And this immediately brought to mind the famous diagram in Charles Darwin's *The Origin of Species*, depicting the evolution of life over thousands upon thousands of generations, in which every line of descent is shown as a sequence of dots! Darwin had drawn life inside each dot, not along the lines. Anthropologists do just the same when they draw genealogical diagrams of kinship and descent. The lines of the kinship chart join up, they connect, but they are not lifelines or even storylines. It seems that what modern thought has done to place – fixing it to spatial locations – it has also done to people, wrapping their lives into temporal moments. If we were but to reverse this procedure, and to imagine life itself not as a fan of dotted lines – as in Darwin's diagram – but as a manifold woven from the countless threads spun by beings of all sorts, both human and non-human, as they find their ways through the tangle of relationships in which they are enmeshed, then our entire understanding of evolution would be irrevocably altered. It would lead us to an open-ended view of the evolutionary process, and of our own history within that process, as one in which inhabitants, through their own activities, continually forge the conditions for their own and each other's lives. Indeed, lines have the power to change the world!

Emboldened by this thought, I returned to the subject of writing. Many scholars have claimed that writing imposed a kind of linearization on human consciousness, unknown to people of preliterate societies. Yet it is surely the case that, ever since people have been speaking and gesturing, they have also been making and following lines. So long as writing is understood in its original sense as a practice of inscription, there cannot then be any hard-and-fast distinction between drawing and writing, or between the craft of the draughtsman and that of the scribe. This led me to think that the kind of linearization that made a break with the consciousness of the past was one of point-to-point connections, that is, of joining the dots. Thus it is that the writer of today is no longer scribe but wordsmith, an author whose verbal assemblies are committed to paper by way of mechanical processes that bypass the work of the hand. In typing and printing, the intimate link between the manual gesture and the inscriptive trace is broken. The author conveys feeling by his choice of words, not by the expressiveness of his lines. There, at last, I began to see a solution to my initial problem, of how it was that language came to be separated from music, and speech from song. And of course, the same logic has driven the contemporary separation of writing from drawing, now placed on opposite sides of an overriding but decidedly modern dichotomy between technology and art.

Finally, then, I wondered what it means to go straight to the point. On the whole, this is not something we do, either in everyday life or in ordinary discourse. We are drawn to certain topics, and meander around them, but by the time we reach them they seem to have disappeared – like a hill we climb that no longer looks like a hill once we have reached the top. How came it, then, that the line that is properly *linear* is assumed to be straight? In modern societies, it seems, straightness has come to epitomize not only rational thought and disputation but also the values of civility and moral rectitude. Although the idea of the straight line as a connection between points that has length but no breadth goes back more than two millennia, to the geometry of Euclid, it was perhaps not until the Renaissance that it began to assume the dominance in our thinking about causes, effects and their relations that it does today. Seeking the historical sources of the straight line, I began looking around for examples of straightness in my own everyday environment. And I began noticing them in obvious places where I had not looked before: in exercise books, floorboards, brick walls and pavements. These lines were puzzling. They ruled surfaces, but did not seem to connect anything with anything else. Their source, I realized, lay not in the geometry – literally 'earth measurement' – of Euclid, but in the taut warp-threads of the weaver's loom. Once more, threads have been turned into traces in the constitution of surfaces: the surfaces of rule, upon which all things can be connected up. But as the certainties of modernity give way to doubt and confusion, lines that once went straight to the point have become fragmented, and the task of life is once more to find a way through the cracks.

There you have it: the path I have followed in writing this book. As I mentioned at the outset, the idea of a book about lines sounds odd at first, even preposterous. Once comprehension dawns, however, it is as though a dam has burst, liberating a torrent of ideas that have previously been locked up within the enclosures of more circumscribed ways of thinking. I have found that in speaking on the subject – not only with academic colleagues but also with friends and relatives – almost everyone has had suggestions to make, from examples of lines I might think about to books I should read that touch on the subject in one way or another. All of these suggestions were good, but for every lead I was able to follow up a hundred were left unexplored. To have pursued them all would have required many lives. Running alongside my life as an anthropologist I would have needed another as an archaeologist, while in still others I would have had to be a classicist, a medieval historian, a historian of art and architecture, a palaeographer, a geographer, a philosopher, a linguist, a musicologist, a psychologist, a cartographer, to name just a few. To experts in those disciplines who, unlike myself, really know what they are talking about, I can only apologize for my ignorance and clumsiness in fields in which I have had to struggle to make my way.

It has not been my purpose, however, even to attempt to cover what is, by any measure, a vast and hitherto unexplored intellectual terrain. In presenting this brief history of the line my intention is much more modest: merely to give the surface of the terrain a little scratch – to write on it a bit. Thus the book should be read as a prolegomenon whose aim is to open up lines of inquiry that others might be inspired to pursue, in whatever directions their knowledge and experience might take them. I have written it as an open invitation to join in an enterprise that, so far as I know, has no name. People who study things call themselves students of material culture. People who study lines call themselves . . . I don't know what they call themselves, but I do know that I have become one of them. And in doing so, I have joined the ranks of draughtsmen, calligraphers, handwriters, storytellers, walkers, thinkers, observers – indeed of practically everyone who has ever lived. For people inhabit a world that consists, in the first place, not of things but of lines. After all, what is a thing, or indeed a person, if not a tying together of the lines – the paths of growth and movement – of all the many constituents gathered there? Originally, 'thing' meant a gathering of people, and a place where they would meet to resolve their affairs. As the derivation of the word suggests, *every thing is a parliament of lines*. What I hope to establish, in this book, is that to study both people and things is to study the lines they are made of.

1 Language, music and notation

> Songs are thoughts which are sung out with the breath when people let themselves be moved by a great force . . . When the words that we need shoot up of themselves, we have a new song.
>
> Orpingalik, an elder of the Netsilingmiut (Netsilik Eskimo) (cited in Adams 1997: 15)

On the distinction between speech and song

The problem I seek to resolve in this chapter stems from a puzzle about the distinction, and the relation, between speech and song. Those of us, like myself, brought up in the Western 'classical' tradition are inclined to contrast these uses of the voice along the axis of a distinction between language and music. When we listen to music, whether vocal or instrumental, it is surely to the sound itself that we attend. And if we were to ask after the meaning of this sound, the answer could only be in terms of the feeling it evokes in us. As musical sound permeates the awareness of listeners, it gives shape or form to their very perception of the world. But most of us, I think, are convinced that when we listen to speech it is quite otherwise. The meanings of spoken words, we say, are to be found neither in their sounds nor in the effects that they have on us. They are rather supposed to lie *behind* the sounds. Thus the attention of listeners is not drawn to the sounds of speech in themselves but rather to the meanings conveyed by them and which they serve, in a sense, to deliver. It seems that, in listening to speech, our awareness penetrates through the sound to reach a world of verbal meaning beyond. And by the same token, that world is absolutely silent – as silent, indeed, as are the pages of a book. In short, whereas sound is of the essence of music, language is mute.

How do we come to have this peculiar view of the silence of language or, for that matter, of the non-verbal nature of musical sound? It is not one that would have made sense to our predecessors of the Middle Ages or classical Antiquity. In an oft-cited passage of *The Republic*, Plato has Socrates assert that music 'is composed of three things, the words, the harmony, and the rhythm'.[1] The words, then, are not just an integral part of music; they are its leading part. 'The harmony and the rhythm', continues Socrates, 'must follow the words.' Evidently for Plato and his contemporaries, serious music was an essentially verbal art. To take the words out of music, they thought, is to reduce it to a mere embellishment or accompaniment. This, in turn, accounts for the lowly status accorded at the time to instrumental music. But by the same token, the sounds of words, whether recited or sung, were central to their meaning.

Jumping ahead in time to the churchmen of the medieval period, we find much the same idea. As Lydia Goehr has observed, most early church music was sung 'in a declamatory style designed to give priority to the word' (Goehr 1992: 131). The human voice, since it was uniquely capable of articulating the Word of God, was considered to be the only properly musical organ. Yet it was, so to speak, a mouthpiece for the word, not its creator. St Jerome, in the fourth century, advised worshippers to sing 'more with the heart than with the voice'. One should sing, he explains, 'not through the voice, but through the words he pronounces' (Strunk 1950: 72). Jerome's point, which strikingly echoes the aphorism of the Netsilingmiut elder Orpingalik that heads this chapter, was that the word is intrinsically sonorous, and that the role of the voice is not so much to produce the sounds of words but, in song, to let them go forth – to 'shoot up of themselves', as Orpingalik put it.

This was a view that persisted throughout, and indeed beyond, the Middle Ages. Plato's rule, for example, was cited with approval by the Venetian choirmaster Gioseffe Zarlino, by far the most influential musical theorist of the Renaissance, in his *Istituzioni armoniche* of 1558, as well as in a text, dating from 1602, of the Florentine Giulio Caccini, composer of the first opera ever to be printed (Strunk 1950: 255–6, 378). It seems strange, however, to modern sensibilities. To exemplify the modern understanding of language and speech, I turn to the work of one of the founding fathers of contemporary linguistics, Ferdinand de Saussure, as set out in his celebrated courses of lectures delivered at the University of Geneva between 1906 and 1911 (Saussure 1959).

At first glance, Saussure seems as committed as his pre-modern forebears to the principle of the sonority of the word. 'The only true bond', he insists, is 'the bond of sound' (1959: 25). By means of a diagram (Figure 1.1), he explains that, in language, thought or consciousness hovers over sound like air over water. But on closer inspection it turns out that words, for Saussure, do not exist in their sounding. After all, he remarks, we can talk to ourselves or recite verse without making any sound, and even without moving the tongue or lips. Understood in a purely physical or material sense, therefore, sound cannot belong to language. It is, says Saussure, 'only a secondary thing, substance to be put to use' (1959: 118). In language, then, there are no sounds as such; there are only what Saussure calls *images* of sound. Whereas sound is physical, the sound-image is a phenomenon of psychology – it

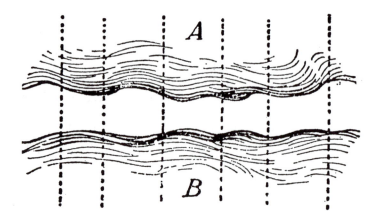

Figure 1.1 Saussure's depiction of language at the interface between a plane of thought (A) and a plane of sound-imagery (B). The role of language is to cut the interface into divisions, indicated by vertical dashed lines, thereby establishing a series of relations between particular ideas and particular sound-images. Reproduced from Saussure (1959: 112).

exists as an 'imprint' of the sound on the surface of the mind (ibid.: 66). Language, according to Saussure, maps one configuration of differences, on the plane of sound-imagery, on to another, on the plane of thought, such that for every segment of thought – or concept – there corresponds a specific image. Every coupling of concept and sound-image is a word. It follows that language, as a system of relations between words, is internal to the mind, and is given independently of its physical instantiation in acts of speech.

The implication of Saussure's argument is that, in so far as words are incorporated into music, as in song, they cease to be words at all. They no longer belong to language. 'When words and music come together in song', writes Susanne Langer, 'music swallows words' (Langer 1953: 152). By the same token, so long as sounds are subservient to verbal expression, they remain alien to music. As the contemporary Japanese composer Toru Takemitsu puts it, 'When sounds are possessed by ideas instead of having their own identity, music suffers' (Takemitsu 1997: 7). In a complete reversal of classical and medieval conceptions, pure music came in the modern era to be regarded as song *without* words, ideally instrumental rather than vocal. Thus the question I posed a moment ago can be rephrased as follows: how did it come about that the essential musicality of song was transferred from its verbal to its non-verbal components of melody, harmony and rhythm? And conversely, how was the sound taken out of language?

One possible answer has been persuasively argued by Walter Ong (1982: 91). It lies, he claims, in our familiarity with the written word. Apprehending words as they are seen on paper, both motionless and open to prolonged inspection, we readily perceive them as objects with an existence and meaning quite apart from their sounding in acts of speech. It is as though listening to speech were a species of vision – a kind of seeing with the ear, or 'earsight' – in which to hear spoken words is akin to looking at them. Take the example of Saussure. As a scholar, immersed in a world of books, it was only natural that he should have modelled the apprehension of spoken words upon his experience of inspecting their written counterparts. Could he, however, possibly have come up with his idea of the sound-image, as a 'psychological imprint', had he never encountered the printed page?

Ong thinks not, and it is on precisely this point that he takes issue with Saussure. In common with a host of other linguists in his wake, Saussure regarded writing as merely an alternative medium to speech for the outward expression of sound-images. What he failed to recognize, Ong thinks, was that the sight of the written word is necessary for the formation of the image in the first place (Ong 1982: 17; Saussure 1959: 119–20). The effects of our familiarity with writing do indeed run so deep that it is quite difficult for us to imagine how speech would be experienced by people among whom writing is completely unknown. Such people, inhabiting a world of what Ong calls 'primary orality', would have no conception whatever of words as existing separately from their actual sounding. For them, words *are* their sounds, not things *conveyed* by sounds. Instead of using their ears to see, in the fashion of people in literate societies, they use them to hear. Listening to words as we would listen to music and song, they concentrate on the sounds themselves rather than on meanings that are supposed to lie behind the sounds. And for precisely this reason, the distinction that *we* – literate people – make between speech and song, and which seems obvious enough to us, would mean nothing to them. In both speech and song, for people at a stage of primary orality, it is the sound that counts.

The script and the score

Now if Ong is right to claim that the effect of writing is to establish language as a separate domain of words and meanings, detached from the sounds of speech, then the division between language and music would have been installed at the very origin of writing itself. Thenceforth the history of writing would have developed along its own path, so that it could reasonably be treated – as it generally has been – as a chapter in the history of language. Ong's claim has, however, been widely disputed. Indeed there is a good deal of evidence to suggest that the distinction between language and music, at least in the form in which it has come down to us, has its source not in the birth of writing but in its demise. I shall explain later what I mean by the end of writing. My immediate point is this. If, during much of the history of writing, music was a verbal art – if the musical essence of song lay in the sonority of the words of which it was composed – then the written word must also have been a form of written music. Today, for those of us schooled in the Western tradition, writing seems very different from musical notation, though as we shall see in a moment it is no easy matter to specify exactly where the difference lies. But it appears that this difference was not given from the outset. It has rather emerged in the course of the history of writing itself. To put it another way, there can be no history of writing that is not also a history of musical notation, and an important part of that history must be about how these two came to be distinguished. What we cannot do is retroject onto the past a modern distinction between language and music, and assume that in understanding how the one came to be written we need take no account of the writing of the other. Yet by and large, this is precisely the assumption that has been made. In my reading on the history of writing, I have rarely found more than marginal reference to musical notation. Usually there is none at all.

My contention, then, is that any history of writing must be part of a more comprehensive history of notation. Before turning to consider the form this history should take, let me first take up the question of how – according to contemporary Western conventions – the written text is distinguished from the notated musical composition, or the script from the score. This question was addressed by the philosopher Nelson Goodman in his lectures on 'Languages of Art' (Goodman 1969). At first glance the answer might seem obvious. Is it not possible to propose, assert or denote by means of written words in a way that would be impossible in a score? And by the same token, does not the decipherment of a script call for a level of understanding beyond what is needed to recognize a performance as issuing from a score? As Goodman shows, however, neither of these criteria of differentiation withstands closer scrutiny. Instead, the issue seems to him to hinge upon where we would locate that essence of a composition or text that allows us to regard it as a 'work'. I shall not dwell on the intricacies of Goodman's argument, but merely restate his conclusion, namely that, whereas 'a musical score is in a notation and defines a work, . . . a literary script is both in a notation and is itself a work' (Goodman 1969: 210). The writer uses a notational system, just as a composer does, and what he writes is a work of literature. But the composer does not write a musical work. He writes a score, which in turn specifies a class of performances compliant with it. The musical work is that class of performances. To complete the picture, Goodman considers the cases of sketch drawing and etching, which are contrasted in the same way: the drawing is a work; with etching the work is a class of impressions compliant with the original plate. But unlike both the script and the score, neither drawing nor etching employs any kind of notation (see Figure 1.2). Setting aside the question, to which I return in Chapter 5, of what it takes for a drawn line to be part of a notation, why should there be this difference between the arts of music and literature in the location of the work?

The answer, I believe, has its roots in the way in which, in the modern era, music came to be purified of its verbal component and language purified of its component of sound. Both the writer, in the production of a script, and the composer, in the production of a score, are making graphic marks of one

	Notational	Non-notational
The work itself	SCRIPT	DRAWING
Work as class of compliant performances	SCORE	ETCHING

Figure 1.2 The differences between script, score, drawing and etching, according to Nelson Goodman.

kind or another on a paper surface. In both cases, these marks could be regarded as representations of sounds. But when we encounter these marks, they take us off in opposite directions. With the script, we recognize the marks as letters and words – that is, as projections of the Saussurian sound-image – imprinted on the surface of the paper just as they are supposed to be imprinted upon the surface of the mind. And they direct us immediately to what they are supposed to stand for, namely ideas or concepts. Recognizing the marks on the musical score, however, as notes and phrases rather than letters and words, they are taken to stand not for ideas or concepts *but for the sounds themselves*. In short, in comparing language and music we find that the direction of signification is reversed. Reading a script is an instance of cognition, of *taking in* the meanings inscribed in the text; reading music is an instance of performance, of *acting out* the instructions inscribed in the score. The former, if you will, takes us ever inward, into the domain of reflective thought; the latter takes us ever outward into the surrounding ambience of sound (Figure 1.3). We may read a text in order to discover the thoughts and intentions of its author, but we read the intentions of the composer, as indicated on the score, in order to experience the music as such. Of course, no system of musical notation can be complete: the orthodox system of notation for Western music, for example, focuses on pitch and rhythm to the exclusion of other features of tone and timbre. These latter features, if they are to be specified, have to be added in another format – for example as written words or abbreviations, or as numbers. Nevertheless the purpose of the notation is to describe the sound with sufficient accuracy to allow a musician reading it to produce a fair copy of the original work.

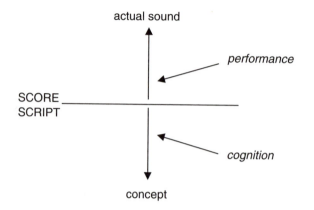

Figure 1.3 Script and score as 'taking in' and 'acting out'.

Once language and music are rigidly partitioned in this way, anomalies inevitably arise on the interface between them. Even Goodman has to admit that, if the script is written for performance as a play, it is halfway to being a score. The actor reads the lines of the play in order to be able to recite them on stage, so that considerations of voice are all-important. And the work, in the case of theatrical production, of course consists not in the script itself but in the class of performances compliant with it (Goodman 1969: 210–11). The same goes for poetry of the kind that has been expressly written to be read aloud. In so far as the poet exploits the sonority of the spoken word to achieve his effects, the poem is closer to music than language, but in so far as it remains an essentially verbal composition, it remains closer to language than music. The poetic text is thus at once script and score, or purely neither the one nor the other. While the anomalous status of dramatic and poetic performance, however, may be a problem for us, it was not a problem for our pre-modern forebears. So far as the musical aspect is concerned, as Lydia Goehr has shown, the very idea of the work as a constructed artefact – with its connotations of monumentality and architectural form – has its roots in a conception of composition, performance and notation that emerged, around the close of the eighteenth century, alongside the separation of music as an autonomous fine art (Goehr 1992: 203). Before that time, the actual *work* of music was understood to lie in the labour of performance, not of pre-composition. The idea that every performance should comply with detailed specifications, set out in advance in the notation, simply did not exist.

Writing that speaks

A parallel shift occurred, around the same time or earlier, in the field of literary production. Michel de Certeau, in *The Practice of Everyday Life* (1984), imagines the modern writer as the isolated Cartesian subject, standing aloof from the world. A master of all he surveys, the writer confronts the blank surface of a sheet of paper much as the colonial conqueror confronts the surface of the earth, or the urban planner confronts a wasteland, in preparation for the superimposition upon it of a construction of his own making. Just as a society is created in the space of colonial rule, or a city erected in the space encompassed by the plan, so the written text is produced in the space of the page (Certeau 1984: 134–6). Thus the text is an artefact – a thing fabricated or made – that is built where before there was nothing (or, if anything was there beforehand, it is eradicated in the process). José Rabasa, commenting on the journals of Christopher Columbus, compares writing on the blank page with sailing in uncharted waters:

> The ship's rostrum and the pen's stylus draw patterns on surfaces devoid of earlier traces. This lack of precedents, the fiction of a 'blank page', enables the writer and mariner, as in the case of Columbus, to claim 'ownership' of both text and territory.
>
> (Rabasa 1993: 56)

But it was not always thus. As Rabasa points out with acknowledgement to de Certeau, the post-Renaissance writing that lays claim to a surface, and to the constructions imposed upon it, is fundamentally different from the scripture of medieval times, for the latter was understood not as something made, but as something that *speaks* (Certeau 1984: 136–7).

At that time the exemplary instance of writing was the Bible. Readers, according to de Certeau, were expected to listen to the voices of the biblical scriptures and thereby to learn from them (1984: 136–7). This was to do no more than follow precedents described in the Old Testament itself. A celebrated instance comes from the book of the prophet Jeremiah, who has his scribe Baruch write down in the 'roll of a book' (that is, a scroll) the words of God that had been spoken to him concerning the punishment to be meted out on the people of Judea for their bad behaviour. Scroll in hand, Baruch went to the people, who promptly asked him to 'read it in their ears'. This he did, much to their discomfort. 'Tell us now', the assembled audience asked him, 'how didst thou write all these words?' To this, Baruch replied: 'He [Jeremiah] pronounced all these words unto me with his mouth, and I wrote them with ink in the book.'[2] The connections here are direct and unmediated: in writing, from the prophet's mouth to the scribe's inky traces; in reading, from the latter to the ears of the people.

If writing *speaks*, and if people *read it in their ears*, then Ong's claim – that a familiarity with the written word necessarily leads people to listen to speech as though they were looking at it – cannot be correct. Indeed literate folk in medieval times, like their predecessors whose stories they were reading in the scriptures, were doing just the opposite of what we do today. Instead of using their ears to look, they were using their eyes to hear, modelling their perception of the written word upon their experience of the spoken one, rather than vice versa. 'Thus it is', wrote St Augustine in the fifth century AD, 'that when a word is written it makes a sign to the eyes whereby that which pertains to the ears enters the mind' (cited in Parkes 1992: 9). If medieval people perceived the word differently from ourselves, this is not because they lived in a world of primary orality, having had only limited exposure to the written forms of either speech or song. It was, to the contrary, because they had a quite different understanding of the activities of reading and writing in themselves. This understanding goes back at least to Greek Antiquity. Eric Havelock has shown how early inscriptions had the quality of oral pronouncements, addressed to particular persons on particular occasions. By having inscriptions placed upon them, even artefacts could be given a voice, allowing them to proclaim to whom they belonged, by whom they were dedicated, or what would happen to anyone who misappropriated them. 'Whoso steals me', says a pot discovered from the Italian coast near Naples and dating from the seventh century BC, 'shall go blind' (Havelock 1982: 190–1, 195).

Now if writing speaks, then to read is to listen. In his inquiry into the etymological derivation of the verb 'to read' from the Anglo-Saxon *ræd* and its Germanic cognates, the medievalist Nicholas Howe shows that its primary meanings centred on the idea of 'giving advice or counsel', from which it was subsequently extended through 'explaining something obscure' (such as solving a riddle) to 'the interpretation of ordinary writing' (Howe 1992: 61–2). Thus, someone who is *ready* is prepared for a situation by virtue of having 'read' it properly or, in other words, of having taken due counsel. That notoriously incompetent Anglo-Saxon king Ethelred the Unready was so nicknamed because he took no counsel, failing in that most basic of kingly obligations. He did not listen. In short, far from being the silent and solitary contemplation of the written word so familiar to us today, reading at that time meant 'a public, spoken act within a community' (ibid.: 74). It was a performance, a matter of reading *out*. Just how well established was this sense of reading in the early Middle Ages is attested by the astonishment that Augustine recorded in his *Confessions* when, arriving in Milan in the fourth century, he observed the reading practices of Ambrose, then Catholic bishop of the city. To Augustine's utter dismay, Ambrose read without making a sound. Though his eyes followed the text, 'his voice and tongue were silent'. Augustine was at a loss to know why, but speculated that it might have been simply 'to preserve his voice, which used easily to become hoarse', for more public occasions (Augustine 1991: 92–3; see also Howe 1992: 60; Parkes 1992: 10). Even Ambrose, moreover, wrote of the *sonus litterarum*, 'the sounds of the letters' (Parkes 1992: 116, fn. 6).

More usually, monastic readers would follow the text with their lips as much as with their eyes, pronouncing or murmuring the word sounds as they went along. The sounds that came forth were known as *voces paginarum* – the 'voices of the pages' (Leclercq 1961: 19; Olson 1994: 183–5). The more they read, the more their heads would be filled with a chorus of such voices. Now present-day readers, accustomed to thinking of sound as a purely physical phenomenon, might be inclined to dismiss these voices as figments of the imagination. Of course, we reassure ourselves, they do not *really* exist. All that exist are images of vocal sound, their psychological imprints upon the surface of the mind. This division between the materiality of sound – its physical substance – and its ideal representation is however a modern construct. It would have made no sense in terms of a philosophy of being according to which, as we shall see, bodily performance and intellectual comprehension are as viscerally linked as eating and digestion. A man who feeds himself will feel as sated, on finishing his meal, as one who has been spoon-fed by another. Who is to say, then, that as the medieval cleric traces the inscriptions written on the page, following them with his eyes and perhaps with his fingers as well, and murmuring to himself as he does so, his mind is not just as much filled with voices as it would have been had the words been read out to him?

Yet of course, he only hears the words because he has heard them sung or spoken before, and because, through their practised reiteration, they have left their mark in both aural and muscular consciousness. To read, then, is not just to listen but to remember. If writing speaks, it does so with the voices of the past, which the reader hears as though he were present in their midst. As the historian Mary Carruthers (1990) has shown with an abundance of examples, from late Antiquity right through to the Renaissance writing was valued above all as an instrument of memory. Its purpose was not to close off the past by providing a complete and objective account of what was said and done, but rather to provide the pathways along which the voices of the past could be retrieved and brought back into the immediacy of present experience, allowing readers to engage directly in dialogue with them and to connect what they have to say to the circumstances of their own lives. In short, writing was read not as a record but as a means of recovery. Carruthers notes that the word used in Greek Antiquity for reading – *anagignosko* – literally meant 'to recollect', and that the corresponding word in Latin – *lego* – likewise referred to a process of gathering or collecting. One classical author after another would describe this process by means of allusions to hunting and fishing, and to tracking down prey (Carruthers 1990: 30, 247). As André Leroi-Gourhan put it, in his massive treatise on *Gesture and Speech*, 'each piece of writing was a compact sequence, rhythmically broken up by seals and marginal notes, around which readers found their way like primitive hunters – by following a trail rather than by studying a plan' (Leroi-Gourhan 1993: 261).

This distinction between trail-following or wayfaring and pre-planned navigation is of critical significance. In brief, the navigator has before him a complete representation of the territory, in the form of a cartographic map, upon which he can plot a course even before setting out. The journey is then no more than an explication of the plot. In wayfaring, by contrast, one follows a path that one has previously travelled in the company of others, or in their footsteps, reconstructing the itinerary as one goes along. Only upon reaching his destination, in this case, can the traveller truly be said to have found his way. A further elaboration of this distinction will have to await Chapter 3, where it will be my main topic. Suffice it to conclude at this point that readers of Antiquity and the Middle Ages were wayfarers and not navigators. They did not interpret the writing on the page as the specification of a plot, already composed and complete in itself, but rather saw it as comprising a set of signposts, direction markers or stepping stones that enabled them to find their way about within the landscape of memory. For this finding of the way – this guided, flowing movement from place to place – medieval readers had a special term, *ductus*. As Carruthers explains, '*ductus* insists upon movement, the con*duct* of a thinking mind on its *way* through a composition' (Carruthers 1998: 77, original emphases).

It would be wrong, however, to think of this mnemonic conduct as an exclusively cognitive operation, as though the text, story or route already existed as a complex composition that had first to be accessed and retrieved in its totality, prior to its bodily execution in writing, speech or locomotion. Though medieval thinkers did imagine that the work of memory inscribes the surface of the mind much as the writer inscribes the surface of the paper with his pen and the traveller inscribes the surface of the earth with his feet, they thought of these surfaces not as spaces to be surveyed but as regions to be inhabited, and which one can get to know not through one single, totalizing gaze, but through the laborious process of moving around. In reading, as in storytelling and travelling, one remembers as one goes along. Thus the act of remembering *was itself conceived as a performance*: the text is remembered by reading it, the story by telling it, the journey by making it. Every text, story or trip, in short, is a journey made rather than an object found. And although with each journey one may cover the same ground, each is nevertheless an original movement. There is no fixed template or specification that underwrites them all, nor can every performance be regarded as a compliant token that is simply 'read off' from the script or route-map (Ingold 2001: 145).

The reader's digest

With this conclusion in mind, let me return to our earlier distinction between the script and the score. Recall that, in terms of this distinction, the graphic marks on the page refer to concepts in the one case, and to actual sounds in the other: thus the script is read 'inwardly' in cognition, whereas the score is read 'outwardly' in performance. It should now be clear that, while the scribes of Antiquity and the Middle Ages were undoubtedly writing letters and words, the resulting literature could hardly qualify as scriptural in this sense. For one thing, the written marks directed readers, in the first place, to audible sounds rather than to abstract verbal meanings lying behind the sounds. For the eleventh-century Benedictine monk Guido d'Arezzo, to whose scheme of musical notation I shall turn shortly, it was perfectly evident that every letter, just like every note of notation, calls up a particular *vox* or sound (Carruthers 1990: 18). For another thing the act of reading, whether it involved the vocal cords or only the silent movement of the tongue and lips, was a performance in which the reader would hear and converse with the voices of his textual interlocutors. There was no idea that reading could be an operation of the solitary intellect, cut off from its grounding in the reader's sensory immersion in the world around him (Howe 1992: 74). Reading, as Dom Leclercq observes, was understood as 'an activity which, like chant and writing, requires the participation of the whole body and the whole mind'. Thus it was that Peter the Venerable, suffering from a cold and having lost his voice, could not read, for 'he could no longer per-form his *lectio*' (Leclercq 1961: 19–20). Granted, then, that the writing was read in performance, and that through this it was experienced as sound, might it not better be regarded as a score?

Once more, the answer has to be negative. It is neither script nor score, for the simple reason that meaning and sound, and cognition and performance, which modern thought aligns on either side of a distinction between lan-guage and music, are in the writing of classical and medieval scribes not opposed at all, but are rather aspects of the same thing. One was expected to read a text, continues Leclercq, 'with one's whole being: with the body, since the mouth pronounced it, with the memory which fixes it, with the intelli-gence that understands its meaning and with the will which desires to put it into practice' (Leclercq 1961: 22). Thus reading was, at one and the same time, both an 'acting out' and a 'taking in'. As I have already intimated, performance and cognition – or declamation and meditation – were as intrinsically linked as eating and digestion. Indeed medieval scholars had frequent resort to gastric metaphor in their commentaries on how writing should be read. Readers were exhorted to mouth the words in a murmur while turning over the text in memory, just as the cow moves her mouth in chewing the cud. In a word, one should *ruminate* (Carruthers 1990: 164–5).

Of a monk much given to prayer, Peter the Venerable exclaimed that, 'without resting, his mouth ruminated the sacred words' (Leclercq 1961: 90). Likewise the cowherd Cædmon, the hero of a tale told by the Venerable Bede, having been miraculously endowed with the gift of poetic composition and taken in for further instruction by the monks of the monastery for which he worked, is said by Bede to have 'learned all he could by listening to them and then, memorizing it and ruminating over it, like some clean animal chewing the cud, he turned it into the most melodious verse' (Colgrave and Mynors 1969: 419). Memory, here, is like a stomach that feeds on the nutrient of masticated words; it is saturated through reading as the stomach is filled through eating. And just as the stomach well filled with rich food finds relief in a sweet-smelling belch or fart, so – according to a statement attributed to St Jerome – 'the cogitations of the inner man bring forth words, and from the abundance of the heart the mouth speaks' (Carruthers

1990: 166). The more divine the words, the sweeter the sound. Recall that it was Jerome who advised his flock to sing 'more with the heart than with the voice'. As with a good belch, the vocal tract does not produce the sound, but merely releases it. What is learned by heart comes from the heart.

The origins of musical notation

We have established that for much of the history of writing, at least in the Western world, speech and song were not yet split into distinct registers. There was but one register, which was described by means of letters and words. Greek Antiquity had a category of vocal art known as *mousike*, but, as Eric Havelock explains and as we have already heard Plato declare, 'music in the melodic sense is only one part of *mousike*, and the lesser part, for melody remained the servant of the words, and its rhythms were framed to obey the quantitative pronunciation of speech' (Havelock 1982: 136). It is for this reason, Havelock surmises, that the Greeks never achieved a workable notation for their 'music'. Since they were unable to conceive of music apart from words, they never had cause to isolate musical notation from writing (ibid.: 345). The possible existence and nature of Ancient Greek musical notation is however a matter of some dispute among classical scholars. Martin West, for example, asserts that, from at least the fourth century BC, the Greeks had not just one but two parallel systems of notation, one for vocal and the other for instrumental music (West 1992: 7). Yet even these notations, if such they were, had very limited functions, and knowledge of them seems to have been restricted to a small minority of professional performers. There would have been no need for a separate notation to specify rhythms or note-values, since these were already intrinsic to the metres of the verses that were sung, with their built-in alternation between sounds of longer and shorter duration (ibid.: 129–30).

Even the melody of song, West admits, was partially based in features of the spoken language, specifically in those variations of pitch that the Greeks called *prosoidia*, or 'singing along'. They described speech by means of the same vocabulary of contrasts, such as high/low and tension/relaxation, which were also applied to melody (West 1992: 198). Commenting on the similarity, Aristoxenus of Tarentumi – a pupil of Aristotle well known for his arrogant and unscrupulous disregard for the works of his predecessors – declared that no one before him had given a thought to how the melodic forms of speech and song ought to be distinguished. The difference, he argued, is that, while in both speech and song the voice moves in pitch as though it were going from place to place, in speech the movement is continuous whereas in song it is intervallic:

> We say that continuous movement is the movement of speech, for when we are conversing the voice moves with respect to place in such a way

that it never seems to stand still. In the other form, which we call inter-vallic, its nature is to move in the opposite way; for it does seem to stand still, and everyone says that the person who appears to be doing this is no longer speaking, but singing.

(Aristoxenus, *Elementa Harmonica*, Book I, in Barker 1989: 133)

Aristoxenus himself had little time for the idea of a distinct musical notation, pouring scorn on the very idea that the writing of melody can contribute anything whatever to its comprehension, which can only come, he declared, 'from two things, perception and memory . . . There is no other way of following the contents of music' (ibid.: 155).

Nevertheless by the third century BC, according to West, an agreed system of melodic notation for vocal music was in general use among professional singers, comprising letter symbols to indicate pitch, placed above the syllables of the text (West 1992: 254). However, their purpose seems to have been largely mnemonic. Singers learned songs simply by hearing them sung, and would not have been helped by note-symbols (ibid.: 270). And the texts of lyrics were normally copied without such symbols, which were only added afterwards, in rather the same way that a contemporary instrumentalist might add fingering and bowing marks to a printed score. This practice of 'marking up' the text, however, had wider application in the field of oratory as well as that of singing, in signs of various kinds that were added above letters and syllables of the text in order to indicate the rise or fall of the voice at important points of declamation. We have already encountered the Greek term, *prosoidia*, for these song-like variations of pitch. The term was translated by the Romans as *ad-cantus*, which subsequently became *accentus* (ibid.: 198). A systematic set of accentuation marks for Greek and Roman literature was developed by Aristophanes of Byzantium, librarian of the Museum of Alexandria, around 200 BC. They were called *neuma*, from the Greek word for 'nod' or 'sign'. There were two basic accents, the acute and the grave, indicating respectively a raising and lowering, and these could be combined, for example into a V or N shape, to represent more complex vocal inflections (Parrish 1957: 4). It was in this form that the 'neumes', as they came to be called, were introduced into the earliest precursor in the history of Western writing for a distinctively musical notation, namely that devised for Gregorian chant.

Precisely when the neumes first came into use is unknown, for, while chants were being written from the fifth century AD, the oldest surviving manuscripts to have been marked up with neumes date from the ninth (see Figure 1.4). Moreover it appears that these markings, placed above letters and syllables, were later additions to the written page. In the Gregorian notation the acute accent kept its original shape, and was called the *virga*, or 'rod', while the grave was reduced to a *punctum*, or 'dot'. By combining these two basic marks in various ways, it was possible to generate a whole vocabulary of further neumes. Thus the *podatus*, or 'foot', comprising a dot followed by

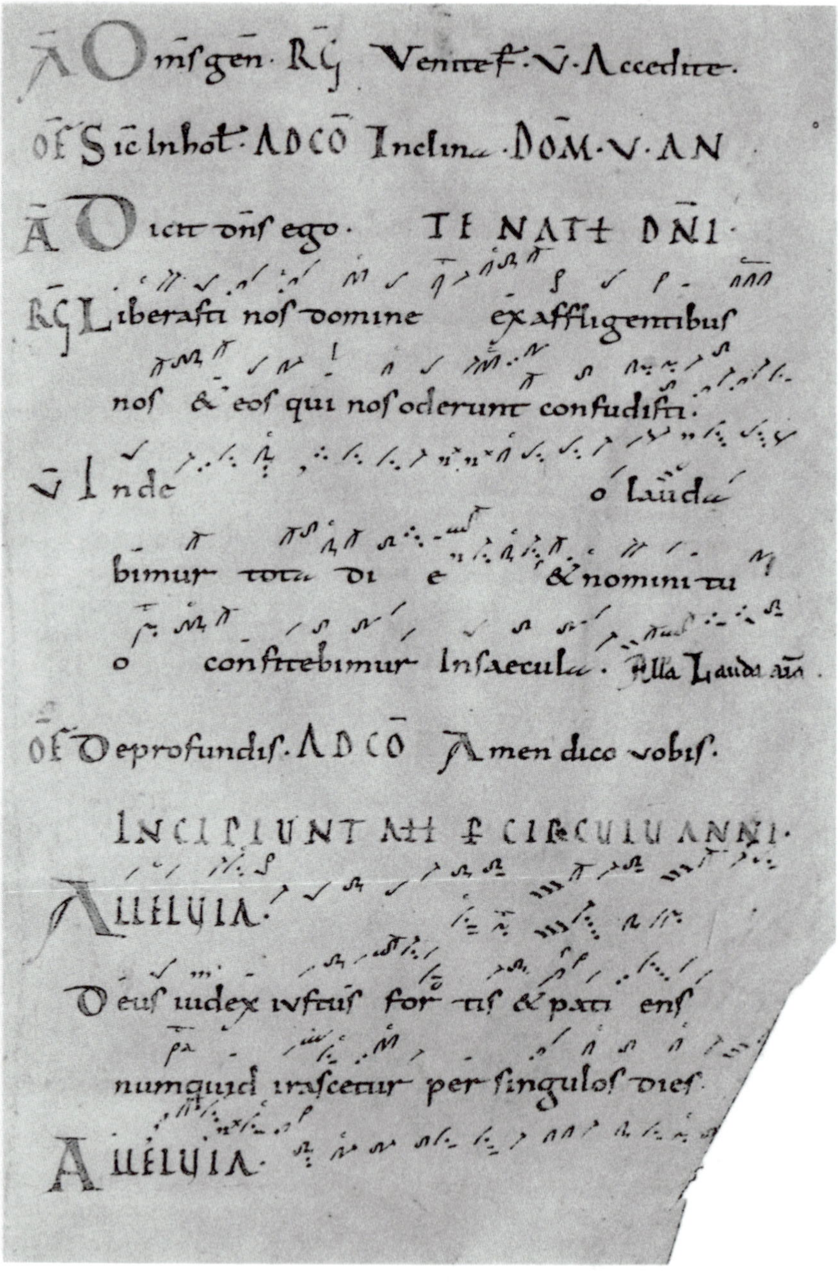

Figure 1.4 A late-ninth-century manuscript marked up with neumes, from the monastery of St Gall (St Gall, Cantatorium, Cod. 359, fol. 125).

a rod, indicated a lower note followed by a higher; the *clivis*, or 'bend', comprising a rod followed by a dot, indicated the reverse; the *scandicus*, or 'climb', comprising two dots and a rod, indicated three ascending notes; the *climacus*, or 'ladder', comprising a rod and two dots, indicated three descending ones; the *torculus*, or 'twist', comprising a dot, a rod, and another dot, indicated a lower, higher and lower note, and so on. There were different schools of neume notation, which are thought to have originated in the course of the ninth century, and these were distinguished in part by the way in which the more complex, multi-note neumes were written, whether by means of points or strokes or some combination of the two. The squaring of the figures, with thin vertical and thick lateral or oblique lines, and with individual notes distinguished as square or diamond-shaped blocks, was a consequence of the replacement of the reed-pen by the quill-pen in the thirteenth century. Figure 1.5, taken from the authoritative work on the subject by Carl Parrish, shows the most commonly used neumes of the principal schools of notation, roughly in chronological order from left to right, and in order of complexity from top to bottom. The far right-hand column shows the equivalent in modern notation.

The earliest notations gave little or no indication to their readers of what notes to sing. Indeed this was a matter of slight importance. The essence of the song, as we have seen, lay in the sonority of its words, and it was assumed that singers would have already known the words of the chants by heart. Just as melody was understood as a mere embellishment of vocal sound, so the neumes were seen as entirely accessory to the written words. They formed what Parrish calls 'a system of melodic reminders', helping the singer to remember the prosodic nuances to be adopted in the pronunciation of each syllable (Parrish 1957: 9). Some schools of notation, however, were at pains to indicate differentials of pitch by placing the neumes at various distances above an imaginary horizontal line. In manuscripts from around the tenth century, the imaginary line was replaced by a real one, actually scratched on the parchment. The decisive step towards the modern system of notation was taken in the eleventh century by Guido d'Arezzo. The neumes, Guido recommended, should be written in such a way that each sound, however often it be repeated in a melody, should always be on its own row. To distinguish these rows, lines are to be drawn close together, so that some rows of sounds are on the lines themselves and others in the intervening spaces. Thus written, a man could learn to sing a verse without ever having heard it beforehand, as Guido demonstrated on a visit to the Pope, John XIX. The Pope was reportedly so excited by Guido's invention that he insisted on trying it out himself, to his evident satisfaction (Strunk 1950: 117–20).

In hindsight, we can readily recognize this system for notating the melodic aspect of song as the precursor of the now familiar stave score. However, it would be wrong to jump to the conclusion that the system was a fully fledged musical notation. For so long as the essential musicality of song was held to lie in the intonation of its words, the neumes remained accessory to the

	SANGALLIAN	FRENCH	AQUITANIAN	BENEVENTAN	NORMAN	MESSINE	GOTHIC	SQUARE
SINGLE NOTES								
VIRGA								
PUNCTUM								
TWO-NOTE NEUMES								
PODATUS								
CLIVIS								
THREE-NOTE NEUMES								
SCANDICUS								
CLIMACUS								
TORCULUS								
PORRECTUS								
COMPOUND NEUMES								
PODATUS SUBBIPUNCTIS								
TORCULUS RESUPINUS								
PORRECTUS FLEXUS								
LIQUESCENT NEUMES								
EPIPHONUS								
CEPHALICUS								
STROPHIC NEUMES								
DISTROPHA & TRISTROPHA								
ORISCUS								
PRESSUS								
SPECIAL NEUMES								
SALICUS								
QUILISMA								

Figure 1.5 The neumes of Gregorian notation. Reproduced from Parrish (1957: 6). From *The Notation of Medieval Music* by Carl Parrish. © 1957 by W. W. Norton & Company Inc. Used by permission of W. W. Norton & Company Inc.

song itself, which was inscribed primarily in the letters of writing. Like the fingerings on a modern instrumental score, they served as annotations to assist the performer, rather than to index the music as such. Just as, on a score, one could erase all the fingerings without losing anything of the music, so one could erase all the neumes from a medieval manuscript without losing anything of the song. What would be lost, in each case, would be something of the player's or singer's ability to perform, due to the removal of the necessary prompts, cues or reminders. Just as with the letter-based note-symbols of Ancient Greece, the written neumes served a wholly mnemonic purpose: they were there to help pupils to learn songs by heart, and especially songs that they had never heard before. 'After I began teaching this procedure to boys', Guido boasted, 'some of them were able to sing an unknown melody before the third day, which by other methods would not have been possible in many weeks' (Strunk 1950: 124). But this was not sight-reading. It still took up to three days, and the pupils could not properly perform until they had committed the song to memory. With the help of the notation, however, they could memorize it that much more quickly.

It would be many centuries before the writing of notes or ligatures upon a stave would emerge as a musical notation in its own right, for this could come about, in Goehr's words, 'only when music liberated itself completely from the text' (Goehr 1992: 133). In the modern score the neumes have undergone an immense elaboration to form a system that has cut loose from its original connection to words. In the script, by contrast, they survive in our time only in its interstices, in the form of punctuation marks. The strange and obscure history of punctuation would deserve a chapter in itself; suffice it to say here that the origins of punctuation lie in the same practices, of marking up already written manuscripts to assist the orator in the phrasing and delivery of texts to be intoned or sung, as those of neumatic notation (Parkes 1992: 36). Indeed it was Aristophanes of Byzantium who first introduced the comma, the colon and the period as part of his general scheme for annotating Greek texts that also included the precursors of the neumes (Brown 1992: 1050). Much later, from around the ninth century AD, these were joined by additional marks – the *punctus elevatus, punctus interrogativus* (precursor of the question mark) and *punctus flexus* – which served to indicate not just a pause but an appropriate inflection of the voice, such as at the end of a question or of a subordinate clause in an as yet unfinished sentence. The source of these new marks, according to T. Julian Brown, was none other than 'the system of musical notation, called neumes, which is known to have been used for Gregorian chant from at least the beginning of the 9th century' (Brown 1992: 1051)!

Once music had been cut loose from words, what had before been an indivisible, poetic unity, namely the song, became a composite of two things, words and sounds. Thenceforth the single register of song, written in letters and words but embellished with accents and inflections indicated by means of both neumes and punctuation marks, was split into two distinct registers, one of language and the other of music, notated respectively by separate lines of script and score which were to be read in parallel. Nowadays, the words of a song are written as a script that accompanies the score. Remove the script and there is still a voice, but it is a voice without words. Remove the score, and there is no sound, no voice, only a chain of words, inert and silent. In the familiar example reproduced in Figure 1.6, the remaining punctuation marks – including commas, inverted commas, parentheses and a semi-colon – serve merely to indicate joints in the syntactical construction of the text and are of no assistance to the singer. Indeed, if anything, they interfere with performance, bearing no obvious relation to the melodic structure or phrasing of the song. To help the singer line up the words with the music, an irregular punctuation has to be introduced in the form of hyphens *within* the words themselves, so as to elongate them beyond their normal printed length. As Havelock puts it, we 'lay words on the rack' of music – stretching them, compressing them and modifying their intonation to conform to its rhythmic and melodic requirements (Havelock 1982: 136). Music has become the master of diction, no longer its servant. Once essential to the musicality of the song, the words are now 'added on' to the music, as accessories. But how did sound come to be expelled from the written word? How did the page lose its voice?

How the page lost its voice

For the answer we have to go back to a distinction I introduced earlier, between wayfaring and navigation. Recall that, for readers of medieval times, the text was like a world one inhabits, and the surface of the page like a country in which one finds one's way about, following the letters and words as the traveller follows footsteps or waymarkers in the terrain. For modern readers, by contrast, the text appears imprinted upon the blank page much as the world appears imprinted upon the paper surface of a cartographic map, ready-made and complete. To follow the plot is like navigating with the map. Yet the map effaces memory. Had it not been for the journeys of travellers, and the knowledge they brought back, it could not have been made. The map itself, however, bears no testimony to these journeys. They have been bracketed out, or consigned to a past that is now superseded. As de Certeau has shown, the map eliminates all trace of the practices that produced it, creating the impression that the structure of the map springs directly from the structure of the world (Certeau 1984: 120–1; Ingold 2000: 234). But the world that is represented in the map is one without inhabitants: no one is there; nothing moves or makes any sound. Now in just the same way that the journeys of inhabitants are eliminated from the cartographic map, the voices of the past are eliminated from the printed text. It bears no witness to the activity of those whose labours brought it into being, appearing rather as a pre-composed artefact, a work. Language is silenced.

This is the point at which to return to my earlier assertion that the silencing of language, and its consequent separation from music, came about not with the birth of writing but with its demise. The end of writing, I believe, was heralded by a radical change in the perception of the surface,

Figure 1.6 The parallel registers of words and music, from a modern book of carols: *While Shepherds Watched*, arranged by Martin Shaw. Reproduced from Dearmer, Vaughan Williams and Shaw (1964: 66). From *The Oxford Book of Carols*. © Oxford University Press 1928. Reproduced by permission.

from something akin to a landscape that one moves *through*, to something more like a screen that one looks *at*, and upon which are projected images from another world. Writing, at least in the sense in which I have been talking about it here, is a handicraft, the art of scribes. The lines inscribed on the page, whether in the form of letters, neumes, punctuation marks or figures, were the visible traces of dextrous movements of the hand. And the eye of the reader, roaming over the page like a hunter on the trail, would follow these traces as it would have followed the trajectories of the hand that made them. For example, *chironomic* neumes, found in many of the oldest manuscripts, were so called because they corresponded to the manual gestures of the choir leader (Parrish 1957: 8). In just the same way as with choral singing, following with the eye and following with the voice were part and parcel of the same process – that of making one's way, actively and attentively, through the text. Looking and listening were not then opposed, as they came to be in modernity, along the axis of a division between visual speculation and aural participation.

It was the technology of print that broke this intimate link between manual gesture and graphic inscription. I would hesitate to claim that printing was the *cause* of the changes in perception I have outlined, since parallel developments were going on in many other fields – for example in engineering and architecture. In every case, however, the outcome was the same: to split skilled handicraft into separate components of 'imaginative' design or composition and 'merely' technical execution, with the consequent reduction of manual labour – whether of the printer, builder or mechanic – to the implementation of pre-determined operational sequences that could just as well be done by machine (Ingold 2000: 349–50). I shall return to this theme in Chapter 5. For the present, we need only observe that in the field of literature the work of composition is attributed to the author. Though we say of the author that he writes, referring archaically to the result of his work as a manuscript, this is evidently the one thing he does not do. Of course he may use pen and paper to assist him in his deliberations. But this scribbling is just one of a plethora of activities entailed in composition, from talking to oneself to pacing the walls of one's study, all of which are antecedent to the transfer of the completed work onto the printed page. And if the author does not write, neither does the printer, for, whereas writing is a process of inscription, printing is one of *impression* – of a pre-composed text upon an empty surface that has been made ready to receive it. Whatever gestures may be involved in the process, whether manual or mechanical, they bear absolutely no relation to the shapes of the graphic marks they serve to deliver.

The word nailed down by print

With this I return to the thesis of Walter Ong, namely that it was writing that laid the word to rest, converting it into a quiescent object for assimilation by vision. Now even Ong has to acknowledge that this is not entirely true, for he cannot deny that, for readers of manuscripts, words were anything but quiescent. They were perceived to throb with sound and movement. Ong attributes this perception to a 'lingering hearing-dominance' that persisted on the margins of manuscript culture and that was only finally expelled with the advent of print. It is as though handwritten lines continued to wriggle around, refusing to be quelled by the objectifying duress of visual surveillance. Only with print, it seems, was the word finally nailed down. As Ong admits, 'print suggests that words are things more than writing ever did, . . . it was print, not writing, that effectively reified the word' (1982: 119–21). Indeed it is hard to avoid the impression that Ong is trying to have it both ways. On the one hand he would have us believe that 'all script represents words as in some way things', and that in this regard print only continued a process of reification that had been initiated thousands of years earlier with the advent of writing (ibid.: 82, 91). Yet if he is right to claim, on the other hand, that it was print and not writing that *effectively* turned words into things, then what happens to his initial thesis, that words become things at the point at which they are rendered in a visible form? Are not handwritten words just as visible as printed ones?

To resolve the contradiction, we need to look again at the distinction between writing and speech. Though frequently debated in terms of a single axis of contrast between orality and literacy, on closer inspection it turns out that speech and writing are really distinguished along two quite separate axes of contrast, the first between aural and visual sensory modalities, the second between bodily gesture (which may be vocal or manual, or both) and its inscription as a trace on some material surface. Compounding these axes gives us not two alternatives but four: (1) aural–gestural, (2) visual–inscriptional, (3) aural–inscriptional and (4) visual–gestural (Figure 1.7). The first and second alternatives correspond to our contemporary under-standings of ordinary speech and writing respectively. We think of speech as comprising vocal gestures that are heard, and of writing as comprising inscribed traces that are seen. Without modern recording equipment the voice does not normally leave any enduring trace, so that the third alterna-tive, taken literally, would have become a practical possibility only in recent times. Yet let us not forget the words of the prophet Jeremiah's scribe, Baruch, who claimed to have rendered in ink the pronouncements mouthed by his mentor. This was an instance of *dictation*, an oral reading out that was indeed expected to yield a durable inscription, albeit in visible form.

The scribe, of course, works with his hands. Were it not for this manual movement nothing would ever be inscribed in writing. Yet following the precedent set by Ong, most discussions of speech and writing have bypassed the hand and its work. Focusing exclusively on the contrast between aural and visual modalities, and their respective properties, they have failed to attend to the relation between gestures and their inscriptions. Thus writing has been understood simply as a visual representation of verbal sound,

	Gesture	Inscription
Aural	SPEECH	DICTATION
Visual	MANUAL GESTURE	WRITING

Figure 1.7 Speech, writing, diction and manual gesture.

rather than as the enduring trace of a dextrous manual movement. This point brings me to the fourth alternative in Figure 1.7, namely the visual apprehension of manual gesture. Such apprehension is characteristic of most human communication in face-to-face situations. All of us gesture with our hands as we speak, and these gestures would be pointless if they could not be seen. Moreover there are forms of language, such as the signed language of the deaf, which are entirely silent and work through manual gesture alone. As the example of signed language shows, however, looking at words can be every bit as active, dynamic and participatory as listening to them. 'The idea that there is a metaphysical gulf dividing communication by visible gestures from communication by audible words', claims Jonathan Rée, 'is a fantasy without foundation, a hallucination rather than a theory' (Rée 1999: 323–4).

He is right. Signed words are no less mobile and active, and no more thing-like, than spoken ones. Moreover so long as the movement of the hand leaves an immediate trace on the page, there is no great difference between looking at signed words and looking at written ones. These observations should dispel once and for all the widespread illusion that there is something inherently reifying about vision.[3] It is not vision that reduces words to things, but rather the disconnection of the technically effective gesture from its graphic outcome that occurs when words are printed instead of written. To read a manuscript, as we have seen, is to follow the trails laid down by a hand that joins with the voice in *pronouncing* the words of a text. But there are no trails to follow on the page of print. The eye of the reader surveys the page, as I show in Chapter 3, but does not inhabit it. And it is precisely because we are already convinced that the words it finds there are things that vision is reduced, in our understanding, to a faculty of disinterested surveillance, set apart from the more dynamic and participatory sense of hearing.

Chanting with (and without) an instrument

I began with a puzzle about the distinction between speech and song. I have shown that we cannot solve this puzzle without also considering the changing relation between writing and musical notation. Both involve lines and surfaces. But in the transition from the medieval manuscript to the modern printed text, and from the ancient neumes to modern musical notation, it is not only the forms of the lines that have changed. There have also been fundamental changes in the understanding of what a line is, and of its relation to surface, to gesture and especially to vision and sound. Thus, starting from the issue of speech and song we have arrived at an entire agenda of inquiry into the nature and history of the line that will occupy us for the remainder of this book. Before proceeding, however, I should like to reassert my disciplinary identity by indulging in a favourite diversion of social anthropologists, namely the invocation of comparative examples from non-Western societies. I do this in full recognition of the dangers of drawing glib and superficial parallels between traditions of knowledge and practice of a complexity and historical depth fully equal to our own. My purpose, however, is merely to indicate that the issues we have confronted in examining the history of notation in the Western world, from Antiquity to the modern era, are by no means confined to this region but have clear resonances elsewhere. My two examples come from Japan and the Peruvian Amazon.

The music that traditionally accompanies performances of the Japanese *noh* theatre is called *shōga*, which literally means to sing or chant. But the same word can refer to the sounds of musical instruments, and to their written notations. While every instrument has its own form of *shōga*, what is common to all of them is that they can be sung or recited with the voice. In what follows I am concerned with one particular instrument, the *fue*, or flute. My information comes from the work of anthropologist Kawori Iguchi, who studied the flute in the course of her ethnographic inquiry into the learning and practice of traditional music in the Japanese city of Kyoto (Iguchi 1999). To anyone familiar with modern Western musical notation, the *shōga* for the *fue* seems very odd indeed, for it is written entirely in characters drawn from the Japanese katakana syllabary. These characters may be read aloud, as word sounds, in a kind of murmur or hum. Since every syllable in the *shōga* is like a vowel, a string of characters reads as an unbroken stream of sound, which nevertheless undergoes continuous modulation with the changes in the positions of the tongue and lips, and hence in the shape of the mouth cavity, entailed in the pronunciation of each successive syllable. For example, the section of notation illustrated in Figure 1.8 reads – from top to bottom – as *o-hya-a-a-a-a-ra*. It is in this flow of vowelic onomatopoeia, of verbal sound, that the essence of the music is held to consist. Yet the katakana syllables are pronounced in just the same way in ordinary speech. It is therefore impossible, as Iguchi points out, to draw a clear division

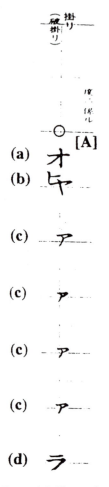

Figure 1.8 Phrase from *kakari* section of *chu-no-mai*: (a) *o*, (b) *hya*, (c) *a*, (d) *ra*. Reproduced from Iguchi (1999: 90), by permission of Kawori Iguchi.

between the sounds of speech and the sounds of music. In the chant, speaking and singing are one and the same (Iguchi 1999: 108).

Where, then, does the flute come into it? The flute is a melodic instrument, yet the melody itself is incidental to the music. It is a decorative embellishment. Thus the music is the same, whether or not the player puts the flute to his lips. If he does not, the music comes out as a vocal hum; if he does, it comes out as the tuneful sound of the flute. When an inexperienced player is called upon to give an important performance, a teacher sits behind him ready to 'stand in' by humming the *shōga* in the event that the player stumbles or fails to keep going. In a *noh* performance, it is critical that the music should continue without interruption, whatever accidents might befall the players. If a performer were to collide on stage with the *fue* player, causing the latter to drop his instrument, he would continue with the vocal recitation of the *shōga* until he managed to pick it up. Even members of the audience may hum the *shōga* to themselves as they hear the *fue* being played (Iguchi 1999: 88, 107).

There is an uncanny parallel here between the Japanese *shōga* and the *mousike* of Greek Antiquity. Where the chant of *shōga* is written by means of the katakana characters for vowel sounds, that of *mousike* was written by means of letters of the alphabet – which were themselves products of the attempt to write the vowel sounds of Greek by means of characters taken from the script for a Semitic language in which vowels were relatively insignificant (Olson 1994: 84). With both *shōga* and *mousike*, the essence of music lay in the sonority of verbal syllables, whereas the melodic aspect was ancillary or even superfluous. It would be tempting to take the parallel one step further, observing that in both cases, too, the principal melodic instrument was the flute. This, however, would be a mistake. The Greek instrument, the *aulos*, though commonly described as a flute, was not really that at all. It was in fact a double-reed instrument, most closely resembling the medieval shawm or modern oboe (Barker 1984: 14–15; West 1992: 81). It was usual for two instruments to be played simultaneously, one held in each hand. However, as with the flute, different notes were obtained by stopping holes with the fingers.

Both Havelock and West describe an Athenian vase from around 480 BC, depicting a series of lessons in music, poetry and recitation. Figure 1.9 reproduces the scenes depicted on the vase as seen from one side. The seated

Figure 1.9 Lessons in reciting, from the Kulix of Douris, c. 480 BC (bpk/ Antikensammlung, Staatliche Museen zu Berlin). Photo: Johannes Laurentius. Reproduced by permission.

figures are evidently grown-ups, while the shorter, standing figures are younger pupils. The seated figure on the right could be a proud parent (Havelock 1982: 201–2) or a slave who has brought the boys to school (West 1992: 37). In the middle, the seated figure holding what every modern reader would immediately identify as a lap-top computer is supposedly writing something while the pupil waits (he cannot be correcting the pupil's work, since he is using the sharp point of the stylus rather than the flat end which would be used for erasure). Havelock (1982: 203) speculates that he is writing a text that the student will then have to recite, and thereby commit to memory. What is going on, then, between the pair of figures on the left? This looks like a music lesson. But notice that it is the teacher, seated, who plays the *auloi*. The pupil, standing, has no instrument at all! Evidently, he is reciting *mousike* to his teacher. Change the instrument, and this could almost be a depiction of a lesson in traditional Japanese music. Here, too, the novice flautist would have to learn to recite the *shōga* before even touching the instrument. Indeed it is common to the melodic instruments of traditional Japan, as Iguchi observes, 'that their melodies can be sung or recited with the mouth' (Iguchi 1999: 87).

Now melody, as we normally understand it, comprises a sequence of notes each with a determinate pitch. Yet the *shōga* gives no indication of pitch. How, then, does the flautist know which notes to play? The answer lies in the fingering. On the *fue*, every fingering – which stops a particular combination of holes – specifies a note. Figure 1.10 shows a page of *shōga* written for Kawori Iguchi by her flute teacher, Sugi Ichikazu, during an introductory lesson. It is to be read from top to bottom, and from right to left. The *shōga* itself has been written with a black pen, and the fingerings in red. To these, Ichikazu has also added diagrams of the holes of the flute, shown as circles that have been filled in for the holes to be stopped. But he never drew these diagrams again. Normally the fingering is written, as here, in Chinese characters, each of which is the name for a particular arrangement of the fingers, a particular finger-hole on the flute, and the particular tone that results. As the *fue* is a solo instrument, there is no attempt to standardize the tuning: thus the same note, played on different instruments, may register quite differently on an absolute scale of pitch. Nor, however, is there any attempt to standardize the fingering (Iguchi 1999: 106). An expert flautist could display his virtuosity by using an elaborate, decorative fingering. The melodic effect would be quite distinctive – so distinctive, indeed, that listeners unfamiliar with the *noh* would probably be unable to recognize it as a realization of the same piece as that effected through conventional fingering. Yet regardless of the fingering adopted, the underlying *shōga* remains identical.

In short, with the *shōga* as with Gregorian chant, melodic inflections embellish the music without fundamentally altering it. And by the same token, the fingerings – with their associated holes and tones – are accessory to the written katakana syllables of the *shōga* notation, just as the neumes

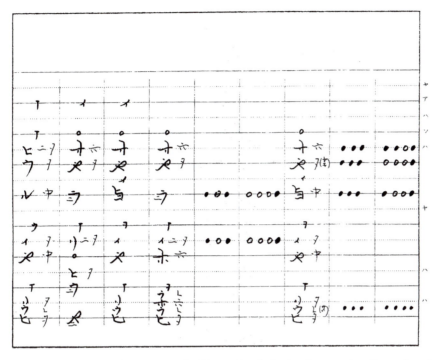

Figure 1.10 The first *shōga* written for Kawori Iguchi by her flute teacher. Reproduced from Iguchi (1999: 94), by permission of Sugi Ichikazu.

were accessory to the words and letters of the medieval song-book. They are merely annotations, and form no part of the music *as such*. As I have already observed, a stave score may be annotated with fingerings in much the same way. Like Japanese *fue* players, Western instrumental musicians, performing from a score, can develop their own idiosyncratic techniques of fingering for playing an identical passage (see Figure 1.11). But there is a critical difference. In Japanese traditional music, as we have seen, both the fingering and the melody produced by it are contingent aspects of performance, while the essence of the music lies in the component of verbal sound. On the stave score, by contrast, every note is specified without reference to how it is fingered. Thus although the fingering remains contingent, the melody is not. It is an aspect of *what* is performed, not of *how* it is performed, pertaining to the music itself rather than the technique of producing it. The difference is very similar to that which divides the Western music of the modern era from its medieval precursor. As the musicality of song was transferred from its verbal to its melodic aspect, so melody was detached from the bodily gestures – whether dextrous or vocal – involved in producing it. And by the same token, the notation of melody ceased to be a notation of gesture.

Figure 1.11 Part of a page from my copy of the score of the sixth suite for solo violoncello by Johann Sebastian Bach, showing pencilled bowings and fingerings.

Lines of sound

My second comparative example comes from eastern Peru, and I begin with a story reported and analysed by the anthropologist Peter Gow (1990), drawn from his fieldwork among the Piro people of this region. The story concerns one individual, Sangama, reputed to be the first Piro man who could read. Told by his younger cousin Moran Zumaeta, and recorded by the missionary Esther Matteson in the 1940s, the events to which the story refers may be dated to around the second decade of the twentieth century. At that time, the Piro were living alongside their white colonial bosses, on *hacienda* plantations, in a condition of debt-slavery. According to Zumaeta's account, Sangama would pick up newspapers discarded by the bosses and read from them. As he read, his eyes would follow the letters and his mouth would move. 'I know how to read the paper', Sangama professed to his cousin Zumaeta. 'It speaks to me . . . The paper has a body; I always see her, cousin . . . She has red lips, with which she speaks.' Zumaeta tells of how he too stared at the paper, but could see no one. But Sangama was insistent, going on to interpret the behaviour of his white bosses in the same terms. 'When the white, our patron, sees a paper, he holds it up all day long, and she talks to him . . . The white does this every day' (Gow 1990: 92–3). As Gow goes on to explain, Sangama's understanding of what it means to read can only be understood if we take account of two particular aspects of Piro culture. The first concerns the significance of design in the control of surfaces; the second has to do with shamanic practice.

The word for writing in the Piro language is *yona*. This term, however, is also used for the intricate, linear designs or patterns that Piro apply to certain surfaces, especially surfaces closely associated with people and, above all, those of the face and body. Evidently for Sangama, the pattern of newsprint on the paper constituted a design in this sense. Thus he perceived the paper as a surface akin to the skin of the body. Now in the healing rituals of the Piro, as among neighbouring Amazonian peoples, the shaman – having taken an infusion of the hallucinogenic vine known as *ayahuasca* – becomes conscious of brilliant snakelike designs that appear to cover his entire field of vision. These are the initial, terrifying manifestations of the spirit of the vine. But as they reach his lips they are converted into songs, through which the spirit reveals herself in her true form as a beautiful woman. It is these songs, as they are wafted through the air and penetrate the body of the patient, that effect the cure. Sangama, it seems, was reading the newspaper with the eye of a shaman. As he gazed at the serpentine patterns formed by the printed letters, the surface of the paper melted away, and there instead was the face of a lovely woman with red painted lips. Zumaeta himself suggests that his elder cousin may have possessed shamanic powers, since he was alleged to have been born one of twins, and twins are supposed to be innately endowed with such powers.

Principles of linear design and shamanic practice very similar to those of the Piro are also found among the Shipibo and Conibo Indians, who inhabit a neighbouring region of the Peruvian Amazon. Shipibo–Conibo designs are composed of continuous angular lines that loosely interlock to form a filigree pattern covering the entire field. The designs are embroidered on textiles, and painted on the surfaces of both ceramic pots and the face. In the past they also appeared on thatched roof interiors, on house posts and beams, and on mosquito tents, boats and paddles, and kitchen and hunting equipment (Gebhart-Sayer 1985: 143–4). Moreover it appears that around the end of the eighteenth century, under the influence of Franciscan missionaries, the Indians had begun to draw their patterns on pages of cotton fabric bound by threads into 'books' with palm-leaf covers. During a stay in Lima in 1802, the explorer Alexander von Humboldt met the missionary Narcissus Gilbar, who told him of the existence of these books. One exemplar was dispatched to Lima and inspected by some of Humboldt's acquaintances, but was subsequently lost. However, a report on the subject that Humboldt published on his return has led scholars to speculate ever since on the possibility that the Indians (known then as Panoans) might have possessed some form of hieroglyphic script. Concluding a review of these speculations some hundred years later, Karl von den Steinen drew particular attention to Gilbar's report that 'for "to read" the Panoans use the charming expression "the paper is talking to him"' (ibid.: 153–4). Unfortunately none of the original books survive today. However, during fieldwork in the Shipibo–Conibo community of Caimito in the early 1980s, the anthropologist Angelika Gebhart-Sayer was told that an old man from a nearby village, the son-in-law of a shaman, had kept a school exercise book whose pages were filled with intricate red and black patterns. One woman remembered how, as a child, she had managed secretly to get hold of the book and to copy four of the designs before being caught and scolded by her grandmother. She claimed never to have forgotten them, and was able to redraw them from memory. One of her drawings is reproduced in Figure 1.12.

As Gebhart-Sayer notes, von den Steinen was probably right to be sceptical of the claim that an indigenous system of hieroglyphic writing existed in the Peruvian Amazon. But could it have been a system of musical notation? In the shamanic healing ceremony of the Shipibo–Conibo, just as among the Piro, the designs which float before the shaman's eyes are – as they touch his lips – at once converted into melodious song. There are evidently certain parallels, in principles of division and symmetry, between the designs and the songs. In the past, women would sometimes work in pairs to decorate large pots. Sitting opposite one another, with the pot between them, neither could see what the other was painting. However, by singing as they worked they were supposedly able to harmonize their performance to such an extent that on completion the two halves of the design, on each side of the pot, would be perfectly matched and joined up. This degree of co-ordination, Gebhart-Sayer surmises, must have involved 'some kind of musical code' (1985: 170). However, in using their song to harmonize the design, Shipibo–Conibo painters were doing just the opposite of European choristers who would use written notation to harmonize their polyphonic song. Indeed from the argument I have developed in this chapter, it should be clear that Shipibo–Conibo designs form neither a script nor a score. They no more represent words or concepts than they do musical sounds. They are rather the phenomenal forms of the voice as they are made present to the listening eye. The songs of the Shipibo–Conibo, as Gebhart-Sayer herself remarks, 'can be heard in a visual way, . . . and the geometric designs may be seen acoustically' (1985: 170). The visible lines of the designs are themselves lines of sound.

We shall consider the Shipibo–Conibo and their designs further in Chapter 2. Let me now return to Sangama. Corroborating Gilbar's report on the Panoans, Sangama believed that the papers he was reading were actually speaking to him. Now in his analysis of Sangama's story, Gow is at pains to contrast Sangama's perception of the written word with conventional Western understandings, and the difference is clearly great. For the modern Western reader, as we have seen, the paper is no more than a screen upon

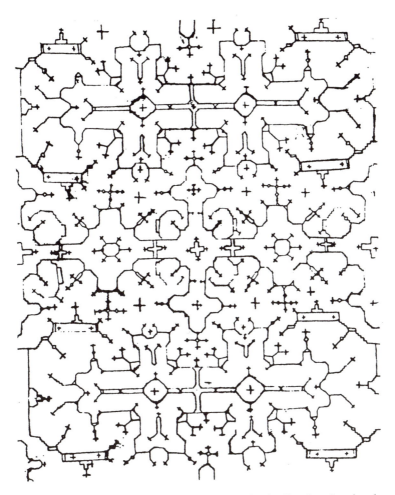

Figure 1.12 One of the designs from the sacred book of a Shipibo–Conibo shaman, drawn from memory by a woman from the village of Caimito in 1981. Reproduced from Gebhart-Sayer (1985: 158).

which are projected graphic images of verbal sound. Sangama, however, did not see images of sounds; he saw the spoken sounds themselves, as they were addressed directly to him. He was listening with his eyes, and the sounds he heard were as real as they surely were to the scribe Baruch as he took down the words of the prophet, his mentor. As Baruch followed with his pen the mouth of the prophet, so Sangama followed the painted lips of the woman he professed to see. In effect, he was lip-reading (Ingold 2000: 281). And so, in their way, were the monks of medieval Europe, as they pored over their liturgical texts. For them, too, otherwise distant voices were not *represented* for the reader on the written page, but were rather brought into his *presence*, so that he could engage with them directly. They would not have been in the least surprised by Sangama's insistence that the page of writing speaks, or by the idea that reading is a matter of listening to what the voices of the pages have to say. The interchangeability of visual and aural perception, which allows for the instant conversion of writing into song, was as central to the monastic practice of medieval monks as to the practice of Amazonian shamans. Moving his mouth and lips as his eyes followed the letters, Sangama ruminated on the text just as would a medieval monk or, for that matter, the traditional Japanese musician performing his *shōga*.

The similarities, however, should not be exaggerated. Monks were not shamans. For them the surface of the page was a landscape or country around which they could roam, picking up the stories of its inhabitants. For the shaman, to the contrary, the surface of the page is a face from which sound pours forth as it does in speech or song. The important conclusion to be drawn from the comparison is that it is in the nature of the *surfaces*, rather than in the nature of the lines themselves, that the crucial differences are to be found. It follows that any history of the line has to start with the relations between lines and surfaces. It is to these relations that I turn in the next chapter.

2 Traces, threads and surfaces

> Points joined together continuously in a row constitute a line. So for us a line
> will be a sign whose length can be divided into parts, but it will be so slender
> that it cannot be split . . . If many lines are joined closely together like threads
> in a cloth, they will create a surface.
>
> Leon Battista Alberti, *De Pictura*, 1435 (Alberti 1972: 37–8)

What is a line?

In the last chapter I argued that a history of writing must be encompassed
within a more inclusive history of notation. In thinking about the form that
such a history might take, what immediately comes to mind is that any
notation consists of lines. Thus a history of notation would have to be
subsumed under a general history of the line. But as I delved into the history
of writing in the Western world, and especially the transition from the
manuscript of medieval times to the modern printed text, it became clear
that what was at stake was not merely the nature of the lines themselves,
and of their production. Most of the lines in question were inscribed on
parchment or paper. Yet the ways in which they were understood depended
critically on whether the plain surface was compared to a landscape to be
travelled or a space to be colonized, or to the skin of the body or the
mirror of the mind. Evidently it is not enough to regard the surface as a
taken-for-granted backdrop for the lines that are inscribed upon it. For just
as the history of writing belongs within the history of notation, and the
history of notation within the history of the line, so there can be no history
of the line that is not also about the changing relations between lines and
surfaces. This chapter is about these relations and their transformations.

Before proceeding, however, some rather fundamental questions have to
be addressed. What *is* a line? For there to be lines, do there *have* to be
surfaces, or can lines exist without any surfaces at all? In a wonderful poem,
simply called *Line*, Matt Donovan captures perfectly the profusion as well as
the confusion of associations that come to mind as soon as you start to think
about what lines might be:

Line

Surface engraved with a narrow stroke, path
imagined between two points. Of singular thickness,
a glib remark, a fragment, an unfinished phrase.
It is any one edge of a shape and its contours
in entirety. Melody arranged, a recitation,
the ways horizons are formed. Think of leveling,
snaring, the body's disposition (both in movement
& repose). It has to do with palms and creases,
with rope wound tight on someone's hand, things
resembling drawn marks: a suture or a mountain ridge,
an incision, this width of light. A razor blade
at a mirror, tapping out a dose, or the churn
of conveyor belts, the scoured, idling machines.
A conduit, a boundary, an exacting
course of thought. And here, the tautness
of tent stakes, earth shoveled, the depth of a trench.

(Donovan 2003: 333)

Some two hundred and fifty years earlier, Dr Samuel Johnson compiled a list of seventeen different meanings of the word 'line' for his *Dictionary of the English Language* of 1755. Here they are:

1   Longitudinal extension
2   A slender string
3   A thread extended to direct any operations
4   The string that sustains the angler's hook
5   Lineaments, or marks in the hands or face
6   Delineation, sketch
7   Contour, outline
8   As much as is written from one margin to the other; a verse
9   Rank
10   Work thrown up; trench
11   Method, disposition
12   Extension, limit
13   Equator, equinoctial circle
14   Progeny, family, ascending or descending
15   A *line* is one tenth of an inch
16   A letter; as in, I read your *lines*
17   Lint or flax

Though perhaps expressed less poetically, there is much in common between Johnson's list and Donovan's, despite the long centuries that separate them. Apart from the several elements that occur in both, they seem equally jumbled and heterogeneous. Taken together, however, they offer a starting point for our inquiry. But how should we proceed? In order to get started I have found it helpful to draw up a rough-and-ready taxonomy of the different kinds of line that we may encounter in everyday life, and to consider a few examples of each. It is with this that I begin.

A taxonomy of lines

The thread

The first distinction I would make is between two major classes of line, which I shall call *threads* and *traces*. By no means all lines fall into either category, but perhaps the majority do, and they will be of most importance for my argument. A thread is a filament of some kind, which may be entangled with other threads or suspended between points in three-dimensional space. At a relatively microscopic level threads have surfaces; however, they are not drawn *on* surfaces. Here are some common examples: a ball of wool, a skein of yarn, a necklace, a cat's cradle, a hammock, a fishing-net, a ship's rigging, a washing line, a plumb-line, an electrical circuit, telephone lines, violin strings, the barbed-wire fence, the tightrope, the suspension bridge. These are all fashioned in one way or another by human hands. Not all threads, however, are artificial. An observant walk through the countryside will reveal any number of thread-like lines, although much of the linear order of nature is hidden underground in the form of roots, rhizomes and fungal mycelia (Figure 2.1). Above ground plants sprout stems and shoots. The leaf of every deciduous tree has its linear network of veins, while every needle of the conifer is a thread-line in itself (Kandinsky 1982: 627–8).

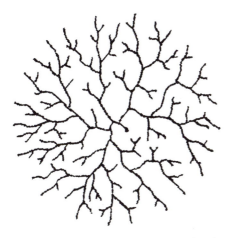

Figure 2.1 Fungal mycelium, drawn by the author's father, the mycologist C. T. Ingold.

The bodies of animals, too, with their external hairs and feathers, antennae and whiskers, and their internal vascular and nervous systems, can be understood as complexly connected bundles of threads. In his *Matter and Memory*, dating from 1896, the philosopher Henri Bergson described the nervous system as 'composed of an enormous number of threads which stretch from the periphery to the centre, and from the centre to the periphery' (Bergson 1991: 45). If animals are made of threads, some make them too: most notoriously the spider, but also the silkworm. The material for these threads, however, is exuded from the body. For the most part the *making* of threads is a human speciality, depending as it does on dextrous movements of the hands, sometimes working in conjunction with the teeth – as in the preparation of sinews for sewing. In most of its uses, too, the thread depends on the human hand's distinctive precision grip, which allows it to be held and manipulated between the thumb and forefinger.[1]

In an essay first published in 1860, the great historian of art and architecture Gottfried Semper argued that the threading, twisting and knotting of fibres were among the most ancient of human arts, from which all else was derived, including both building and textiles (Semper 1989: 254). Even before they were building houses with walls, Semper maintained, humans were weaving enclosures – fences and pens – from sticks and branches; and even before they were weaving cloth they were sewing and stitching nets and corselets (ibid.: 218–19, 231). Though subsequently reviled by the art historical establishment, Semper's arguments have much to commend them. Indeed, I am inclined to agree that the making and use of threads could be a good index of the emergence of characteristically human forms of life, which would have brought such critical innovations in their wake as the garment, the net and the tent. Elizabeth Barber (1994: 45) goes so far as to call it the 'String Revolution'. If threads have not received the attention they deserve from historians and archaeologists, this is undoubtedly in part because they are typically made from organic materials that do not preserve well. But, as Barber suggests, it may also have something to do with the association of the manipulation of threads, at least in the minds of many male prehistorians, with women's work.

Semper's most vociferous opponent was the Austrian art historian Alois Riegl. In his *Problems of Style* of 1893, Riegl rejected out of hand the idea that the line of art originated with the thread. Prehistoric people, he argued, were drawing lines long before they became familiar with weaving and textiles (Riegl 1992: 32, fn. 9). The line was invented, Riegl insisted, not on the back of materials and technique, but in 'the natural course of an essentially artistic process'. This dispute is of interest for our present purposes not for which side might have won the argument but because it hinged on alternative notions of the line. For Semper the prototypical line was a thread; for Riegl it was a *trace*, 'the basic component of all two-dimensional drawing and surface decoration' (1992: 32). And this brings us to the second major class in our taxonomy.

The trace

In our terms the trace is any enduring mark left in or on a solid surface by a continuous movement. Most traces are of one or other of two kinds: additive and reductive. A line drawn with charcoal on paper, or with chalk on a blackboard, is additive, since the material of the charcoal or chalk forms an extra layer that is superimposed upon the substrate. Lines that are scratched, scored or etched into a surface are reductive, since in this case they are formed by removal of material from the surface itself. Like threads, traces abound in the non-human world. They most commonly result from the movements of animals, appearing as paths or tracks. The snail leaves an additive trace of slime, but animal tracks are usually reductive, caused by boring in wood or bark, imprinting in the soft surface of mud, sand or snow or, on harder ground, the wear and tear of many feet. Sometimes these traces are fossilized in the rock, allowing geologists to reconstruct the movements of long extinct creatures. Human beings also leave reductive traces in the landscape, through frequent movement along the same route on foot or horseback or, more recently, by wheeled vehicles. Some traces, however, entail neither the addition nor the subtraction of material. In his celebrated work 'A line made by walking' (1967), artist Richard Long paced up and down in a field until a line appeared in the grass (Figure 2.2). Though scarcely any material was removed by this activity, and none was added, the line shows up in the pattern of reflected light from countless stems of grass bent underfoot (Fuchs 1986: 43–7).

But just as humans are, *par excellence*, makers and users of threads, so have they also come into their own as makers of traces with the hands. It is revealing that we use the same verb, to *draw*, to refer to the activity of the hand both in the manipulation of threads and in the inscription of traces. As we shall see, the two are more intimately linked than we might have supposed. Unaided by any tool or material, humans can make reductive traces – for example in the sand – with their fingers. With an inscribing implement such as a burin or chisel, they can produce traces in much harder material such as wood, bone or stone. The word *writing* originally referred to incisive trace-making of this kind. In Old English the term *writan* carried the specific meaning 'to incise runic letters in stone' (Howe 1992: 61). Thus one would *write* a line by *drawing* a sharp point over a surface: the relation between drawing and writing is here between the gesture – of pulling or dragging the implement – and the line traced by it, rather than, as it is conventionally understood today, between lines of fundamentally different sense and meaning (see Chapter 5). Additive traces can be produced by means of a range of manual implements that deliver a material pigment to the surface, including pens and brushes. In the case of sandpainting no tool is required, as the material is allowed to run between the fingers. However, with the aforementioned instances of chalk and charcoal, as well as with pencils and crayons, the tool doubles up as a source of pigment.

Figure 2.2 'A line made by walking', England, 1967, by Richard Long. Reproduced by permission of Richard Long.

The material of the trace, and the implement with which it is put on, are one and the same.

The cut, the crack and the crease

In what follows I shall concentrate on threads and traces, and on the relations between them. There is, however, a third major class of line, created not by adding material to surfaces, or by scratching it away, but by ruptures in the surfaces themselves. These are cuts, cracks and creases. In his essay of 1926 on 'Point and line to plane', Vasily Kandinsky noted that 'a particular capacity of line [is] its capacity to *create* surface' (Kandinsky 1982: 576, my emphasis). We shall return, in Chapter 6, to the capacity of the straight line to create a level two-dimensional plane, by way of its lateral displacement. The example Kandinsky uses is of how the moving, linear edge of the spade cuts the surface of the soil, as in an archaeological section, creating a new, vertical surface in the process. Then there are, of course, the furrowed lines of the farmer's field, cut in the earth with a ploughshare which not only creates a new surface but turns it face upwards. Cutting a sheet of material rather than the ground itself does not create a surface but divides the material: thus the dressmaker cuts lines in her material with scissors, as does the puzzle-maker with his jig-saw. A kind of cut that is familiar to me through my own fieldwork in Lapland is made with a knife in the ears of the reindeer, creating a pattern of notches of various shapes that serve to identify each animal's owner. Saami people would traditionally describe each pattern as a word, and the cutting of the mark as an act of writing (Figure 2.3).

While cuts can be accidental, as in the obvious case of a wounded finger, cracks are usually so. They result from the fracture of brittle surfaces caused by stress, collision or wear and tear. Because the forces that create cracks are generally both irregular and transverse to lines of breakage, rather than running along them, these lines are typically zigzags rather than curves (Kandinsky 1982: 602–3). Cracks may be commonly observed in nature – in breaking ice, sun-baked mud, stressed rock, dead wood and the bark of ancient trees (Figure 2.4). But of course they are common in artefacts too, whether made of clay, wood, glass or concrete. Unless scratch marks are the ultimate cause of fracture, cracks show no respect for the traces that may have been drawn over a surface. Thus cracks interrupt traces rather as, in the landscape, a path of travel may be interrupted by a precipitous gorge in an otherwise level plateau. To get across, you have to construct a bridge, whereupon the trace becomes a thread. The most extreme case of this would be walking a tightrope.

If the surface is pliant, then it may be folded without breaking, creating creases rather than cracks. The lines on a letter that has been unfolded after having been removed from the envelope are creases, as are the lines of pleated fabric on curtains, upholstery or clothing. So, too, are the lines on the face and hands, caused by folds of the skin. Crease-lines on the palms of the hands have traditionally been read by clairvoyants in the interpretation and anticipation of life histories (Figure 2.5). For the palm-reader, as Elizabeth Hallam explains, 'the hand carries a visual map of life, representing time as a series of interlocking paths, routes and journeys' (Hallam 2002: 181). This example is of particular interest to us for two reasons. The first lies in the observation that the sense in which the clairvoyant 'reads' these lines conforms quite precisely to the medieval conception, already explored in the last chapter, according to which to read was in the first place to speak out, to give

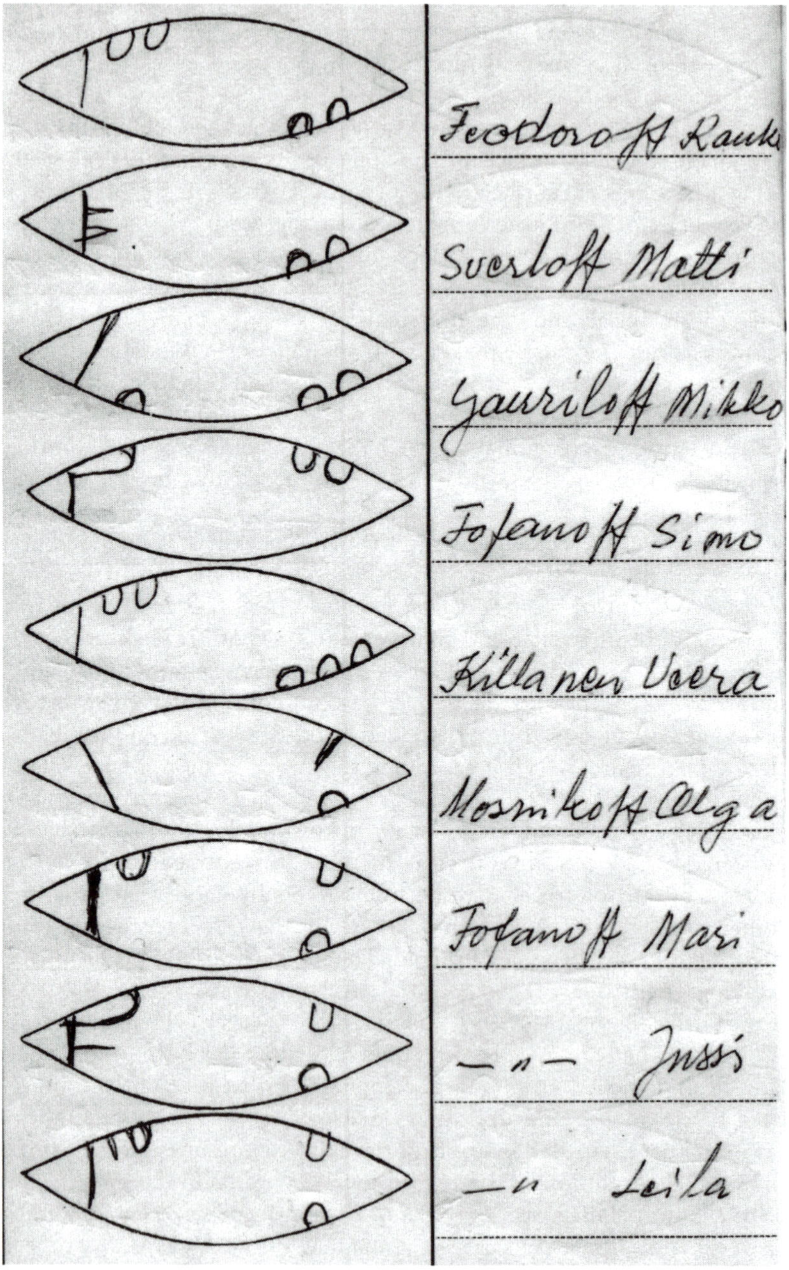

Figure 2.3 A page from a book of reindeer earmarks, collected by the author during fieldwork in Finnish Lapland, 1971–72. The pattern to be cut in the left and right ears is drawn in the book on a standard, double-pointed template, beside each of which is recorded the owner's name.

Figure 2.4 Bark of mature sweet chestnut tree, showing characteristic diagonal twisting cracks. Gunnersbury Park, London. Photograph: Ian Alexander. Reproduced by permission.

counsel, and to explicate matters that would remain otherwise obscure. The second reason lies in the intimate relation between the pattern of crease-lines and the habitual gestures of the hand. This is another means, apart from writing or drawing, by which gestures leave their trace, enfolding *into* the hand the very ways of life that it points or carries *out* in the person's manoeuvring through the world.

Ghostly lines

Up to now we have been speaking of lines that have a real phenomenal presence in the environment, or in the bodies of those organisms that inhabit it – our human selves included. These are, indeed, our principal concern. However, it is also possible to think of the line in a sense that is more visionary or metaphysical. Thus the line of Euclidean geometry, in the words of Jean-François Billeter, 'has neither body nor colour nor texture, nor any other tangible quality: its nature is abstract, conceptual, rational' (Billeter 1990: 47). Infinitely thin, drawn upon a plane that is both transparent and without substance, it is – as James Gibson puts it in his study of the ecology of visual perception – a kind of 'ghost' of the lines, including

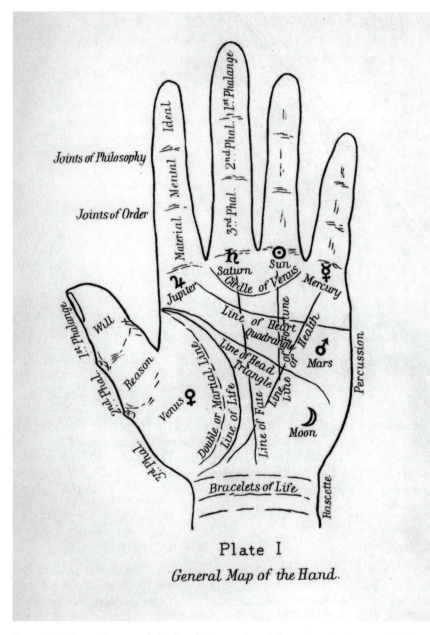

Plate I

General Map of the Hand.

Figure 2.5 'General map of the hand'. Reproduced from Louise Cotton, *Palmistry and its Practical Uses* (1896). By permission of Historic Collections, King's College, University of Aberdeen.

fissures, *sticks* and *fibres* in Gibson's classification, that we actually perceive in the world we inhabit (Gibson 1979: 34–5).

Looking up at the night sky, we imagine the stars to be invisibly connected by ghostly lines into constellations (Figure 2.6). Only by doing so can we tell stories about them (Berger 1982: 284). Survey lines, such as those linking triangulation points, are of an equally ghostly nature, as are geodesic lines such as the grid of latitude and longitude, and the lines of the equator, the tropics, and the polar circles. It is *as if* we had stretched a taut string between points, or traced an arc overland between them, as indeed was done in the earliest practical attempts to measure the earth. Lines of this sort may of course appear on maps and charts as traces drawn with pen and ink, using a ruler and compass. But they have no physical counterpart in the world that is represented on these maps. Some kinds of ghostly line, however, can have very real consequences for people's movements. I came across one such line while herding reindeer along the border between Finland and Russia, some

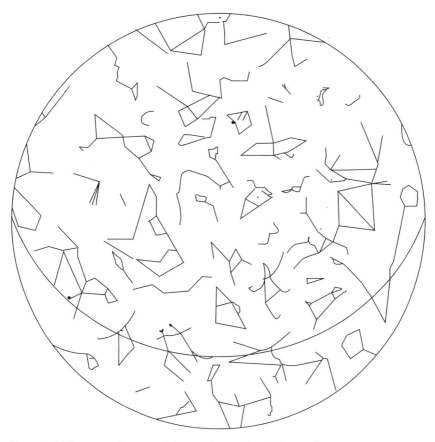

Figure 2.6 The constellations of the northern celestial hemisphere.

twenty-five years ago. The border was marked by a clear-cut strip of forest, down the mid-line of which the actual frontier was supposed to run. It was marked in no other way save by occasional posts. Had I attempted to cross it, however, I would have been shot at from one of the many observation towers on the Soviet side. Equally imaginary but consequential lines partition air-space and fishing waters, and demarcate time-zones.

Whether however a line is real or a ghost – whether, in other words, it is a phenomenon of experience or an apparition – cannot always be unequivocally determined, and I have to confess that the distinction is decidedly problematic. For example the so-called songlines (Chatwin 1987) that, in Aboriginal cosmology, criss-cross the entire continent of Australia are said to have been traced out by ancestral creator beings as they roamed the country during the formative era known as the Dreaming, leaving their mark in such landscape features as hills, rocky outcrops, waterholes and gullies. But these traces, which for Aboriginal people are intrinsic to the constitution of the landscape itself, are for Western observers but part of an imaginary construction that is 'pinned on' to it (Wilson 1988: 50). Likewise, so far as the Western doctor is concerned, the meridian lines that, according to the principles of acupuncture, run like veins through the body, conducting its vital forces and emerging at its surfaces, are entirely fictitious. But for the practitioner of traditional Chinese medicine, they are real threads. In the hands of the calligrapher, according to practitioners, the energy conducted along these threads is conveyed through the dance of the brush to the absorbent paper, where it is manifested in the equally energetic traces of handwriting (Yen 2005: 78).

Lines that don't fit

I admit that this taxonomy of lines is far from satisfactory. The world we inhabit is one of such profuse linearity that it is virtually impossible to accommodate it all within some neatly ordered system. Indeed it is in the very nature of lines that they always seem to wriggle free of any classification one might seek to impose on them, trailing loose ends in every direction. It is not hard to think of instances that do not fit the categories I have suggested. Where would we place the vapour trail left by a flying aircraft, or by a sub-atomic particle in an experimental cloud-chamber? Or forked lightning? Or a trail of scent? These are surely traces of a kind, yet since they are not inscribed on solid surfaces they have the appearance of threads. The Aboriginal people of Yarralin in Australia's Northern Territory, according to their ethnographer Deborah Bird Rose, describe both lightning and the long streaks that sometimes appear across the sky at sunset as 'strings', along which the feared *kaya* beings, mediators between earth and sky and between life and death, drop down to earth or pull people up. Yet the strings of the Aboriginal cosmos also include the tracks of ancestral Dreamings on the surface of the earth (Rose 2000: 52–6, 92–5). Thus the string, for Yarralin people, is both thread and trace, or neither one nor the other. So it is, too,

I am hunting down CST

for Khoisan hunters of the Kalahari, according to anthropologist Chris Low. To track an animal, one follows not only its traces on the ground but also the thread of its scent, carried on the wind. It is as if hunter and quarry were joined by a string, trailing at once on the earth and through the air (Low 2007). Tom Brown, an American trapper taught by an old Apache scout, echoes this Khoisan understanding. 'The first track', he writes, 'is the end of a string' (Brown 1978: 1).

Rather similarly, as we have seen, the energetic lines of traditional Chinese medicine can be at once vein-like threads, coursing through the body, and inked traces on the surface of the page. Can lines, then, like veins, be *tubes* through which material flows – as in pipelines for oil, gas and water, or the proboscises of insects and elephants? Do we perhaps need a separate category of *rods*, to denote lines in three-dimensional space whose rigidity allows for the engineering of stable structures? Apart from the obvious case of angling, the combination of rod and line is basic to the construction of the tent. Kandinsky singles out the Eiffel Tower as an 'early attempt to create a particularly tall building out of lines – line having ousted surface' (1982: 621). Buckminster Fuller's geodesic dome is a more recent application of the same architectural principle, known as tensegrity, by which the stability of a structure is engineered by distributing and balancing counteracting forces of compression and tension along its component lines. Tensegrity is common to both artefacts and living organisms, and is found in the latter at every level from the cytoskeletal architecture of the cell to the bones, muscles, tendons and ligaments of the whole body (Ingber 1998). Indeed lines are everywhere, and they raise more questions than I can possibly answer here.

From traces to threads and back again

My present concern, however, is more limited, and this is to develop an argument concerning the relation between lines and surfaces. Perhaps I could introduce it with a little vignette. On a recent ferry-crossing from Norway to Sweden I observed three ladies sitting around a table in the ship's lounge. One was writing a letter with a fountain pen, the second was knitting, and the third was using a needle and thread to embroider a design from a pattern book upon a plain white fabric. As they worked they chatted among themselves. What struck me about this scene was that, while the life-histories of the three women were momentarily entangled in their conversation, the activity in which each was engaged involved a different use of the line, and a different relation between line and surface. In her writing, the first was inscribing an additive trace upon the surface of the page. The second had a hank of wool beside her, but as she worked, threading the wool through her fingers and picking up the loops with her knitting needles, she was turning the thread into an evenly textured surface. For the third, the embroiderer, the surface was pre-prepared, as indeed it was for her friend the letter-writer. Yet like the knitter, she was threading her lines and not tracing them.

Watching these women at work, I began to reflect on the similarities and differences between writing, knitting and embroidery. It occurred to me that, while as a form of trace-making writing is equally opposed to embroidery and knitting which both work with threads, these latter two are also opposed to one another. The knitter binds her lines into a surface, upon which the original threads now figure as traces, namely in the regular pattern formed by their entwining. The embroiderer, to the contrary, starts with traces on a surface, as on the page of her pattern book, but in her activity with the needle she translates those traces into threads. In so doing, moreover, she contrives to make the surface of the fabric disappear. For when we look at embroidered cloth we see the lines as threads, not as traces, almost as though the cloth had itself been rendered transparent. 'Embroidery', as Semper declared, 'is, in fact, *a kind of mosaic in threads*' (1989: 228).

In this sense it imitates the making of lace, and it is no wonder that embroidery and lacework appear so often together, the first in the central field and the second around the periphery of a finely wrought scarf, kerchief or table covering. In the oldest form of needle-point lacework, most famously centred on the city of Venice, the pattern was first traced out on a sheet of parchment, on to which the threads were sewn. When the work was finished the parchment was detached and discarded, leaving only the pattern of threads (Semper 1989: 222–3). In her study of traditional lace-making on the Venetian island of Burano, Lidia Sciama explains how the pattern is nowadays picked out with needle and thread on a cotton lining, following an outline traced on paper, prior to the removal of both the lining and the paper to leave what is called *punto in aria*, 'stitching in the air' (Sciama 2003: 156). Contrary to official history, which claims that lacework was derived from embroidery, Burano women insist that it is modelled on the techniques used by their menfolk to make fishing nets. The body postures and techniques involved in both cases are strikingly similar (ibid.: 188).

Though I started out by presenting threads and traces as though they were categorically differentiated, these examples of knitting, embroidery and lacework suggest that, in reality, each stands as a transform of the other. Threads may be transformed into traces, and traces into threads. It is through the transformation of threads into traces, I argue, that surfaces are brought into being. And conversely, it is through the transformation of traces into threads that surfaces are dissolved. In what follows I present examples to illustrate both directions of transformation. I shall consider the latter first, and then proceed to the former.

Traces to threads: mazes, loops and designs

Mazes and labyrinths

I begin with what is perhaps the most archetypal use of the thread to be found not just in the history of Western civilization but throughout the world. We are all familiar with the story of how the Athenian hero Theseus, cast by the Cretan king Minos into the Labyrinth of Knossos, found his way out again having slain the dreaded Minotaur at its centre. He did so, of course, by means of a thread presented to him by Minos's daughter Ariadne. Now the great artificer Daedalus, who devised the Labyrinth, is alleged to have modelled it upon the maze that leads to the Underworld. Many classical authors went on to identify the original labyrinth with one or other of the many systems of natural caverns riddling the mountainsides of Crete (Figure 2.7; see Matthews 1922: 23–8). Be that as it may, the labyrinth or maze has remained a powerful image of movement and wayfaring in a world of the dead that is believed to lie beneath the surface of the world of quotidian experience.

Just to give an indication of the generality of this image, I reproduce a sketch (Figure 2.8) from the classic monograph by Waldemar Bogoras on the Chukchi of north-eastern Siberia. It depicts the paths in the underground world of the dead as they were claimed to have been seen, in a deep swoon, by the man who drew it. This world, it is said, is full of intricate passages that are supposed to puzzle newcomers. The circles represent holes through which they enter. These pathways, it seems, are imagined not as tracks etched upon a landscape but rather as narrow channels that run deep below its surface. The dead, like potholers, are doomed to wander these channels, and recent arrivals are as liable to lose their way in them as are travellers in a maze. The ghostly traveller, unlike his living counterpart, does not have the perception of walking upon solid ground, with the earth beneath his feet and the sky above, nor does he have the advantage of all-around vision and hearing. He is not, as we would say, 'out in the open'. To the contrary, he is fully enclosed within the earth, shut up in a medium that affords movement only along its cracks and crevices, and that insulates him from sensory contact with his surroundings. Unable to see where he is going he can have no idea, when paths diverge, of which to take. In short, whereas the living, in making their way in the world, follow the traces left by their predecessors *upon* the surface of the earth, the dead have to thread their way *through* its interstices.

For many decades, and despite its cross-cultural resonance, the maze has been a neglected topic in anthropology. However, it has been recently revived in the work of Alfred Gell. In his influential book *Art and Agency*, Gell treats the maze as a prime example of what he calls 'the apotropaic use of patterns' (Gell 1998: 83–90). By this he means the practice of inscribing complex and visually puzzling designs upon surfaces in order to protect those sheltered behind them from attack by evil spirits or demons. The idea is that the demons are lured to the surface by their fascination with the pattern, but are so tantalized by it that they cannot bear to pass without first having unravelled it, or solved the puzzle it presents. In this they are bound to get stuck, failing ever to arrive at a solution that would allow them through to the other side. Apotropaic patterns, Gell suggests, function as 'demonic

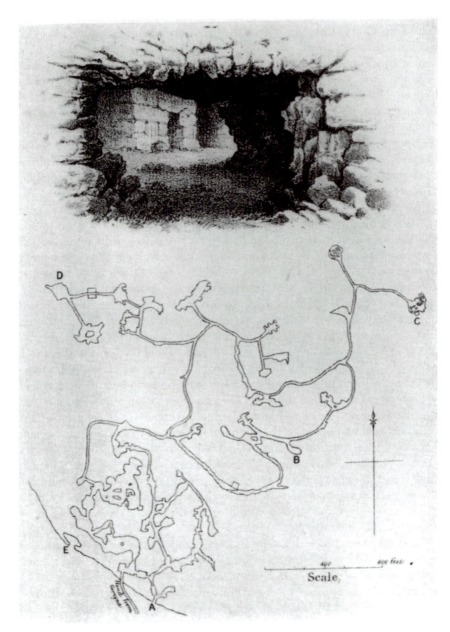

Figure 2.7 A sketch of the Caverns of Gortyna, on the side of Mount Ida in southern Crete, considered by some to have been the original Labyrinth of the Minotaur. The sketch was made by the artist-traveller F. W. Sieber in 1817, and reputedly took him three days to make. Reproduced from Matthews (1922: facing p. 28). By permission of Historic Collections, King's College, University of Aberdeen.

Figure 2.8 Chukchee sketch representing paths in the world of the dead. Reproduced
from Bogoras (1904–09: 335).

fly-paper' (ibid.: 84). The idea is an attractive one, and it is of course possible
that certain kinds of pattern are or were used in this way. One of the examples that Gell adduces is of Celtic knotwork patterns, in which a continuous
line, though traced on a surface, is made to appear as though it loops over
and under to form a tight weave that covers the entire field. Another example
is of the designs known as *kōlam*, drawn by women in Tamil Nadu, South
India, on the thresholds of houses and temples. These likewise consist of
one or several lines that meander around a grid of dots (without however
joining them), crossing over themselves and one another, but nevertheless
returning to where they begin so that each forms a closed loop (Figure 2.9). In
both cases, ethnographic evidence points to the significance of the patterns
in affording protection from demonic attack (ibid.: 84–6).

Figure 2.9 Above: *kōlam* designs from Tamil Nadu, South India, drawn from a
     photograph by Amar Mall. The one on the left is a *kampi kōlam* (Mall 2007).
     Below: Celtic spiral knot from Tara Brooch pin head, drawn following
     instructions in Meehan (1991: 111).

But as an explanation of the labyrinth, Gell's suggestion is wide of the
mark. This is because it assumes from the outset a kind of 'demon's eye
view' – an aerial perspective from which the overall layout of the maze
may be surveyed and represented in a pattern-like form. Such a perspective,
however, is not available to the terrestrial traveller who is already embarked
upon a journey across the earth's surface – a journey that is tantamount to
life itself. The entrance to the maze marks the point not at which he touches
down upon the surface, but at which he *goes underground*. Now as an interface
between earth and air, the ground is a kind of surface that is visible from
above, but not from below. It does not have another side. Thus at the very
moment of going underground, of entering the labyrinth, the surface itself
disappears from sight. It appears to dissolve. This moment marks the transition from life to death. Thenceforth – and quite unlike Gell's demon which,
caught in the contemplation of an apotropaic pattern, is glued to a surface –
the ghostly traveller finds himself in a world without any surface at all. Every
path is now a thread rather than a trace. And the maze of passages, never
visible in its totality, can only be reconstructed by those few – such as the

hero Theseus, or the Chukchi shaman who drew the sketch for Bogoras – who have visited the world of the dead and made it back again.

Indeed this conversion of traces into threads, and the consequent dissolution of surface, may hold the key to the protective functions of Celtic knotwork and the South Indian *kōlam*. In a recent study, Amar Mall (2007) has shown that *kōlam* actually come in two forms. In one, the lines of the pattern actually join the dots of the grid on which they are drawn; in the other they loop around them (Figure 2.9). The lines of the latter, known as *kampi*, are clearly distinguished from those of the former, and it is specifically to the *kampi kōlam* that protective functions are attributed. Lines that join dots mark the outlines of a mosaic of shapes. Such lines are not only drawn on a surface; they actually *define* that surface as a geometrical plane – a point that the painter Paul Klee made in his notebooks (Klee 1961: 109). But the *kampi* line, Mall argues, 'has precisely the opposite effect, dissolving the very surface upon which it is drawn so that it appears as a labyrinthine mesh of threads along which all of life and existence is constrained to run' (Mall 2007: 76). Rather than ambushing demons with an insoluble speculative conundrum, as Gell suggests, and causing them to get stuck in their attempts to figure out from the completed pattern the principles of its construction, the *kampi kōlam* more likely exercises its protective functions by catching them in the labyrinth, from which they can no more escape than ghosts in the world of the dead. For at the very moment when the demon alights on the surface, it ceases to be a surface at all, and the lines apparently drawn on it become threads that trap the demon as if in a spider's web. Perhaps Celtic knotwork designs functioned in the same way to ward off the Devil.

Looping and open-work

My second example of the way in which surfaces are dissolved through the transformation of traces into threads comes from a study by Brigitta Hauser-Schäublin of the decorative art of the Abelam, a people of East Sepik Province in Papua New Guinea (Hauser-Schäublin 1996). Abelam decorations are assembled from strings, strips and fronds, mainly of plant material, so as to form an open mesh of flowing or intersecting lines. This approach to decoration, which the Abelam share in common with most other Melanesian peoples, is radically different from that of the 'cloth cultures' of Polynesia and Indonesia, which make use of woven textiles, plaited mats or bark cloth to wrap things up so that they can be alternately concealed and revealed. The aesthetic focus of the Abelam is not on the surface but on the line. 'All patterns', according to Hauser-Schäublin, 'are perceived from the perspective of the line, or "visual open-work", rather than from that of the homogeneous plane so abundantly displayed and represented in cloth' (1996: 82). Besides making things from strips of leaves or lengths of string, however, Abelam also paint. These paintings are done on spathes of the sago palm that have been covered in grey or black mud. A line is first painted on the spathe, using a feather dipped in white pigment. This is the most important line, which acts as a template for the rest of the pattern. Once it is done, additional lines are added in red, yellow and black. In a large, complex painting, such as for the façade of a ceremonial house, the painter starts from the top and works in rows. However, he always leaves a white line hanging like a string from the bottom of the designs on each row, so that he can take it up and continue it on commencing the next (Figure 2.10). As a result, all the rows of the complete work are connected together by continuous white lines (called *maindshe*). The lines in the other colours, by contrast, are discontinuous and serve only to highlight the white *maindshe* (ibid.: 89).

Figure 2.10 Abelam men at work on a painting. In the row on which they are currently working, the painters are picking up and continuing the white lines left hanging from the previous row. Photograph: Jörg Hauser. Reproduced by permission of Jörg Hauser and Brigitta Hauser-Schäublin.

Now what is remarkable is that exactly the same principle is involved in making the net bag or *bilum*, one of the most ubiquitous and multifunctional accessories to everyday life among the peoples of inland Melanesia. The string of the *bilum*, made from the bast of various trees and shrubs, is naturally of a beige colour, but it is taken to be white. Just as in the painting, where the artist picks up the 'loose end' of the *maindshe* from the previous row in proceeding with the next, so in the making of net bags every additional length of string is attached to the one before – by twining the fibres and rolling them on the thigh – so as to form one continuous line from which the whole bag is produced. This line is known by the same term, *maindshe*. Patterns are formed through the addition of strings dyed in red and black. Although we might be inclined to see the coloured designs as standing out against a white background, for the Abelam it is the other way around, as it is in their paintings. Indeed, Abelam men say that the designs painted on their ceremonial house façades have their origin in women's net bag patterns. Evidently, the *maindshe* of the painting, though it is formed as an additive trace upon an opaque surface, is treated as a thread of the same kind as the *maindshe* of the bag. And in the transformation of the painted line into a looped thread the surface is contrived to disappear, so that the painting has the same texture of 'open-work' that is so characteristic of all Abelam art. Another way of dissolving a surface, of course, is by cutting it up. This is exactly what happened when Hauser-Schäublin, at the request of some Abelam women, brought back some plain black and red cloth from a shopping trip to a nearby town. Instead of using it as cloth, they first cut it into strips and went on to unravel the shredded fabric into its individual threads. These were then twined and rolled to form strings, from which they made colourfully patterned net bags (ibid.: 96).

Designs for the body

For a third example of the transformation of traces into threads I return to the study by Angelika Gebhart-Sayer (1985) of the Shipibo–Conibo Indians of the Peruvian Amazon, already introduced in the last chapter. Until about two centuries ago, according to Gebhart-Sayer, Shipibo and Conibo villages were covered in continuous zigzag lines. They spread over the interior surfaces of houses, over the outer surfaces of ceramic pottery, over boats, hunting gear and cooking utensils, over finely woven cotton garments, and over the faces, hands and legs of their wearers. Today this preoccupation with the line continues in textile embroidery, ceramic painting, plaited beadwork and occasional facial marking (Gebhart-Sayer 1985: 143–4). Line-making is exclusively the province of women, and is perceived by them as a matter of tracing visible lines across opaque surfaces. The painter or embroiderer commences by drawing the basic formlines. These are relatively thick, but twist and turn like snakes so that they have no clear direction. Secondary lines are then drawn parallel to the formlines, on either side. Any vacant space is filled with tertiary lines, to ensure that the surface is covered in its entirety (ibid.: 147). The regular repetition of the formlines lends the overall pattern a certain symmetry (Figure 2.11).

These surface patterns, however, are only the visible manifestations of design. In addition, Shipibo–Conibo people hold that every individual is invisibly marked with designs that are bestowed, from early childhood onwards, in the course of shamanic healing sessions. These designs, which are permanent, are understood to permeate and saturate the entire living body, and remain after death with a person's spirit (ibid.: 144–5). In the healing ceremony the shaman – who is generally but not invariably male – 'sings' the design, but as the vocal sound meanders through the air he sees it transformed into a pattern that *sinks into* the patient's body. It is a transformation, however, that is visible only to the shaman himself. In this vision the lines are seen to be spun by the spirit of the humming bird, Pino. Hovering above the patient, the spirit busily swishes and whirrs with his beak in rapid, tiny movements. Though Pino is described as a 'writer' or 'secretary' among spirits, it is clear that the lines that issue from his restless beak are threads and not traces. For the patterns he writes, far from being inscribed across the surface of the patient's body, are said to drop down upon it, and to penetrate it (ibid.: 162–4). Thus as traces are transformed in the shaman's vision into threads, it is the very surface of the body that is dissolved, allowing the lines to penetrate its interiority where the cure becomes effective.

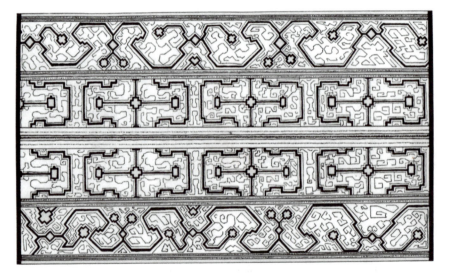

Figure 2.11 Shipibo–Conibo woman's mantle (*racoti*). Reproduced from Tessmann (1928: Plate II, facing p. 40), by permission of the Bodleian Library, University of Oxford, shelfmark 247236 d.13.

From threads to traces: knotting, weaving, brocade, text

In the examples I have presented – of the labyrinthine underworld of the Siberian Chukchi, the painting of ceremonial house façades among the Abelam of New Guinea, and the shamanic healing of the Shipibo–Conibo Indians of eastern Peru – we have seen how the transformation of traces into threads dissolves the surfaces of the earth, the house and the body respectively. It is now time to turn to the reverse transformation: that of threads into traces in the constitution of surfaces. The etymology of 'line' itself offers an exemplary instance of this transformation. As Samuel Johnson reminds us in his *Dictionary*, one of the meanings of the word (the seventeenth and final entry in his list) is 'lint or flax'. *Lint* is derived from the Latin *linea*, which originally meant a thread made from flax, *linum*. These threads were woven into cloth that we now call *linen*, and that could be used to *line* garments by providing an extra layer of warmth. And if 'line' began as a thread rather than a trace, so did 'text' begin as a meshwork of interwoven threads rather than of inscribed traces. The verb 'to weave', in Latin, was *texere*, from which are derived our words 'textile' and – by way of the French *tistre* – 'tissue', meaning a delicately woven fabric composed of a myriad of interlaced threads.

Anatomists would go on to adopt this compositional metaphor to describe the organs of the body, said to consist of epithelial, connective, muscular and nervous tissues. They would write of how the surfaces of these organs, illuminated by skilled anatomical vision, are rendered transparent, revealing their underlying linear structure. In his *Introduction to Science* of 1911, J. Arthur Thomson wrote:

> When we work long at a thing and come to know it up and down, in and out, through and through, it becomes in a quite remarkable way translucent. The botanist can see through his tree, see wood and bast . . . The zoologist can in the same way see through the snail on the thorn, seeing as in a glass model everything in its place, the nerve-centres, the muscles, the stomach, the beating heart, the coursing blood, and the filtering kidney. So the human body becomes translucent to the skilled anatomist . . .
>
> (Thomson 1911: 27–8)[2]

Thus the anatomical gaze, not unlike that of the shaman, resolves bodily surfaces into their constituent threads. But whereas the shaman heals by dropping lines into the body, the Western surgeon proceeds in the opposite direction, stitching up the lines he already finds within the body and whose ruptures are the cause of the malaise, so as to reconstitute the surfaces of the whole.

Knotting and weaving

As our little excursion into the etymological derivation of line and tissue suggests, it is perhaps in stitching and weaving that we find the most obvious examples of how surfaces are constituted from threads, and of how traces are generated in the process. In essence, as Semper pointed out (1989: 219), the stitch is a knot through whose iteration – as in knitting and crocheting – an unbroken surface can be formed from a continuous line of yarn. The knotted surface is, in a sense, the obverse of the looped open-work of people like the Abelam, described above. Where the loop is surface-destroying, the knot is surface-creating. The surface we perceive, however, is not the knot but the space taken up by it. It is, as Susanne Küchler explains, 'everything but the knot, with the knot lying within or beneath the surfaces which make it visible to the eye' (Küchler 2001: 65). The more securely the knots are drawn, the more impenetrable the surface appears to be. In Tahiti, for example, special wooden sticks known as *to'o*, held to be embodiments of divine power, were tightly wrapped in knotted sennit cordage, in order to protect them from view. The *to'o* would only be revealed in periodic rituals of 'wrapping the gods', and then only to personages of rank. Such was their power that for anyone else to see them would have resulted in certain death (ibid.: 66–7; Gell 1998: 111). The surface, then, is absolutely sealed; nevertheless its original constitution from threads remains evident in its textured tracery (Figure 2.12). The texture, in short, proclaims that the surface is not merely a passive container for divine power, but actively *binds it up*.

Turning from knotting to weaving, the weaver starts not with a single, continuous line of yarn but with one set of parallel lines, the warp, strung lengthwise, through which another line, the weft, is threaded crosswise, alternately over and under the warp strings. If the weft is all of one colour, then the finished cloth will appear as an unbroken, homogeneous surface. However, by introducing wefts of different colours it is easy to produce straight, transverse stripes of any desired thickness. From a distance, these look like lines drawn across the material. Thus as the textile is built up through the process of weaving, the coloured threads of the weft gradually give rise to the appearance of a trace upon its surface. The production of diagonal or longitudinal lines is more complex. In her classic account of how to weave a Navajo blanket, Gladys Reichard shows how diagonals may be made at inclinations of 40 or 52.5 degrees to the transverse direction by carrying the weft in the base colour one warp-line further either in every row or in every second row, while the contrasting colour, coming in from the other side, correspondingly loses a warp (Reichard 1936: 89–94) (Figure 2.13). The point at which the two colours meet, known as the lock, accordingly shifts from row to row at regular intervals. To produce longitudinal stripes the two weft colours, coming in from opposite sides, always loop back around the same warps, so that the transverse position of the lock remains constant.

Figure 2.12 Tahitian *to'o*, with knotted binding. Reproduced by permission of University of Cambridge Museum of Archaeology and Anthropology E 1907.342 (Z 6067).

What is most striking about the Navajo blanket, however, is that, while the coloured designs on its surface are strongly linear, these lines are not themselves threads. Nor are they really traces. Indeed when we look for the line in the blanket, however closely, we find only differences – namely, variations in the colour of the threads, and row-by-row displacements in the locking position of the weft for each colour. We could say that the line on the blanket exists not as a composite of the threads of which it is made, but as

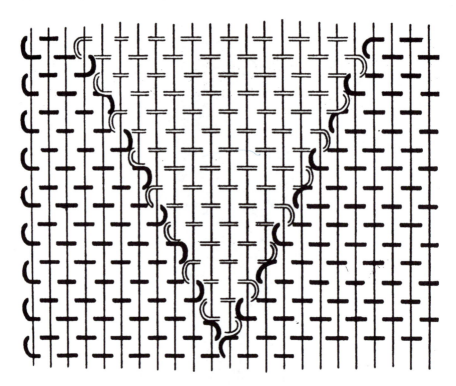

Figure 2.13 Forming the side of a triangle in a Navajo blanket with two colours, with the first (black) advancing one warp farther in each row and the second (white) losing a warp. The effect is to produce a smooth line at an inclination of 40 degrees. Reproduced from Reichard (1936: 90).

an ordered system of differences among them. Taken together, however, these differences add up to something positive, namely the perception of a continuous line on a coherent surface. And it is this perception that gives the line the appearance of a trace. Nevertheless the line formed on a woven surface as it is built up from threads is in reality quite unlike a line that is drawn on a surface that already exists. The difference may be highlighted by contrasting the blanket with another major focus of Navajo artistic practice, the sandpainting. This is made by dribbling a fine stream of dyed sand, first in one colour and then in another, to form a linear design upon the naturally earth-coloured sand of a smooth, pre-prepared floor. The sand is allowed to trickle between the index and middle finger, while controlling the flow with the thumb. In this case, the line is clearly an additive trace, a crystallization of the precise movements and gestures involved in producing it. Some Navajo weavers, under pressure to produce 'authentically Navajo' designs for the tourist market, have taken to copying the sandpainting designs on their blankets. But the results, Reichard tells us, are generally unsatisfactory, not only because it is virtually impossible to achieve the right colours, but also because the technique of weaving is inappropriate to producing designs of this kind. They are too intricate (Reichard 1936: 156).

In short, whereas the line on a pre-existent surface – such as that of the sandpainting – is the trace of a movement, the line on a surface that is being woven from threads – such as that of the blanket – grows organically, in one direction, through the accumulation of transverse, back-and-forth movements in the other. This distinction, in turn, provides the key to understanding the relation between weaving and writing. The common derivation, noted above, of the words 'text' and 'textile' from *texere*, 'to weave', points to the significance of this relation. How was it that writing, which generally involves the inscription of traces upon a surface, came to be modelled on weaving, which involves the manipulation of threads? How did the thread of the weaver become the trace of the writer? The Chinese philosopher Liu Hsieh, who lived in the fifth century AD, placed this question at the very birth of writing in his intriguing but enigmatic remark that 'when bird's markings replaced knotted cords, writing first emerged'.[3] What he had in mind, apparently, was the replacement of a notational system based on the knotting and looping of threads or strings with one based on inscriptive traces analogous to the footprints of birds and animals.

From knotted cords to brocaded letters

Not everything that is done in a notation, after all, need consist of traces. For example, among the people of Kandingei, on the Middle Sepik River, Papua New Guinea, the most important man in every group keeps a knotted cord – some six to eight metres long and three centimetres thick – which is said to represent the primal migration in which the founder of the clan, following in the path of a crocodile, journeyed from place to place (Figure 2.14). Each large knot in the cord, into which is woven a dried piece of betel-nut shell, represents a primal place, while the smaller knots preceding it stand for the secret names of the totem dwelling in that place. In important ceremonies, the owner of the cord lets it run through his fingers, rather as though he were handling a rosary, 'singing' each place and its associated totems. Thus the movement of slipping the cord through the fingers corresponds to the movement of the clan founder as he journeyed from one settlement to the next. In mortuary ceremonies it also corresponds to the movement of the ghost as it travels to the land of the dead, borne on a grass island that nevertheless runs aground at one place after another along the way (Wassmann 1991: 51–60, 70–1, 103–5, 114; on the nearby Iatmul, see also Silverman 1998: 429).

The most celebrated example of a notational device that consists entirely of threads is of course the Inka *khipu*. The *khipu* comprises a plied cord to which secondary cords are attached with knots (Figure 2.15). Further, tertiary cords may be knotted to secondary ones, fourth-order to tertiary, fifth-order to fourth-order, and so on. Scholars still argue about the function of the

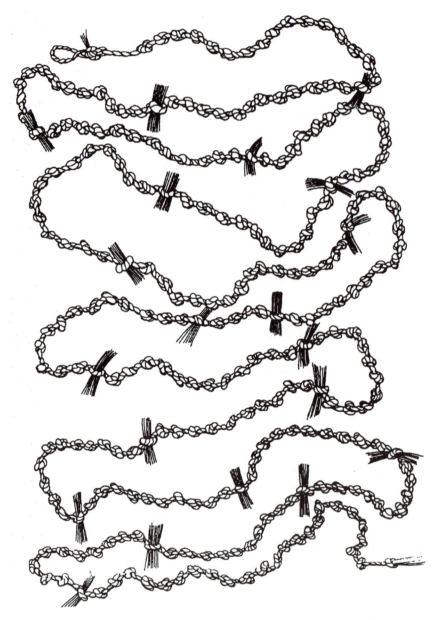

Figure 2.14 Palingawi knotted cord, Kandingei, Middle Sepik River, Papua New Guinea. Reproduced from Wassmann (1991: 71).

Figure 2.15 Khipukamayuq, or 'keeper of the *khipu*', depicted by Felipe Guaman Poma de Ayala around the turn of the seventeenth century. He is shown holding the *khipu*, while in the lower left-hand corner is depicted a *taptana*, or stone calculating device. Reproduced from Guaman Poma de Ayala (1987: 365).

khipu, whether it served to prompt the memory or to record information, and – if the latter – whether that information was merely numerical or involved elements of narrative (Quilter and Urton 2002). It seems beyond doubt, however, that almost every element of its construction carried meanings of one sort or another, including the types of knots and their placement on the cords, the ways the cords are plied, and the colour combinations used. More-over as a kind of fabric the *khipu* is constructed on the same principle, involv-ing the combination of a suspension line with pendants, as many other kinds of Inka fabric including necklaces, headbands and of course, on a larger scale, the suspension bridge. But although the weaving of textiles was highly developed among the Inka, the *khipu* is not woven, and it is not a textile. It has no surface apart from the surfaces of the cords from which it is made.

For an example of writing that is actually woven into textiles we can move from the Andes to Mesoamerica, and to the Maya peoples of Guatemala. In the *Popol Vuh*, a chronicle of the creation of man, the actions of the gods, the origins and history of the Quiché people and the chronology of their kings, written (in Spanish letters but in the indigenous Quiché language) in the sixteenth century, it is said of the monkey gods that 'they are flautists, they are singers, and they are writers; and they are also engravers, they are jewel-lers, they are metalworkers' (Tedlock and Tedlock 1985: 123). In this passage the writer is called *ajtz'ib*, from the word for written characters, *tz'ib*. But according to Barbara and Dennis Tedlock, on whose authoritative work I draw for this discussion, *tz'ib* could also refer to 'figures, designs, and dia-grams in general, whether they be drawn, painted, engraved, embroidered, or woven' (ibid.: 124). Scarves woven in recent times by the Quiché Maya include brocaded zoomorphic figures, together with additional designs that indicate the identity of the weaver. These are all *tz'ib* (whereas the vertical bands of colour that run through the textiles are not). An example is shown in Figure 2.16. This particular scarf also carries the name of its owner, embroidered in alphabetic capitals. Though the juxtaposition of letters and designs seems incongruous to us, for contemporary Quiché it is entirely unremarkable, for both are instances of *tz'ib*. Critically, however, whereas the embroidered letters were added after the weaving was complete the brocaded designs were incorporated, during the weaving process itself, through the addition of supplementary wefts. Thus although they look like traces on the surface of the scarf, these *tz'ib* are actually built up – along with the surface itself – from threads, through their cumulative displacement. In the technique of brocading, weaving and writing become one and the same.

Weaving text

I turn finally to the kinds of texts that have come down to us within the Western tradition. The idea of the text as a woven tapestry may seem strange to modern readers accustomed to seeing letters and words in print. For reasons that will become apparent in the next chapter, they are

Figure 2.16 Quiché Maya woven scarf. Photograph: Barbara and Dennis Tedlock, reproduced with their permission.

more likely to treat the metaphor in a much looser sense, referring to the 'weaving' of the narrative that the text relates, rather than of the actual lines of writing on the page. But it would have seemed perfectly natural to the citizens of ancient Greece and Rome when, thanks to the introduction of papyrus from Egypt and the ink-filled reed-pen as an instrument of writing, they first began to employ the cursive script. Until then, letters could only be scratched or incised on hard surfaces with short, separate strokes (recall that the Old English *writan* referred specifically to incision of this kind). With pen on papyrus, however, it was possible to produce a continuous line. The subsequent introduction of the more durable and smooth-surfaced parchment or vellum, in the fourth and fifth centuries AD, allowed this line, now made with a quill-pen, to flow even more freely. Figure 2.17 shows an example of a script from the ninth century: it comes from a charter written by one Walto, notary to the father of the Frankish emperor Charles the Fat.

One has only to glance at this example to appreciate the force of the analogy between writing and weaving. Just as the weaver's shuttle moves back and forth as it lays down the weft, so the writer's pen moves up and down, leaving a trail of ink behind it. But this trail, the letter-line, is no

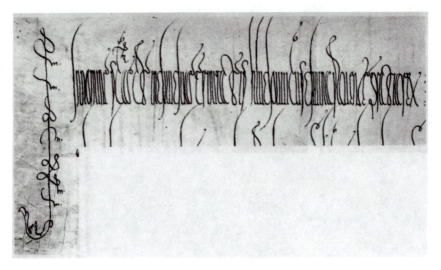

Figure 2.17 Ninth-century charter script. Reproduced from Gray (1971: 19). By permission of Oxford University Press.

more the same as the line of text than is the line on a tapestry the same as the lines of its constituent threads. As with the woven tapestry, when we look for the text-line we do not find it. It exists neither as a visible trace nor as a thread. Rather, it emerges through the progressive lengthwise displacement of the letter-line as it oscillates up and down within a determinate 'band-width' (though with many trailing ends), in much the same way that the woven stripe is built up through the longitudinal displacement of the weft as it oscillates transversely between selected warp-lines. In the fifteenth-century Gothic book-hand known as 'textura', this parallel was drawn quite explicitly: the hand was so called on account of the resemblance of a page of writing to the texture of a woven blanket. Just as the letter-line had its figurative source in the weaver's yarn, so – as we shall see in Chapter 6 – the prototype for the straight, ruled lines of the manuscript, between which the letters were arrayed, lay in the warp strings stretched taut on the loom. Originally these ruled lines were scored, and – as with warp-lines – were faint or invisible. When Gutenberg adopted textura for his first printed type, the lines disappeared altogether. What had begun with the interweaving of warp and weft ended with the impression of preformed letter-shapes, pre-arranged in rows, upon a pre-prepared surface (Figure 2.18). From that point on, the text was no longer woven but assembled, pieced together from discrete graphic elements. The transformation was complete. In the next chapter we shall explore some of its consequences.

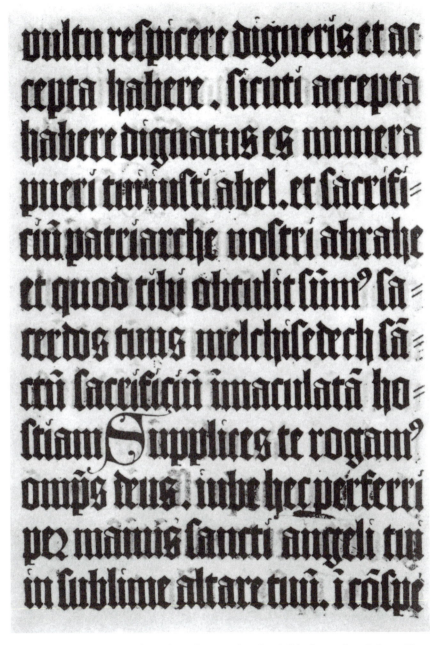

Figure 2.18 Textura type by Johan Sensenschmidt, 1481. Reproduced from Kapr (1983: 80).

3   Up, across and along

The trace and the connector

> Whilst a man is free – cried the Corporal, giving a flourish with his stick thus –

Here is the line traced in the air by the Corporal, as depicted in Laurence Sterne's narrative of 1762, *The Life and Opinions of Tristram Shandy, Gentleman*:

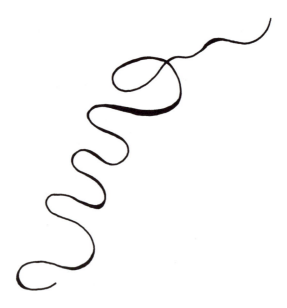

Like any other gesture, the Corporal's flourish embodies a certain duration. The line to which it gives rise is, therefore, intrinsically dynamic and temporal. When, pen in hand, Sterne recreated the flourish on the page, his gesture left an enduring trace that we can still read (Sterne 1978: 743). The artist Paul Klee described this kind of line as the most active and authentic.

Whether traced in the air or on paper, whether by the tip of th
pen, it arises from the movement of a point that – just as t
intended – is free to go where it will, for movement's sake. As K
ably put it, the line that develops freely, and in its own time, 'goe
walk' (1961: 105). And in reading it, the eyes follow the same path
hand in drawing it.

Another kind of line, however, is in a hurry. It wants to get from one
location to another, and then to another, but has little time to do so. The
appearance of this line, says Klee, is 'more like a series of appointments than
a walk'. It goes from point to point, in sequence, as quickly as possible, and
in principle in no time at all, for every successive destination is already fixed
prior to setting out, and each segment of the line is pre-determined by the
points it connects. Whereas the active line on a walk is dynamic, the line that
connects adjacent points in series is, according to Klee, 'the quintessence of
the static' (ibid.: 109). If the former takes us on a journey that has no obvious
beginning or end, the latter presents us with an array of interconnected
destinations that can, as on a route-map, be viewed all at once.

Retracing the Corporal's stick-waving gesture, Sterne evidently took his
line for a walk. But now let me suggest a simple experiment. Take this line,
and cut it up into short segments of roughly equal length. Now imagine that
every segment could be wound up like a thread, and packed into the confines
of a spot located around the mid-point of the original segment. The result
would be a scatter of dots, as shown below:

I have in fact drawn each dot by hand. To do this I had to bring the tip
of my pencil into contact with the paper at a pre-determined point, and

then to jiggle it about on that point so as to form the dot. All the energy, and all the movement, was focused there – almost as if I were drilling a hole. In the spaces between the dots, however, there remains no trace of movement. Although the dots are located on the path of the original gesture they are not connected by its trace, since what is left of the trace and of the movement that gave rise to it is wound up in the dots. Each appears as an isolated and compact moment, broken off from those preceding and following. To be sure, in order to proceed from the execution of one dot to the next I had to lift my pencil and shift my hand a little, before returning the tip to the paper surface. But this transverse movement plays no part in the process of inscription itself which, as we have seen, is wholly confined to drawing the dots. Had I wished, I could have withdrawn my hand altogether from the work and laid down my pencil, only to resume the task at a later time.

Where then, in this scatter of dots, is the line? It can only exist as a chain of connections between fixed points. To recover the original trajectory of the Corporal's stick, we have to *join them up*. This I have done below:

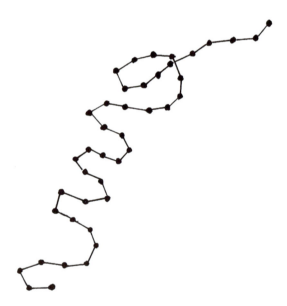

Although the connecting lines have to be executed in a determinate sequence, the pattern they eventually form – much as in a child's join-the-dots puzzle – is already given as a virtual object from the outset. To complete the pattern is not to take a line for a walk but rather to engage in a process of construction or assembly, in which every linear segment serves as a joint, welding together the elements of the pattern into a totality of a higher order. Once the construction is complete there is nowhere further for the line to go. What we see is no longer the *trace of a gesture* but an assembly of *point-to-point connectors*. The composition stands as a finished object, an artefact. Its constituent lines join things up, but they do not grow or develop.

This distinction between the *walk* and the *assembly* is the key to my argument in this chapter. I aim to show how the line, in the course of its history, has been gradually shorn of the movement that gave rise to it. Once the trace of a continuous gesture, the line has been fragmented – under the sway of modernity – into a succession of points or dots. This fragmentation, as I shall explain, has taken place in the related fields of *travel*, where wayfaring is replaced by destination-oriented transport, *mapping*, where the drawn sketch is replaced by the route-plan, and *textuality*, where storytelling is replaced by the pre-composed plot. It has also transformed our understanding of *place*: once a knot tied from multiple and interlaced strands of movement and growth, it now figures as a node in a static network of connectors. To an ever-increasing extent, people in modern metropolitan societies find themselves in environments built as assemblies of connected elements. Yet in practice they continue to thread their own ways through these environments, tracing paths as they go. I suggest that to understand how people do not just occupy but *inhabit* the environments in which they dwell, we might do better to revert from the paradigm of the assembly to that of the walk.

Trails and routes

In his contemplation on the Arctic, *Playing Dead* (1989), the Canadian writer Rudy Wiebe compares native Inuit understandings of movement and travel over land or sea ice with those of the Royal Navy in its search for the elusive North-West Passage to the Orient. For the Inuit, *as soon as a person moves he becomes a line*. To hunt for an animal, or to find another human being who may be lost, you lay one line of tracks through the expanse, looking for signs of another line that might lead you to your quarry. Thus the entire country is perceived as a mesh of interweaving lines rather than a continuous surface.[1] The British, however, 'accustomed to the fluid, trackless seas, moved in terms of area' (ibid.: 16). The ship, supplied for the voyage before setting sail, was conceived by its naval commanders as a mobile vessel that would carry its crew across the seas on a course determined by the latitude and longitude of successive points *en route* to the intended destination. In brief, whereas the Inuit moved through the world *along* paths of travel, the British sailed *across* what they saw as the surface of the globe. Both kinds of movement, along and across, may be described by lines, but they are lines of fundamentally different kinds. The line that goes along has, in Klee's terms, gone out for a walk. The line that goes across, by contrast, is a connector, linking a series of points arrayed in two-dimensional space. In what follows I shall link this difference to one between two modalities of travel that I shall call, respectively, *wayfaring* and *transport*.

The wayfarer is continually on the move. More strictly, he is his movement. As with the Inuit in the example presented above, the wayfarer is instantiated in the world as a line of travel. Claudio Aporta, who carried out ethnographic fieldwork in the community of Igloolik, reports that for its Inuit inhabitants 'travelling . . . was not a transitional activity between one place and another, but a way of being . . . The act of travelling from or to a particular location plays a part in defining who the traveller is' (Aporta 2004: 13). The traveller and his line are, in this case, one and the same. It is a line that advances from the tip as he presses on in an ongoing process of growth and development, or of self-renewal. An example from the other side of the world will help to reinforce the point. Batek women from Pahang, Malaysia, according to Tuck Po Lye (1997: 159), say that the roots of the wild tubers they collect for food 'walk' as humans and other animals do. If this idea seems odd to us, it is only because we are inclined to reduce the activity of walking to the mechanics of locomotion, as though the walker were a passenger in his own body and carried by his legs from point to point. For the Batek, however, walking is a matter of laying a trail as one goes along. And this is exactly what roots do as they issue forth along lines of growth, threading their ways through the soil. The wayfarer's trail, and the trailing root, are phenomena of the same kind. Both exemplify Klee's dictum that it is the line itself that 'goes out for a walk'.

As he proceeds, however, the wayfarer has to sustain himself, both perceptually and materially, through an active engagement with the country that opens up along his path. 'Walking on a trail', as Lye observes, 'the Batek are actively monitoring it', looking out for useful plant materials to gather, and for the spoors and traces of animals (Lye 2004: 64). Likewise among the Foi of Papua New Guinea, according to James Weiner, journeying on foot 'is never merely a matter of getting from one point to another'. Always on the lookout for fruiting trees, quality rattan or edible insect larvae, the Foi *work* their paths, turning them into 'conduits of inscribed activity' (Weiner 1991: 38). To outsiders these paths, unless well worn, may be barely perceptible. In dense tropical forest, vegetation can close up behind the traveller as if he had never been. On the open tundra or sea ice of the Arctic, traces may be quickly buried under falling or blowing snow. When the ice melts and Inuit take to their kayaks or whaling boats, the trails they leave are instantly erased in the watery medium. Yet however faint or ephemeral their traces on land and water, these trails remain etched in the memories of those who follow them (Aporta 2004: 15). For the Inuit, as Aporta observes, 'life happens while travelling. Other travellers are met, children are born, and hunting, fishing and other subsistence activities are performed' (ibid.: 13).

Even seafarers make their way along invisible lines. Ever attentive to wind and weather, to swell and tide, to the flight of birds and a host of other signs, the experienced mariner can guide his ship through the deepest of waters without having resort to charts or instruments of any kind. Samuel Johnson illustrated the third of his seventeen senses of the word 'line ('a thread extended to direct any operations'), to which I referred in the last chapter, with a verse from the historical poem 'Annus Mirabilis' (1666) by John

Dryden, in which the poet interrupts a vivid account of a battle between the English and Dutch fleets with a section on the history of shipping and navigation:

> The Ebbs of Tydes, and their mysterious flow,
> We, as Arts Elements shall understand:
> And as by Line upon the Ocean go,
> Whose paths shall be as familiar as the Land.
>   (Dryden 1958: 81)[2]

What Dryden is celebrating here is the unparalleled capacity of English seafarers to find their way in the open sea, rather than having to hug the land as their predecessors did.

But while there is a certain parallel in this regard between wayfaring and seafaring, there is a world of difference between the experience of the mariner for whom seafaring is a way of life, and the perspective of the naval high command, in my earlier example, whose aim was to link home ports with dominions overseas, facilitating the global expansion of trade, settlement and empire. The key distinction, if you will, is between lines of seafaring and of shipping, or between life *at* sea and routeing *across* it. Driven by imperial ambition, the Royal Navy sought to dispatch its ships towards destinations fixed within a global system of co-ordinates, sidelining traditional seafaring skills in favour of an instrumental calculus of point-to-point navigation. From the command perspective the ship was seen not as an organ of seafaring but as a vehicle of transport.

Unlike wayfaring or seafaring, transport is destination-oriented. It is not so much a development *along* a way of life as a carrying *across*, from location to location, of people and goods in such a way as to leave their basic natures unaffected. Even the wayfarer, of course, goes from place to place, as does the mariner from harbour to harbour. He must periodically pause to rest, and may even return repeatedly to the same abode or haven to do so. Each pause, however, is a moment of tension that – like holding one's breath – becomes ever more intense and less sustainable the longer it lasts. Indeed the wayfarer or seafarer has no final destination, for wherever he is, and so long as life goes on, there is somewhere further he can go. For the transported traveller and his baggage, by contrast, every destination is a terminus, every port a point of re-entry into a world from which he has been temporarily exiled whilst in transit. This point marks a moment not of tension but of completion. Here is a further example to illustrate the contrast, which also shows how the two modalities of travel may operate side by side in a delicate balance.

Orochon people of north-central Sakhalin, in the Russian Far East, draw a livelihood from hunting wild reindeer. Yet they ride to the hunt on the saddled backs of domestic animals of the same species, and collect their kills by means of reindeer-drawn sledges. The path of the saddle-back rider, according to anthropologist Heonik Kwon, is 'visceral in shape, full of sharp turns and detours'. As they go on their way, hunters are ever attentive to the landscape that unfolds along the path, and to its living animal inhabitants. Here and there, animals may be killed. But every kill is left where it lies, to be retrieved later, while the path itself meanders on, eventually winding back at camp. When however the hunter subsequently goes to collect his kill, he drives his sledge directly to the site where the carcass has been cached. The sledge path, Kwon reports, 'is approximately a straight line, the shortest distance between the camp and the destination' (1998: 118). Not only is the sledge path clearly distinguished from the saddle path: the two paths depart from opposite sides of the camp and never intersect. It is along the saddle path that life is lived: it has no beginning or ending but carries on indefinitely. This path is a line of wayfaring. The sledge path, by contrast, is a line of transport. It has a starting point and an end point, and connects the two. On the sledge the body of the dead animal is carried from one site, where it was killed, to another, where it will be distributed and consumed. Eventually, too, the sledge will carry the body of the hunter, when he dies, to his final burial place in the forest.

As this example suggests, it is not merely the harnessing of sources of energy beyond the human body that turns wayfaring into transport. The Orochon hunter does not cease to be a wayfarer when he mounts his riding deer, nor does the European mariner cease to be a seafarer when he hoists a sail. Although the former relies on animal power, and the latter on the wind, in both cases the traveller's movement – his orientation and pace – is continually responsive to his perceptual monitoring of the environment that is revealed along the way. He watches, listens and feels as he goes, his entire being alert to the countless cues that, at every moment, prompt the slightest adjustments to his bearing. Today the wayfarer may even drive a machine, such as a motor-bike, all-terrain vehicle or snowmobile, as Saami herdsmen do in gathering their reindeer. In the Australian Western Desert Aboriginal people have turned the car into an organ of wayfaring. Out in the bush, as Diana Young explains, cars are driven *gesturally*. The driver manoeuvres skilfully around rocks, tree stumps and rabbit holes, leaving tyre tracks that are understood and interpreted in just the same way as the tracks of those travelling on foot. Thus 'the marks a vehicle's passage makes on the land are conceived as the gestures of the driver' (Young 2001: 45).

Transport, then, is distinguished not by the employment of mechanical means but by the dissolution of the intimate bond that, in wayfaring, couples locomotion and perception. The transported traveller becomes a passenger, who does not himself move but is rather *moved* from place to place. The sights, sounds and feelings that accost him during the passage have absolutely no bearing on the motion that carries him forth. For the soldier on parade, eyes turned to the right as his legs beat out an oscillation of metronomic regularity, marching is transport. Comparing marching with peripatetic walking, historical geographer Kenneth Olwig argues that marching presupposes an 'open', placeless space – a *utopia*. It obliterates the places it leaves behind. Peripatetic walking, by contrast, is *topian*. It 'does not parade us linearly to the steady beat of its drum but, like the spiral of a harmonic progression, allows us to return to, and regenerate, the places that give us sustenance' (Olwig 2002: 23). As a form of transport on foot, marching implies a sense of progress that goes not around from place to place but onwards *from stage to stage* (ibid.: 41–2). This same sense of progress, which came into regular use in the course of the seventeenth century, also applied to travel by stage-coach. While on the road the traveller, cocooned in his carriage, would draw for subsistence on his own supplies and do all he could to shield himself from direct contact with passers-by or their places of abode. For he would undertake the journey not for its own sake, or for the experience it might afford, but for the sole purpose of witnessing the sights to be seen at his destination (Wallace 1993: 39). A tour would consist of a series of such destinations. Only upon arrival at each stop, and when his means of transport come to a halt, does the tourist begin to move.

Thus the very places where the wayfarer pauses for rest are, for the transported passenger, sites of activity. But this activity, confined within a place, is all concentrated on one spot. In between sites he barely skims the surface of the world, if not skipping it entirely, leaving no trace of having passed by or even any recollection of the journey. Indeed the tourist may be advised to expunge from memory the experience of getting there, however arduous or eventful it may have been, lest it should bias or detract from the appreciation of what he has come to see. In effect, the practice of transport converts every trail into the equivalent of a dotted line. Just as in drawing the dotted line I lower my pencil on to the paper and jiggle its tip on the spot, so the tourist alights at each destination on his itinerary and casts around from where he stands, before taking off for the next. The lines that link successive destinations, like those that join the dots, are not traces of movement but point-to-point connectors. These are the lines of transport. They differ from lines of wayfaring in precisely the same way that the connector differs from the gestural trace. They are not trails but routes.

Drawing freehand, I take my line for a walk. Likewise the wayfarer, in his perambulations, lays a trail on the ground in the form of footprints, paths and tracks. Writing of the Walbiri, an Aboriginal people of the Australian Central Desert, Roy Wagner notes that 'the life of a person is the sum of his tracks, the total inscription of his movements, something that can be traced out along the ground' (Wagner 1986: 21). It is no different when travelling by car, as Young found among neighbouring Pitjantjatjara people. Hunters are known and recognized by their roads, and the history of a road would be told only as people '*went along*' (Young 2001: 46, original emphasis). To go along, however, is to thread one's way *through* the world rather than routeing from point to point *across* its surface. Indeed for the wayfarer the world, as such, has no surface. Of course he encounters surfaces of diverse kinds – of solid ground, water, vegetation and so on. Indeed it is largely thanks to the way these surfaces respond to light, sound and the pressure of touch that he perceives the world in the way he does. They are surfaces, however, *in* the world, not *of* it (Ingold 2000: 241). And woven into their very texture, and thence into the country itself, are the lines of growth and movement of its inhabitants. Every such line is tantamount to a way of life.

Australian Aboriginal people, writes Bruce Chatwin, imagine their country not as a surface area that can be divided into blocks but as an 'interlocking network' of lines or 'ways through'. 'All our words for "country"', Chatwin's Aboriginal interlocutor told him, 'are the same as the words for "line"' (Chatwin 1987: 62). These are the lines along which ancestral beings sang the world into existence in the Dreaming, and they are retraced in the comings and goings, as well as the singing and storytelling, of their contemporary reincarnations. Taken together, they form a tangle of interwoven and complexly knotted strings. But is this tangle really a *network*, as Chatwin claims? It is indeed something like a net in its original sense of an open-work fabric of entwined threads or cords. It was in this sense, for example, that Gottfried Semper – in his essay of 1860 to which I referred in the last chapter – wrote of the 'invention of the network' among primitive people who made and used it for fishing and hunting (Semper 1989: 218). But through its metaphorical extension to the realms of modern transport and communications, and especially information technology, the meaning of 'the net' has changed. We are now more inclined to think of it as a complex of interconnected points than of interwoven lines. For this reason I find Chatwin's characterization of Aboriginal country slightly misleading. It is more a *meshwork* than a network.

I borrow the term 'meshwork' from the philosopher Henri Lefebvre, who speaks of 'the reticular patterns left by animals, both wild and domestic, and by people (in and around the houses of village or small town, as in the town's immediate environs)', whose movements weave an environment that is more 'archi-textural' than architectural (Lefebvre 1991: 117–18). Benjamin Orlove, in his study of life and land around Lake Titicaca in the Peruvian Andes, offers a vivid depiction of such an archi-textural meshwork – a 'web of lines on the land' that covers the altiplano. Most of these lines, Orlove reports,

> are barely a meter wide, beaten or trodden by the feet of animals and men and women, and also of children, who, by the ages of three or four, trot along uncomplainingly to keep up with the adults, whether for a short walk to a relative's house or a field, or for half a day's hike to a distant pasture or market. Some of the lines are quite literally drawn in the earth by villagers working with picks and shovels. A few of them are broader, as much as five meters wide, and receive the passage of an occasional car or truck.
>
> (Orlove 2002: 210)

The lines of a network, in its contemporary sense, join the dots. They are connectors. However, the lines that Orlove describes in this passage form a meshwork of interwoven trails rather than a network of intersecting routes. The lines of the meshwork are the trails *along* which life is lived. And as I show schematically in Figure 3.1, it is in the entanglement of lines, not in the connecting of points, that the mesh is constituted.

Wayfaring, I believe, is the most fundamental mode by which living beings, both human and non-human, inhabit the earth. By habitation I do not mean taking one's place in a world that has been prepared in advance for the populations that arrive to reside there. The inhabitant is rather one who participates from within in the very process of the world's continual coming into being and who, in laying a trail of life, contributes to its weave and texture. These lines are typically winding and irregular, yet comprehensively entangled into a close-knit tissue. 'In describing their past lives', writes anthropologist Renato Rosaldo of the Ilongot people of the Philippines, 'Ilongots speak of walking on paths that meander, like the courses of the streams they follow, in ways that cannot be foreseen' (Rosaldo 1993: 257). They have no ultimate destination, no final point with which they are seeking to link up. This is not to deny that inhabitants also engage in practices of transport, as the example of Orochon reindeer hunters shows. But the lines of transport, in this and comparable cases, link points in a world constituted by the movements of wayfaring. The Orochon sledge path is held within the mesh, and never crosses the ways of life traced by the saddle.

From time to time in the course of history, however, imperial powers have sought to occupy the inhabited world, throwing a network of connections across what appears, in their eyes, to be not a tissue of trails but a blank surface. These connections are lines of occupation. They facilitate the outward passage of personnel and equipment to sites of settlement and extraction, and the return of the riches drawn therefrom. Unlike paths formed through the practices of wayfaring, such lines are surveyed and built in advance of the traffic that comes to pass up and down them. They are typically straight and regular, and intersect only at nodal points of power. Drawn cross-country, they are inclined to ride roughshod over the lines of habitation that are woven into it, cutting them as, for example, a trunk road, railway or pipeline cuts the byways frequented by humans and animals in the vicinity through which it passes (see Figure 3.2). But lines of occupation do not only connect. They also divide, cutting the occupied surface into territorial blocks. These frontier lines, too, built to restrict movement rather than to facilitate it, can seriously disrupt the lives of inhabitants whose trails they happen to cross. They are lines, as the novelist Georges Perec has observed, 'for which millions of people have died' (cited in Paasi 2004: 176).

To sum up so far: I have established a contrast between two modalities of travel, namely wayfaring and transport. Like the line that goes out for a walk, the path of the wayfarer wends hither and thither, and may even pause here and there before moving on. But it has no beginning or end. While on the trail the wayfarer is always somewhere, yet every 'somewhere' is on the way to somewhere else. The inhabited world is a reticulate meshwork of

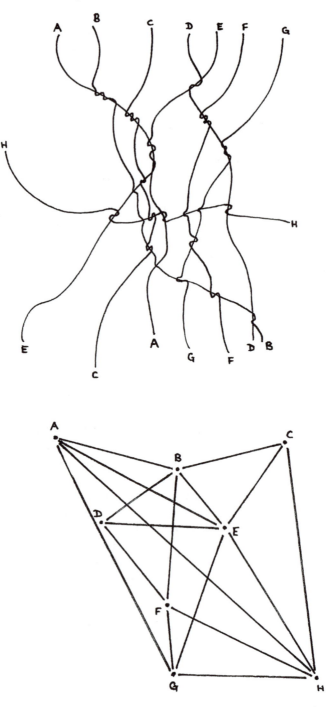

Figure 3.1 The meshwork of entangled lines (above) and the network of connected points (below).

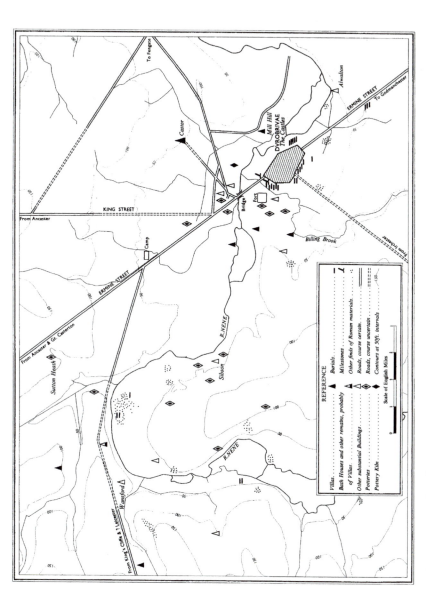

Figure 3.2 Lines of occupation. Roads converging on the town of Durobrivae, one of the principal industrial centres during the Roman occupation of Britain. Reproduced from the Ordnance Survey *Map of Roman Britain* (third edition), 1956, by permission of Ordnance Survey on behalf of HMSO. © Crown Copyright 2006. Ordnance Survey Licence Number 100014649.

such trails, which is continually being woven as life goes on along them. Transport, by contrast, is tied to specific locations. Every move serves the purpose of relocating persons and their effects, and is oriented to a specific destination. The traveller who departs from one location and arrives at another is, in between, nowhere at all. Taken together, the lines of transport form a network of point-to-point connections. In the colonial project of occupation, this network, once an undercurrent to life and constrained by its ways, becomes ascendant, spreading across the territory and overriding the tangled trails of inhabitants. I shall now go on to show how the distinction between the walk and the connector underlies a fundamental difference not only in the dynamics of movement but also in the integration of knowledge. I begin with a discussion of the ways in which lines may be drawn on maps.

Mapping and knowing

The vast majority of maps that have ever been drawn by human beings have scarcely survived the immediate contexts of their production. These are usually contexts of storytelling in which people describe the journeys they have made, or that have been made by characters of legend or myth, often with the purpose of providing directions so that others can follow along the same paths. Retracing their steps in narrative, storytellers may also gesture with their hands and fingers, and these gestures may in turn give rise to lines. For the most part such lines are entirely ephemeral, consisting of traces either scratched in sand, mud or snow, using the fingers or a simple tool, or sketched on any readily available surface such as bark or paper, or even the back of the hand. Usually they are no sooner made than rubbed out, washed off, or scrunched up and thrown away (Wood 1993: 83). You may of course keep the sketch map I have drawn to help you find your way to my house, but only for so long as it takes you to arrive there, since it has little use except for that particular journey which, once made, you are unlikely to forget. The map does not tell you where things are, allowing you to navigate from any spatial location you choose to any other. Rather, the lines on the sketch map are formed through the gestural re-enactment of journeys *actually made*, to and from places that are already known for their histories of previous com- ings and goings. The joins, splits and intersections of these lines indicate which paths to follow, and which can lead you astray, depending on where you want to go. They are lines of movement. In effect, the 'walk' of the line retraces your own 'walk' through the terrain.

For this reason sketch maps are not generally surrounded by frames or borders (Belyea 1996: 6). The map makes no claim to represent a certain territory, or to mark the spatial locations of features included within its frontiers. What count are the lines, not the spaces around them. Just as the country through which the wayfarer passes is composed of the meshwork of paths of travel, so the sketch map consists – no more and no less – of the lines that make it up. They are drawn *along*, in the evolution of a gesture, rather than *across* the surfaces on which they are traced. Indeed in principle the lines of a sketch map need not be traced on any surface at all. The gesturing hand can as well weave as draw, creating something more like a cat's cradle than a diagram. In the past, Australian Aboriginal people used string figures to describe the 'strings' or tracks of ancestral Dreamings (Rose 2000: 52), while Micronesian seafarers used coconut-leaf ribs to map the intersecting courses of ocean swells (Turnbull 1991: 24; see Ingold 2000: 241). Modern cartographic maps, however, are quite different. Such maps always have borders separating the space inside, which is part of the map, from the space outside, which is not. Of course there are many lines on the map, representing such things as roads and railways, as well as administrative boundaries. But these lines, drawn across the surface of the cartographic map, signify occupation, not habitation. They betoken as appropriation of the space surrounding the points that the lines connect or – if they are frontier lines – that they enclose.

Nothing better illustrates this difference between the lines of the sketch map and those of the cartographic map than our habit of drawing *on* maps of each kind (Orlove 1993: 29–30). To draw on a sketch map is merely to add the trace of one further gesture to the traces of previous ones. Such a map may be the conversational product of many hands, in which participants take turns to add lines as they describe their various journeys. The map grows line by line as the conversation proceeds, and there is no point at which it can ever be said to be truly complete. For in every intervention, as Barbara Belyea notes, 'the gesture becomes part of the map' (1996: 11). To draw on a carto-graphic map, however, is quite another matter. The marine navigator may plot his course on a chart, using a ruler and pencil, but the ruled line forms no part of the chart and should be rubbed out once the voyage is completed. Were I, on the other hand, to take a pen and – while recounting the story of a trip – to retrace in ink my path across the surface of the map, I would be judged to have committed an offence tantamount to writing all over the printed text of a book! I shall return below to the parallel between the map and the book, for the line of writing has – as I shall show – undergone a historical transformation precisely akin to that of the drawn line on the map. My present point is that the gestural trace, or the line that has gone out for a walk, has no business in the discipline of cartography. Far from becoming a part of the map, it is considered an excrescence that should be removed (Ingold 2000: 234). For the cartographic line is not the trace of a gesture, nor does the eye, in reading it, follow the line as it would follow a gesture. These lines are not traces but connectors.

Michel de Certeau has shown how the maps of medieval times, which were really illustrated stories telling of journeys made and of memorable encounters along the way, were gradually supplanted during the early history of modernity by spatial representations of the earth's surface (Certeau 1984: 120–1). In this process the original tales were broken into iconic fragments that, in turn, were reduced to mere decorative embellishments included, alongside place-names, among the contents of particular sites. The fragmentation of the narrative, and the compression of each piece within the confines of a marked location, strikingly parallel the impact of destination-oriented transport on earlier practices of wayfaring. In mapping as in travel, the trail left as the trace of a gesture is converted into the equivalent of a dotted line. Drawing a line on a cartographic map is like joining the dots. Such lines, as on a marine navigation chart or an air traffic route-map, form a network of point-to-point connections. They enable the prospective traveller to assemble a route-plan, in the form of a chain of connections, and thereby *virtually* to reach his destination even before setting out. As a cognitive artefact or assembly, the plan pre-exists its enactment 'on the ground'.

The same principle applies in the making of the map itself. To chart the course of a river, for example, you would use survey data to plot locations on the banks at a series of points. Marking each point with a dot or cross, you would then connect them up. Figure 3.3 is taken from a map of the stream Skælbækken, which forms part of the frontier between Germany and Denmark, included in a 1920 frontier survey atlas. On the map the course of the stream is reconstructed as two chains of connected points, roughly parallel, corresponding to its banks. The course traced by Skælbækken's waters, as they flow *along* towards the sea, has become a double dividing line that cuts *across* the plane of the map, marking a hard-and-fast international

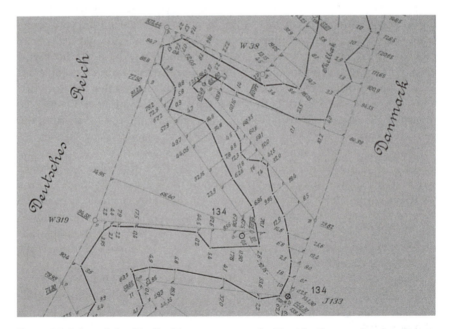

Figure 3.3 Map of the Skælbækken stream on the Danish–German border. Reproduced by permission of Sonderjyllands Statsamt from the *Grænseatlas* of 1920.

boundary. Whereas on the map the intermediate space indicates a relation between the territories on either side, in the world – as Gilles Deleuze and Félix Guattari say – this midst is precisely 'where things take on speed'. The real stream carries on in a direction orthogonal to the territorial relation, 'gnawing away at its two banks and picking up speed in the middle' (Deleuze and Guattari 1983: 58).

Another example comes from Charles Goodwin's (1994) account of the map-making practices of archaeologists. In this case the map is of a profile – that is, of a vertical section cut through the earth at a site of excavation. In the following extract, Goodwin describes the procedure involved:

> To demarcate what the archaeologist believes are two different layers of dirt, a line is drawn between them with a trowel. The line and the ground surface above it are then transferred to a piece of graph paper. This is a task that involves two people. One measures the length and depth co-ordinates of the points to be mapped, using a ruler and tape measure. He or she reports the measurements as pairs of numbers, such as 'At forty, plus eleven point five' . . . A second archaeologist transfers the numbers provided by the measurer to a piece of graph paper. After plotting a set of points, he or she makes the map by drawing the lines between them.
>
> (Goodwin 1994: 612)

The line drawn with a trowel in the earth, just like that etched by a stream in the landscape, is of course the trace of a movement. But the line on graph paper is a chain of point-to-point connections (Figure 3.4). These lines are distinguished precisely as Laurence Sterne's tracing of the Corporal's flourish, with which I began, is distinguished from my 'join the dots' reconstruction of it. Both kinds of line embody in their formation a certain way of knowing. But these ways, as I shall now show, are fundamentally different.

When, drawing a sketch map for a friend, I take my line for a walk, I retrace in gesture the walk that I made in the countryside and that was originally traced out as a trail along the ground. Telling the story of the journey as I draw, I weave a narrative thread that wanders from topic to topic, just as in my walk I wandered from place to place. This story recounts just one chapter in the never-ending journey that is life itself, and it is through this journey – with all its twists and turns – that we grow into a knowledge of the world about us. As James Gibson argued, in laying out his ecological psychology, we perceive the world along a 'path of observation' (1979: 197). Proceeding on our way things fall into and out of sight, as new vistas open up and others are closed off. By way of these modulations in the array of reflected light reaching the eyes, the structure of our environment is progressively disclosed. It is no different, in principle, with the senses of touch and hearing, for together with vision these are but aspects of a total system of bodily orientation. Thus the knowledge we have of our surroundings is

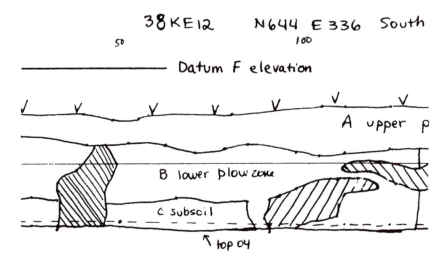

Figure 3.4 Profile map of layers of dirt exposed on the side of a square pit dug in the excavation of an archaeological site. Reproduced from Goodwin (1994: 611). Charles Goodwin, 'Professional Vision', *American Anthropologist*, Vol. 96, No. 3: 606–633. © 1994, American Anthropological Association. Used by permission. All rights reserved.

forged in the very course of our moving through them, in the passage from place to place and the changing horizons along the way (Ingold 2000: 227). As wayfarers we experience what Robin Jarvis (1997: 69) has called a 'progressional ordering of reality', or the integration of knowledge *along* a path of travel.

That is not, however, how the matter is understood within the dominant framework of modern thought. It is rather supposed that knowledge is assembled by joining up, into a complete picture, observations taken from a number of fixed points. As we have seen, this is how the surveyor proceeds in the construction of a cartographic map. Many geographers and psychologists have argued that we are all surveyors in our everyday lives, and that we use our bodies, as the surveyor uses his instruments, to obtain data from multiple points of observation that are then passed to the mind, and from which it assembles a comprehensive representation of the world – the so-called cognitive map. 'The problem of perception', writes psychologist Keith Oatley, is to understand the processes 'that allow us to create in our minds a representation . . . of what it is like out there, given a fragmentary, changing two-dimensional set of receptor excitations' (Oatley 1978: 167). According to this view, knowledge is integrated not by going *along* but by building *up*, that is by fitting these site-specific fragments into structures of progressively greater inclusiveness. In effect the surveyor's walk (if indeed he *does* walk, rather than take a vehicle) is broken up and reduced to the geographical counterpart of the dotted line. Just as in drawing the dotted line the pencil tip has to be carried across from one point to the next, so to obtain his data the surveyor has to be transported from site to site. But if the transverse movements of the hand, in the former case, are ancillary to the process of inscription, so those of the surveyor, in the latter, are ancillary to the process of observation. Serving merely to relocate the agent and his equipment – or the mind and its body – from one stationary locus of observation to another, they play no part in the integration of the information obtained.

I have argued that it is fundamentally through the practices of wayfaring that beings inhabit the world. By the same token, the ways of knowing of inhabitants go along, and not up. Or in a word, inhabitant knowledge – as I shall call it – is *alongly* integrated. Consider, for example, the knowledge of place-names. Steven Feld describes how, for the Kaluli of Papua New Guinea, every place lies on a path (*tok*), so that the naming of places is always a part of a remembrance, in speech or song, of travelling the *tok* along which they lie (Feld 1996: 103). Among the Navajo of the south-western United States, according to Klara Kelley and Harris Francis (2005), place-names that index specific landmarks are told in sequence to form stories or 'verbal maps' describing lines of travel for people to follow. These however were guidelines rather than actual trails on the ground, for the latter, responsive to variations in the distribution of natural resources and other contingencies, 'would wind back and forth along the guideline in the verbal map' (ibid.: 99). In a study of the Saami of the district of Inari, in north-eastern Finland, Nuccio Mazzullo (2005: 173) shows how names are assigned, recalled or invoked in the course of undertaking particular journeys, or as they are recounted in narrative. Each name draws its meaning from this narrative context. Thus along a certain river there is a name for every twist and bend, and for every pool and rapids. The name, however, far from being affixed to a specific location on the river, denotes a moment in the journey upstream – a journey habitually made by those who live along its banks. To list these names is to tell a story of the entire journey.

Such names, however, mean nothing on their own, and rarely appear on cartographic maps. For surveying is a mode of occupation, not habitation. The names the surveyor seeks are indexed to locations in terms of their distinctive features, but without regard to how one arrives there. These named locations are the components that are then assembled into a larger totality. Occupant knowledge, in short, is *upwardly* integrated. And this finally brings us to the crux of the difference between these two knowledge systems, of habitation and occupation respectively. In the first, a way of knowing is itself a path of movement through the world: the wayfarer literally 'knows as he goes' (Ingold 2000: 229–30), along a line of travel. The second, by contrast, is founded upon a categorical distinction between the mechanics of movement and the formation of knowledge, or between locomotion and cognition. Whereas the former cuts from point to point *across* the world, the latter builds *up*, from the array of points and the materials collected therefrom, into an integrated assembly.

Storylines and plots

I have suggested that drawing a line on a sketch map is much like telling a story. Indeed the two commonly proceed in tandem as complementary strands of one and the same performance. Thus the storyline goes *along*, as does the line on the map. The things of which the story tells, let us say, do not so much exist as occur; each is a moment of ongoing activity. These things, in a word, are not objects but topics. Lying at the confluence of actions and responses, every topic is identified by its relations to the things that paved the way for it, that presently concur with it and that follow it into the world. Here the meaning of the 'relation' has to be understood quite literally, not as a connection between pre-located entities but as a path traced through the terrain of lived experience. Far from connecting points in a network, every relation is one line in a meshwork of interwoven trails. To tell a story, then, is to *relate*, in narrative, the occurrences of the past, retracing a path through the world that others, recursively picking up the threads of past lives, can follow in the process of spinning out their own. But rather as in looping or knitting, the thread being spun now and the thread picked up from the past are both of the same yarn. There is no point at which the story ends and life begins. Thus:

In a recent conference, the Russian anthropologist Natalia Novikova introduced a paper on the meaning of self-determination for the Khanty people of western Siberia by explaining how old Khanty storytellers would keep going in the evenings until everyone else was asleep, so that no one would ever know how their stories really finished (Novikova 2002: 83). The Khanty word usually translated as 'story' literally means a *way* – not in the sense of a prescribed code of conduct, sanctioned by tradition, but in the sense of a path to be followed, along which one can keep on going rather than coming to a dead end or being caught in a loop of ever-repeating cycles (Kurttila and Ingold 2001: 192). Likewise the stories told by Orochon hunters, on returning every evening to the encampment, rarely conclude with the death of the prey, but rather elaborate on everything of interest witnessed or encountered along the trail. Stories, for the Orochon, should not end for the same reason that life should not. They are rather carried on for as long as the saddle, the embodiment of the unison of a man and his riding deer, continues to thread a path through the forest. And since saddles are inherited, each generation takes up and carries on the stories of its predecessors (Kwon 1998: 118–21). As with the line that goes out for a walk, in the story as in life there is always somewhere further one can go. And in storytelling as in wayfaring, it is in the movement from place to place – or from topic to topic – that knowledge is integrated.

But now let us suppose that the story is told not with the voice but in writing. Instead of a stream of vocal sound we have a line of handwritten text. Does not this line, too, go out for a walk, continually advancing from the tip as the story proceeds? In her discussion of the parallels between walking and narrative writing, Rebecca Solnit draws just such an analogy:

> To write is to carve a new path through the terrain of the imagination, or to point out new features on a familiar route. To read is to travel through that terrain with the author as guide ... I have often wished that my sentences could be written out as a single line running into the distance so that it would be clear that a sentence is likewise a road and reading is travelling.
>
> (Solnit 2001: 72)

As I shall show below, Solnit's wish is somewhat thwarted by her perception that writing consists of sentences and by its appearance on the page in the form of the discrete letters and evenly spaced words of typescript. To readers of medieval Europe, however, the analogy between reading and trav-elling would have been self-evident, even though the lines of the handwritten manuscript advanced row by row rather than along one continuous path.

Commentators from the Middle Ages, as we saw in Chapter 1, would time and again compare reading to wayfaring, and the surface of the page to an inhabited landscape. Just as to travel is to remember the path, or to tell a story is to remember how it goes, so to read, in this fashion, was to retrace a trail through the text. One remembered the text in much the same way as one would remember a story or a journey. The reader, in short, would *inhabit* the world of the page, proceeding from word to word as the storyteller proceeds from topic to topic, or the traveller from place to place. We have seen that, for the inhabitant, the line of his walking is a way of knowing. Likewise the line of writing is, for him, a way of remembering. In both cases, knowledge is integrated *along* a path of movement. And in this respect, there is no differ-ence in principle between the handwritten manuscript and the story voiced in speech or song. There is however, as I shall now show, a fundamental difference between the line that is written or voiced and that of a modern typed or printed composition. It is not, then, writing itself that makes the difference. It is rather what happens to writing when the flowing letter-line of the manuscript is replaced by the connecting lines of a pre-composed plot.

Writing as conceived in the modern project is not a practice of inscription or line-making. It has little if anything to do with the craft of the scribe. As we observed in Chapter 1, with acknowledgement to de Certeau, the modern writer encounters the blank surface of the page as an empty space awaiting the imposition of a construction of which he alone is the author (Certeau 1984: 134). Upon this space he lays out linguistic fragments – letters, words, sentences – which, nesting hierarchically, can be integrated to form a complete composition. Indeed his practice is not unlike that of the cartographer who likewise positions iconic fragments on the paper surface to mark the locations of objects in the world. Neither on the page of the book nor on the surface of the map do the gestures of the author leave any trace beyond these discrete and compacted marks. They are all that is left of the original lines, respectively, of the manuscript and the sketch map. The elements of the page may be joined in the imagination so as to form a plot – the literary equivalent of the scientist's graph or the tourist's route-plan. But the lines of the plot are not traced by the reader as he moves through the text. They are rather supposed to be laid out already before the journey begins. These lines are connectors. To read them, as André Leroi-Gourhan realized (1993: 261), is to study a plan rather than to follow a trail. Unlike his medieval predecessor – an inhabitant of the page myopically entangled in its inked traces – the modern reader *surveys* the page as if from a great height. Routeing across it from point to point, like the Royal Navy on the high seas, he moves in terms of area. In so doing he occupies the page and asserts his mastery over it. But he does not inhabit it.

Though I have drawn inspiration from de Certeau's account of the transformation of writing that accompanied the onset of modernity, he is wrong about one thing. Depositing verbal fragments at points across the space of the page, de Certeau tells us, the modern writer performs 'an itinerant, progressive, and regulated practice – a "walk" ' (1984: 134). The one thing walking does *not* do, however, is leave fragments in its wake. Thus a practice of writing that deposits fragments cannot be tantamount to walking. Of course the walker proceeds by plantigrade steps, impressing on the ground a sequence of discrete footprints rather than a continuous trail. The storyteller does much the same, as John Berger has emphasized. 'No story', he writes,

> is like a wheeled vehicle whose contact with the road is continuous. Stories walk, like animals and men. And their steps are not only between narrated events but between each sentence, sometimes each word. Every step is a stride over something not said.
>
> (Berger 1982: 284–5)

Indeed the same could also be said of the handwriting of a manuscript. Even with a cursive script, the writer has to lift his pen from time to time from the paper surface, between words and sometimes between letters.

But although the traces of the handwriter may be discontinuous, even punctual, the movement that generates them is a continuous one that tolerates no interruption. We may recall from Chapter 1 that medieval scholars referred to this movement, which they compared to wayfaring, by the concept of *ductus* – a concept still used by palaeographers with reference to the movement of the hand in writing. The *ductus* of handwriting, Rosemary Sassoon explains, combines 'the visible trace of a hand movement while the pen is on the paper and the invisible trace of the movements when the pen is not in contact with the paper' (Sassoon 2000: 39). Thus the handwriter is like the embroiderer of running stitch, whose thread continues even though its appearance on the surface takes the form of evenly spaced dashes, or like a boatman who continues to row even as he lifts his oars from the water, or indeed like the walker, who does not cease to walk as he lifts each foot, alternately, from the ground. Thus footprints are not fragments, and no more are the letters and words of the manuscript. They are not broken off from the line of movement but enplanted along it.

It was when writers *ceased* to perform the equivalent of a walk, I contend, that their words were reduced to fragments and in turn fragmented. In a thesis on walking, movement and perception, Wendy Gunn (1996) poses the question: 'How do the traces of a footprint in the sand differ from records of walking measured by the instruments of gait analysis?' The scientific study of gait treats walking as a mechanical process of locomotion, and records the bodily kinesis of experimental subjects by plotting the position of selected joints at regular intervals and joining the points of the plot to form a graph. Although the resulting lines are continuous, these lines are connectors and, as such, are devoid of movement. They are lines of locomotion, not of movement, and go *across*, from point to point, rather than *along* the trail of the walker's own way of life. There is more movement, Gunn observes, in a single footprint than in all these lines put together, even though the print itself is one of a discontinuous series (ibid.: 37–8). Likewise, there is more movement in a single trace of handwriting than in a whole page of printed text. If handwriting is like walking, then the line of print (joining evenly spaced letters) is like the record of gait analysis (joining equidistant plots).

Today when we look at the printed page we see row upon row of compact and self-contained graphic marks. In the kind of handwriting that imitates print – such as is required when we fill up bureaucratic forms – the line goes nowhere. It performs a miniature pirouette on one spot, whereupon the pen is withdrawn and shifted a little to the right, where it does the same again. These transverse movements are not part of the act of writing; they serve only to transport the pen from spot to spot. The typewriter works on precisely the same principle: the keys, tapped with the fingers, deliver readymade letter-forms to the page, but the machine takes care of the lateral displacement. Here the original connection between the manual gesture and its graphic trace is finally broken altogether, for the punctual movements of the digits on the keys are wholly unrelated to the marks engraved on them, and which they impress upon the page. In the typed or printed text, every letter or punctuation mark is wrapped up in itself, totally detached from its neighbours to left and right. Thus the letter-line of print or typescript does not go out for a walk. Indeed it does not go out at all, but remains confined to its point of origin.

In that epitome of modern bureaucracy, the dotted line, the same principle is taken to its logical extreme. Upon this line that is not a line the movement of life is collapsed into a series of instants. Lifeless and inert, it neither moves nor speaks. It has no personality whatsoever. It is, if you will, the perfect negation of the signature that comes to stand above it. Unlike the wayfarer who signs his presence on the land in the ever-growing sum of his trails, and the scribe who signs his presence on the page in his ever-extending letter-line, the modern author signs his work with the trace of a gesture so truncated and condensed, and so deeply sedimented in motor memory, that he carries it within him wherever he goes as a mark of his unique and unchanging identity. It is, as the graphologist H. J. Jacoby put it, his 'psychological visiting card' (cited in Sassoon 2000: 76). To sign on the dotted line is not to lay a trail but to execute this mark on the things to be found and appropriated at successive sites of occupation (Figure 3.5). Nothing better illustrates the opposition, central to the modern constitution, between individual idiosyncrasy and the determinations of the social order.

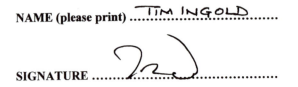

Figure 3.5 The author's printed name and signature, on the dotted line.

Now if the modern writer does not lay a trail, neither does the modern reader follow it. Scanning the page, his cognitive task is rather to reassemble the fragments he finds there into larger wholes – letters into words, words into sentences and sentences into the complete composition. Reading *across* the page rather than *along* its lines, he joins *up* the components distributed on its surface through a hierarchy of levels of integration (see Figure 3.6). The procedure is formally equivalent to that of the assembly line in industrial manufacture, where the transverse motion of the conveyor belt allows for the piecing together of components added at fixed intervals to the finished product (Ong 1982: 118). In both cases, integration proceeds not alongly but upwards. This is why, returning to Solnit's dream of writing along a single, continuous line, its fulfilment is inevitably frustrated by the premise that the text consists of *sentences*. For the sentence is an artefact of language, constructed in accordance with those rules of assembly we call 'grammar'. Every sentence is made up of words. But once words are treated as the building blocks of sentences – that is, as the components of an assembly – they are no longer perceived to *occur*, as they do for the storyteller

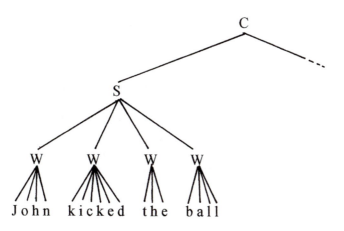

Figure 3.6 The hierarchy of levels of integration in a modern printed text. Letters are assembled into words (W), which are assembled into sentences (S), which in turn are assembled into the overall composition (C).

or scribe, in places along a path, but rather to *exist* as discrete entities located on the space of the page. They too are made up of elements, namely individual letters. And so Solnit's line, which has the appearance of a string of letters, interrupted at intervals by spaces and punctuation marks, can never even get underway. It is not a movement along a path but an immobile chain of connectors.

To round off the argument of this section, let me return to the irascible Aristoxenus of Tarentumi, pupil of Aristotle, whom we first met in Chapter 1. Recall that Aristoxenus described the prosody of the voice, in both speech and song, as a movement from place (*topos*) to place. But whereas the spoken voice, he thought, continually wanders, never settling anywhere for more than a moment, the voice of the singer moves with a lilt, as though holding its balance for as long as it can in one place before sliding away, only to restore its poise at another. The errant gait of the walker and the lilt of the dancer might be compared in the same terms. When, subsequently, Greek texts were 'marked up' for the purposes of oratorical performance or intonation, these dynamics of movement and rest in the melodic line were indicated by means of accents and punctuation marks. The purpose of punctuation, in particular, was to show where the orator could pause for breath. Crucially, however, these were pauses in an otherwise ongoing flow, like stopping off for a breather along the way from place to place. We have seen how this flow came to be understood by early medieval writers in terms of the notion of *ductus*, as a *way through* a composition. 'The rhetorical concept of *ductus*', Mary Carruthers explains, 'emphasizes way-finding by organizing the structure of any composition as a journey through a linked series of stages, each of which has its own characteristic flow' (Carruthers 1998: 80).

The flow, here, is like that of the contours of the land as, proceeding along a path, variously textured surfaces come into and pass out of sight. Thus the 'stages' of the composition are to be compared not to steps in the march of progress but to the successive vistas that open up along the way towards a goal. Going from stage to stage is like turning a corner, to reveal new horizons ahead (Ingold 2000: 238). But as handwriting gave way to print, as the page lost its voice and as the task of the reader turned from wayfaring to navigation – to joining up the components of the plot – so the flow of the *ductus* was stilled, leaving in its place a myriad of tiny fragments. The role of punctuation, then, was no longer to assist readers in modulating the flow, but rather to help them in reassembling the elements of the text. Punctuation marks, which once signposted turning points on a walk or pauses along the way, have come instead to indicate the joints of an assembly, marking off the segments of a vertically integrated, syntactic structure. They have nothing to do with performance, and everything to do with cognition.

Around the place

One prominent casualty of the fragmentation of lines of movement, knowledge and description that we have set out in the foregoing, and of their compression into confined spots, has been the concept of place. Once a moment of rest along a path of movement, place has been reconfigured in modernity as a nexus within which all life, growth and activity are *contained*. Between places, so conceived, there are only connections. On a cartographic map each such place is conventionally marked with a dot. To show that it is occupied, however, it may be depicted as an open circle, with its manifold occupants – the persons and things to be found there – indicated as smaller dots enclosed within. Thus:

Just who or what these occupants are, in this depiction, has nothing to do with where they are or how they came to be there. The picture resembles one of those games in which players compete to move their counters from position to position across a board (Figure 3.7). The identity of each counter is fixed before the game begins and remains unchanged throughout, regardless of the number of moves it makes. Likewise, as we have seen, the substantive identities of people and goods – that is, the characteristics that determine their particular natures – are not in principle supposed to be affected by their transport from site to site. But conversely, just as the positions on the board are laid out in advance of play, so the locational identity of each place is specified independently of the identities of its more or less transient

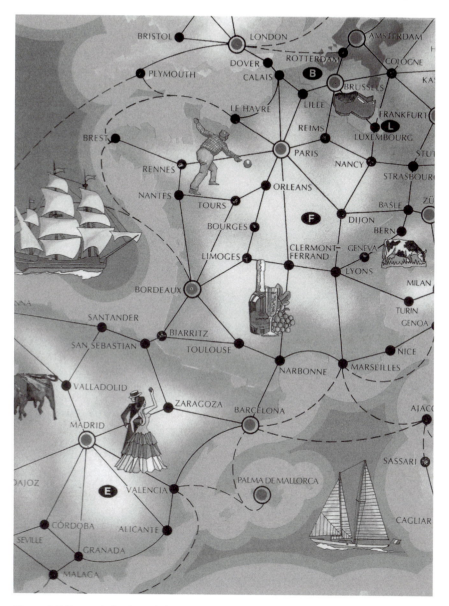

Figure 3.7 Part of the board for the game *Journey through Europe*. Players have to transport their pieces from one city to another, depending on cards they have been dealt, with a number of moves determined by the throw of a dice, but only by way of the marked lines.

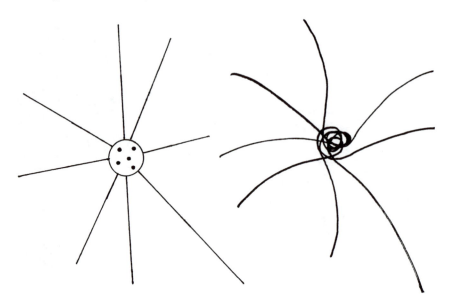

Figure 3.8 The hub-and-spokes model of place (left) compared with the place as a knot of entangled lifelines (right). In the diagram on the left, the circle represents a place, the dots are its living occupants and the straight lines indicate the connectors of a transport network. In the diagram on the right, the lines are living inhabitants, and the knot in the middle is a place.

occupants. On a map as on the game-board, locations or positions may be joined by lines to indicate possible moves. These lines are, of course, static point-to-point connectors. Together they form a network in which every place figures as a hub, from which connections fan out like the spokes of a wheel (see Figure 3.8, left).

Now there is, at first glance, a striking resemblance between this kind of picture and the patterns that Walbiri people of Central Australia draw, often with their fingers in the sand, as they tell of the earth-forming journeys of their ancestors in the Dreaming. The places from which the ancestors emerged, or through which they travelled, are depicted by circles, and the paths between them are depicted by connecting lines. In the example reproduced in Figure 3.9, taken from a drawing done on paper, the ancestor is shown coming up from the ground at A, travelling to nearby B, and then on through C, D, E and F, before returning into the ground at A. Each place looks to us – as indeed it did to the ethnographer of the Walbiri, Nancy Munn – like a container for life, linked to other places as nodes in a network (Munn 1973a: 213–15). But the appearance is deceptive. A vital clue is offered by the fact that the place is commonly depicted, as in our illustration, not by a single circle but by either a series of concentric rings or a spiral winding in towards the centre. Moreover Munn tells us that the concentric rings and the spiral are treated as equivalent forms (1973a: 202). These forms

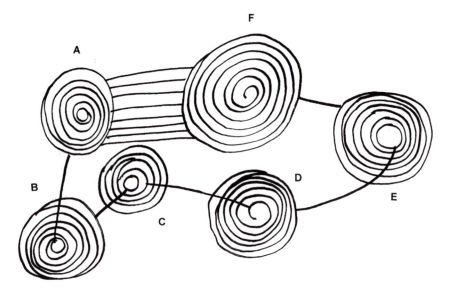

Figure 3.9 Site-path figure, from a Walbiri paper drawing. Redrawn from Munn (1973a: 194). By permission of Oxford University Press.

are not static nor, strictly speaking, do they enclose. They surround nothing but themselves. What they describe is not an external boundary within which life is contained, but rather the current of life itself as it circles around a focus. The place, in Walbiri thinking, is like a vortex. Although it is conventional to draw the rings or spirals and the lines between them with separate strokes, so that they appear to intersect, the movement they are meant to convey is continuous. Emerging from the ground at the focal point, the ancestor 'walks around' making camp, describing an ever-widening spiral, until he eventually heads off and away. Returning, he would conduct the same movement in reverse. Thus:

For the same reason that the circular lines of Walbiri drawings do not contain, the straight lines do not connect. Both kinds of line, circular and straight, are the traces of gestural movements of the inscribing hand as it re-enacts the movements of the ancestors along their original paths. Every such path, according to Munn, is 'a kind of life-line' (1973a: 214), tracing an alternating progression of 'coming out' and 'going in'. While coming out the movement around bends into a movement away; while going in the movement towards bends into a movement around. At the very heart of the place however, as in the eye of the vortex, nothing moves at all. This is the point of absolute rest where, in the Walbiri conception, the ancestor sinks back into the ground whence he originally came. Yet the return is never final, for the ancestral potency that animates the place is periodically re-embodied in the generations of living people it brings forth, that come from the ground when they are born and go back in when they die. As inhabitants of the places from which they come these living generations retrace in their everyday activities the perambulations of their ancestors, albeit at a finer scale, leaving a myriad of capillary trails where the latter left arterial tracks. For them, too, life goes on *around* places, as well as *towards* and *away from* places elsewhere. You make camp by walking around it; you sustain yourself and your companions by hunting and gathering along the paths that lead from one camp site to another. But you only go *inside* a place to die.

The life of a Walbiri person, as I have already noted in my earlier discussion of wayfaring, is laid out on the ground as the sum of his trails. Suppose, then, that we were to draw just one stretch of a person's trails, showing his coming to a place, his hanging around for a while and his eventual departure. It might look something like this:

He is not of course the only person to spend time in the place, for he encounters others there who may have arrived along different trails and will in turn go their separate ways. If we add their trails to the picture, it becomes a good deal more convoluted. The place now has the appearance of a complex knot. My concern is not to unravel the knot, but to compare it to the hub-and-spokes model with which I began this section (see Figure 3.8). In this latter model the hub, as a container for life, is clearly distinguished from the individuals it contains – each represented by a mobile dot – as well as from the lines connecting it to other hubs in the network. The knot, by contrast, does not contain life but is rather formed of the very lines along which life is lived. These lines are bound together *in* the knot, but they are not bound *by* it. To the contrary they trail beyond it, only to become caught up with other lines in other knots. Together they make up what I have called a meshwork. Every place, then, is a knot in the meshwork, and the threads from which it is traced are lines of wayfaring.

It is for this reason that I have consistently referred to wayfarers as *inhabitants* rather than *locals*, and to what they know as inhabitant rather than local knowledge. For it would be quite wrong to suppose that such people are confined within a particular place, or that their experience is circumscribed by the restricted horizons of a life lived only there. It would be equally wrong, however, to suppose that the wayfarer wanders aimlessly over the surface of the earth, with no place or places of abode. The experience of habitation cannot be comprehended within the terms of the conventional opposition between the settler and the nomad, since this opposition is itself founded on the contrary principle of occupation. Settlers occupy places; nomads fail to do so. Wayfarers, however, are not failed or reluctant occupants but successful inhabitants. They may indeed be widely travelled, moving from place to place – often over considerable distances – and con-tributing through these movements to the ongoing formation of each of the places through which they pass. Wayfaring, in short, is neither placeless nor place-bound but place-*making*. It could be described as a flowing line proceeding through a succession of places, thus:

But now let me return to that *other* kind of line, the one Klee described as having to keep a series of appointments. Strictly speaking, of course, it is not the line that keeps these appointments but a dot. Following a chain of connections, it hops from one pre-determined location to another, thus:

Suppose that this dot represents an individual with a busy schedule. As he goes from each appointment to the next, he is always in a hurry. Why should this be so?

For the wayfarer whose line goes out for a walk, speed is not an issue. It makes no more sense to ask about the speed of wayfaring than it does to ask about the speed of life. What matters is not how fast one moves, in terms of the ratio of distance to elapsed time, but that this movement should be in phase with, or attuned to, the movements of other phenomena of the inhabited world. The question 'How long does it take?' only becomes rele-vant when the duration of a journey is measured out towards a pre-determined destination. Once however the dynamics of movement have been reduced, as in destination-oriented transport, to the mechanics of locomotion, the speed of travel arises as a key concern. The traveller whose business of life is conducted at successive stopping-off points wants to spend his time *in* places, not *between* them. While in transit he has nothing to do. Much of the history of transport has been taken up with attempts to attenuate these liminal, in-between periods, by devising ever-faster mechanical means. In principle the speed of transport can be increased indefinitely; indeed in a perfect system the traveller could arrive at his destination in no time at all. But in practice transport is never perfect, just as it is impossible to be in several places at the same time. There is always some friction in the system. Thus unlike the wayfarer who moves *with* time, the transported traveller races *against* it, seeing in its passage not an organic potential for growth but the mechanical limitations of his equipment. If he had his way, every point in his entire network of connections, laid out on the plane of the present, could be accessed simultaneously. And so, driven by an unattainable ideal, our individual hurries from point to point, both trying and inevitably failing to be everywhere at once. The time it takes is a measure of his impatience.

The possibility of pure transport is, in short, an illusion. We cannot get from location to location by leap-frogging the world, nor can the traveller ever be quite the same on arrival at a place as when he set out. It is precisely because perfect transport is impossible – because all travel is movement in real time – that places do not just have locations but histories. Since, moreover, no one can be everywhere at once, it is not possible wholly to detach the dynamics of movement from the formation of knowledge, as though they lay on orthogonal axes running respectively laterally and vertically, across and upwards. There is no way, in practice, that the mind can ascend from the surface of the world while leaving the body to route across it, merely collecting data for the mind to assemble into structures of objective knowledge. Pure objectivity is as illusory as pure transport, and for much the same reasons. The illusion can only be sustained by suppressing the embodied experience of place-to-place movement that is intrinsic to life, growth and knowledge. To do his job even the surveyor has to get around, and must perforce allow his eyes to wander over the landscape just as the modern reader, while turning the pages, lets his eyes wander over the printed text. In both cases the experience of movement is bound to intrude upon observational practice. For all of us, in reality, knowledge is not built up as we go across, but rather grows as we go along.

Perhaps what truly distinguishes the predicament of people in modern metropolitan societies is the extent to which they are compelled to inhabit an environment that has been planned and built expressly for the purposes of occupation. The architecture and public spaces of the built environment enclose and contain; its roads and highways connect. Transport systems nowadays span the globe in a vast network of destination-to-destination links. For passengers, strapped to their seats, travel is no longer an experience of movement in which action and perception are intimately coupled, but has become one of enforced immobility and sensory deprivation. On arrival, the traveller is released from his bonds only to find that his freedom of movement is circumscribed within the limits of the site. Yet the structures that confine, channel and contain are not immutable. They are ceaselessly eroded by the tactical manoeuvring of inhabitants whose 'wandering lines' (*lignes d'erre*) or 'efficacious meanderings' – in de Certeau's words (1984: xviii) – undercut the strategic designs of society's master-builders, causing them gradually to wear out and disintegrate. Quite apart from human beings who may or may not respect the rules of play, these inhabitants include countless non-humans that have no heed for them at all. Flying, crawling, wriggling and burrowing all over and under the regular, linearized infrastructure of the occupied world, creatures of every sort continually reincorporate and rearrange its crumbling fragments into their own ways of life.

Indeed nothing can escape the tentacles of the meshwork of habitation as its ever-extending lines probe every crack or crevice that might potentially afford growth and movement. Life will not be contained, but rather threads its way through the world along the myriad lines of its relations. But if life is not enclosed within a boundary, neither can it be surrounded. What then becomes of our concept of environment? Literally an environment is that which surrounds. For inhabitants, however, the environment does not consist of the surroundings of a bounded place but of a zone in which their several pathways are thoroughly entangled. In this zone of entanglement – this meshwork of interwoven lines – there are no insides or outsides, only openings and ways through. An ecology of life, in short, must be one of threads and traces, not of nodes and connectors. And its subject of inquiry must consist not of the relations *between* organisms and their external environments but of the relations *along* their severally enmeshed ways of life. Ecology, in short, is the study of the life of lines.

4   The genealogical line

Life, I have argued, is not confined within points but proceeds along lines. But does it grow or flow? Should we liken its movement to that of a stream or river as it cuts through the landscape on its way to the sea, or would it better be compared to the stems of plants as they push upwards towards the light? Perhaps these alternatives are not mutually exclusive: after all, the growth of a tree depends on the flow of sap through the bark that sustains it, just as a river brings nourishment and fertility to the land along its banks. Nevertheless throughout the history of the Western world, from classical Antiquity to the present day, hydraulic and arboricultural metaphors have struggled for supremacy, or have sought compromise in the most bizarre and improbable of solutions. Nowhere has this been more apparent than in the practices of genealogy, of tracing the paths of human life from their ancestral sources or roots to their contemporary manifestations. In this brief interlude I turn my attention to the genealogical line.

Mention the word *line* to a social anthropologist, and kinship or genealogical connection is probably the first thing he or she will think of. No other kind of line has exercised such a hold on the disciplinary imagination. And it is in charts of kinship and descent, too, that lines are most frequently drawn in anthropological notebooks and texts. Yet as I aim to show, in its co-optation as an instrument of scientific method, the genealogical line has undergone a profound transformation. For the line of the chart neither grows nor flows but *connects*. And by the same token, the lives it connects are compressed into points. I begin, however, with a little history, for which I am principally indebted to the remarkable work of Christiane Klapisch-Zuber (1991).

Upside-down trees

The Romans, according to literary sources, were given to ornamenting the halls of their houses with decorations that would link portraits of their forebears with wavy lines or ribbons (*stemmata*). These genealogies were to be read from the top, where the founding ancestor would be placed, and down through the sequence of descendant generations. The Latin terminology of filiation carries 'the implicit metaphor of a stream – of blood, of wealth, of values – flowing from the same source situated on high, down to a group of individuals placed much lower' (Klapisch-Zuber 1991: 112). Progeny were descendants, and descent runs downhill. For this reason, Roman authors were not attracted by the image of the tree as a means of depicting genealogical pedigree. If your purpose is to demonstrate an unequivocal claim to noble ancestry, then an arboreal depiction is doubly inappropriate. Not only does it place the ancestors at the base where descendants ought to be; it also presents a proliferation of divergent branches rather than emphasizing the lineal continuity of hereditary succession. Though there are occasional references to 'branches' (*rami*) in Roman genealogical texts, the term was used to denote the side-lines that linked portraits or names to the *stemmata*, rather than the lines of the genealogy itself.

However, to clerics of the Early Middle Ages, seeking precedents in Roman law for the definition of degrees of kinship governing inheritance and the prohibition of marriage, the image of branches appeared in another guise. Their abstract kinship diagrams took the generic form of an overhanging triangle mounted on a central pillar. Centrally situated at the base of the triangle was the notional individual, *ego*, whose complement of theoretically possible kinship relations was to be depicted. His lineal ancestors were placed at the apex, his collateral relatives off to each side, and his lineal descendants down the pillar. To be sure, these diagrams did not look much like trees, and they could have been (and sometimes were) dressed up in other guises, for example as bodies or houses. But from the ninth century, tables of consanguinity began to be called *arbores juris*, imagined in the outline of a tree with the central pillar as the trunk, the overhanging triangle as the canopy and the apex as the treetop. The branches, in this image, led off from the trunk – which depicted lineal ancestry and descent – to collateral kin on either side. But while convention dictated that the *arbor juris* took the shape of a tree – in other words, that there was an iconic resemblance between the outline of the diagram and the outline of a tree – illustrators of the time were reluctant to go so far as to suggest any resemblance between a living tree and what the diagram purported to represent, namely the lines of consanguinity themselves. This was for a very simple reason. Any tree resembling the *arbor juris* would have to grow *upside down*, from the ancestors at the top to their descendants at the base! Figure 4.1, taken from a much more recent, eighteenth-century source, aptly illustrates the paradox involved.

The feudal nobility of the later Middle Ages, concerned above all to guarantee their hereditary titles to land and privilege, preferred to perpetuate the ancient practice of reading genealogical lines from top to bottom. The lines were depicted as channels down which the dynastic blood would flow, and along them were placed personages represented by miniature portraits, crests or medallions. Resistance to tree imagery was further reinforced by the practice of chronicling dynastic histories on long rolls of parchment. To read a scroll, line by line, is to read downwards. Trees, however, grow upwards.

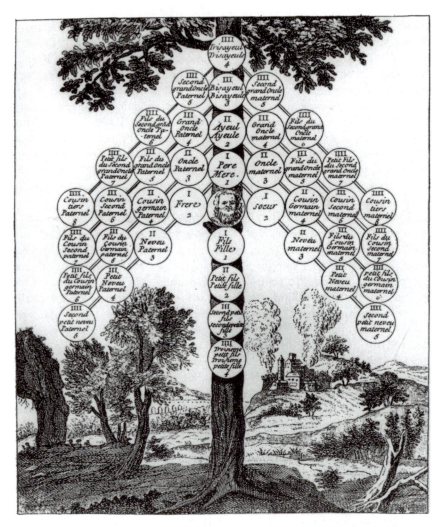

Figure 4.1 An eighteenth-century French *arbor consanguinitatis*. The face halfway up
the trunk represents *ego*. Below him, down the trunk, are four generations
of descendants, and above four generations of ancestors. Patrilateral kin
are arrayed on the left, and matrilateral kin on the right. Arabic and roman
numerals indicate degrees of consanguinity according to Roman civil law
and Christian canon law respectively. Reproduced from Domat (1777,
I: 405).

There could be no way, therefore, of combining textual description with
arboreal depiction of genealogical succession, save by having the tree grow
from top to bottom. Some illustrators did indeed attempt this, with a tree
trunk that looked more like a stalk of bamboo, never varying in thickness,
and with ivy-like foliage that seemed unsure whether it wanted to grow

upwards or downwards (Klapisch-Zuber 1991: Fig. 15). However, for the image of the genealogical tree to become established it had to be separable from the text and to make sense on its own without the benefit of accompanying description. The major impetus behind this development was the growing popularity, in late medieval times, of images of the biblical Tree of Jesse.

The source of the image lies in a specific interpretation of the prophecy of Isaiah (Chapter XI), that 'there shall come forth a rod out of the stem of Jesse, and a Branch shall grow out of his roots'. In this interpretation, the stem (or root) was Jesse's son King David and the rod (or shoot) led up to the Virgin Mary, from whose womb budded the flower of Christ (Bouquet 1996: 48–50). Depictions of the Tree frequently had the trunk issuing from the figure of a recumbent Jesse, who is dreaming of what will come to pass, and proceed through a series of ascendant generations to the figure of the Saviour at the top. The upward thrust of the tree, straining towards the sky, conveyed an ideal of moral and spiritual perfection, and it was in this, rather than in any precise delineation of genealogical relationships and their entailments with regard to inheritance, that its significance initially resided. The potency of the image, however, was not lost on ruling families who saw in it an opportunity to lay claim to divine origin. The problem they faced was how to marry the *upward growing* image of the Tree of Jesse with the *downward flowing* image of the aristocratic bloodline. They solved it by the very trick that their predecessors had deemed impossible, namely by representing the *arbor juris*, with its lines of descent running vertically and diagonally downwards from an apical ancestor, as a real, living tree, but one whose roots – unlike those of any ordinary tree, which are planted in the earth – are actually placed in the heavens.

Thus the first genealogical trees were literally upside down. The *arbor juris* became an *arbor inversa*, an 'inverted tree', nourished by the light of heaven rather than the strength of the earth. In some depictions, even 'poor Jesse found himself uncomfortably lying upside down, in a landscape that was equally topsy-turvy' (Klapisch-Zuber 1991: 124). Before the tree could be turned right way up again, it was necessary to accept the principle that future generations, far from merely passing on the flow of ancestral substance, could exceed the reach of their ancestors in growing towards higher states of fulfilment, and that the future could even be superior to the past. In its upright form – still harking back to the Tree of Jesse – the genealogical tree combined a declaration of ancestry with a statement of ambition (Figure 4.2). Thus at the dawn of the modern era, the tree became an icon of progress. But the contradictions between ascendant growth and descendant flow were never fully resolved, as we can see today in tree-pictures that are marketed to feed an insatiable popular appetite for tracing family connections, which place the customer's numerous ancestors – doubling in number with each ascendant generation – up in the canopy and foliage. These trees are not so much upside down as growing backwards, pushing further into the past

Figure 4.2 Genealogy of the House of France, 1350–1589, from Jean II to Henri III, Château de Chambord. Photograph: Éditions Gaud. By permission of Éditions Gaud.

with every new shoot. They present a precise inversion of the temporal experience of modernity, according to which the present continually over-tops and overshadows the past.

Crane's foot to circuit board

It was W. H. R. Rivers, in the first decade of the twentieth century, who took the decisive step in converting the genealogical line into an element of scientific notation. Rivers's background was in the natural sciences: he had trained in medicine but had been drawn to the physiology and psychology of sensory perception. His anthropological interests were kindled by way of his participation in the Cambridge University Expedition to the Torres Straits in 1898–99. Though he had joined the expedition as its physician-cum-psychologist, his determination to establish rigorous scientific protocols for the collection of ethnological materials led him to formulate what, in a celebrated article published in 1910, he called 'the genealogical method of anthropological inquiry'. The method comprised, in essence, instructions for the collection of information from native informants on the full com-plement of individuals with whom they might have kinship connections, up to the limits of their knowledge and memory. The ethnologist was advised to proceed systematically, starting with the informant's own immediate kin and going on to elicit the connections of each of the latter, one by one, in ascend-ing and descending generations. By putting all this information together, Rivers thought, it should be possible to construct an entire network through which the precise connection between any pair of individuals could be traced.

Significantly, Rivers introduced his 1910 article by noting the 'familiar fact that many peoples preserve long pedigrees of their ancestors' (Rivers 1968: 97). While the notion of pedigree would have been entirely familiar to his mainly British middle-class readers, and would no doubt have appealed to their ingrained snobbery (Bouquet 1993: 38–9, 188–9), it did not have any intrinsic connection with the image of the tree. The word itself comes from the Latin *pes* (foot) and *grus* (crane), originally referring to a diagram of three lines, arranged in the form of an arrow and resembling the imprint of a crane's foot, which was used to indicate lines of descent in early European genealogies. The principal connotation of the word is one of undiluted succession along a single line, rather than of the unity of divergent lines in a common root. In that sense it comes much closer to the classical Roman *stemma* or ribbon. A usage recorded in the *Oxford English Dictionary*, dated to 1532, describes the pedigree as 'a *string* of people'. If comparisons were drawn with the natural world, they were with the animal rather than the vegetable kingdom. For pedigree was above all about controlling the flow of blood and ensuring its continued purity, as much in the domain of animal breeding (such as of horses and cattle) as in that of the breeding of human beings. And as a flow rather than a growth, pedigree ran down rather than climbing up.

The charts that Rivers constructed according to his method – and by and large those that anthropologists have constructed ever since – placed ancestors above and descendants below. Far from overturning, yet again, the image of the family tree, it is more likely that Rivers was appealing to the much older tradition of the ribbon-like *stemma*.[1] Yet while in his 1910 article he used the terms 'pedigree' and 'genealogy' more or less interchangeably, at the back of his mind was a concern to differentiate between them on the lines of a distinction between the stories that people tell about themselves and the information gleaned from them by systematic forensic inquiry (Bouquet 1993: 140). It would be more than fifty years, however, before the distinction would be spelled out precisely and unequivocally. In an article published in 1967 social anthropologist John Barnes sought once again to give detailed instructions for the systematic collection of genealogical data, while acknowledging that the method first set out by Rivers 'can scarcely be improved' (Barnes 1967: 106). But upon the distinction between pedigree and genealogy, he was insistent. 'Pedigree' was to be used for 'a genealogical statement made orally, diagrammatically or in writing by an actor or informant', whereas 'genealogy' was to be taken to mean 'a genealogical statement made by an ethnographer as part of his field record or of its analysis'. And between the two lay all the difference between culture and science. 'The cultural milieu of the actors marks the method of construction of the pedigree, whereas the demands of science determine how the genealogy is recorded' (ibid.: 103).

Anthropologists have argued interminably over whether it is really possible to distinguish people's 'home-made models' of origin and descent from the records of objective science. Even Barnes had to admit that 'no clear dividing line' can be drawn between genealogical links memorialized in pedigree and those that, while they can be elicited by the ethnographer, will sooner or later be forgotten by the people. Nevertheless, he assures us, 'the transition is real' (ibid.: 119). Critics have noted that the genealogical method itself taps into such deep-seated precedents in the history of European cultures that any scientific claim to have definitively purified genealogy of its connotations of pedigree is at the very least questionable (Bouquet 1996: 62). Somewhat related to this is an equally interminable argument over whether genealogical connections have an underlying biogenetic reality or whether they exist only as social or cultural constructs that are effectively 'cut loose' from their physical underpinning. These arguments have been as turgid as they have been inconclusive, and I have no intention of reviving them here. My concern is different. Might it be that the contrast between the pedigree and the genealogy has to do neither with the range of people bound by its lines, nor with the ways in which information on these people has been obtained, but with the nature of the lines themselves?

When Barnes's article appeared in print I had just begun my undergraduate studies in social anthropology at the University of Cambridge, and was receiving my initial indoctrination into kinship theory.[2] One of the first things drummed into me was that on no account should kin ever be described as 'blood relations'. They were to be known as 'consanguines'. Any objection that these were two ways of saying exactly the same thing, using words of Germanic and Latin origin respectively, was summarily brushed aside. For my teachers something very fundamental was clearly at stake, though for a neophyte like myself it was hard to figure out what it was. Perhaps, by recalling the argument of the previous chapter, we can now be a little clearer. Blood is the real material stuff that pumps through people's veins, and that used to be thought to flow from parents to their offspring. Consanguinity, by contrast, is an abstraction – at least within the context of kinship theory. Just as the geometrical line, as we saw in Chapter 2, is the 'ghost' of a real trace or thread, so the line of consanguineal kinship is the ghost of the allegedly real bloodline. And it is produced by a procedure precisely analogous to that by which the dotted line is evolved from the gestural trace. To recapitulate: take a line described by a movement, cut it up into segments, roll each segment tightly into a dot, and finally join the dots. This is exactly how the line of the 'scientific' genealogy is derived from the thread of pedigree. The consanguineal line is not a thread or a trace but a connector.

From this follow a suite of differences that we would expect from the argument already adduced in Chapter 3. The genealogical diagram takes the form of a chart whose lines connect points. Like a map on which one can plot the route from any one destination to any other (or vice versa) even before setting out, the chart – as Pierre Bourdieu was the first to observe – 'can be taken in at a glance, *uno intuitu*, and scanned indifferently from any point in any direction', thus presenting 'the complete network of kinship relations over several generations . . . as a totality present in simultaneity' (Bourdieu 1977: 38). Purged of the elegant tracery and ornamentation of the pedigree, it has the sterile austerity of an electrical circuit board. Indeed many charts show more than a passing resemblance to wiring diagrams (see Figure 4.3). That the lines on the chart are the ghosts of threads rather than of traces is evident from Barnes's recommendation (1967: 122) that where unconnected lines have to cross one another, as is often the case, one should draw a little hump just as electrical engineers do in notating their circuits. Though it has been conventional to array persons of successive generations on a vertical axis, and of the same generation on a horizontal one, Barnes also recommends, in the interests of clarity (ibid.: 114), that the intergenerational axis be laid horizontally. Since the chart itself is constructed as an assembly of connecting lines, its actual orientation is immaterial. Both recommendations have been widely adopted.

The lines of the genealogical chart do not go out for a walk, as those of the traditional pedigree do. Reading a pedigree, we follow its trails rather as we would the lines of a sketch map or itinerary, either 'downstream' towards descendants or 'upstream' towards ancestors. The personages we encounter along the way are like places on the river. Just as the names of places, told in

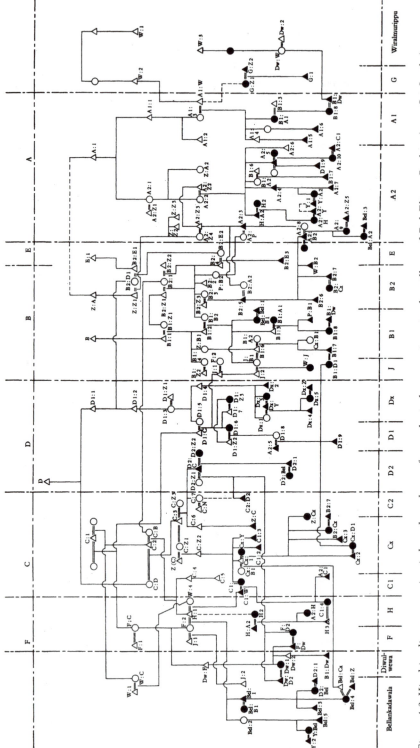

Figure 4.3 Kinship diagram as circuit board: a chart of genealogical connections in the village of Pul Eliya, Ceylon (now Sri Lanka), as documented by Edmund Leach in the late 1950s. Reproduced from Leach (1961). By permission of Cambridge University Press.

sequence, narrate the journey along the course on which they lie, so the names of persons, similarly recited in order, tell the story of the line. Each person, in turn, is a topic of the story. The lines of the genealogical chart, by contrast, are read not along but up and across. Reading the chart is a matter not of following a storyline but of reconstructing a plot. The cognitive task of the reader, as we have already seen in the case of the printed text, is not to find a way through the landscape of memory but to assemble into a coherent structure the fragments distributed over the surface of the blank page. These fragments are conventionally indicated by little triangles and circles, standing symbolically for males and females respectively. But far from picking up a story from ancestors and carrying it onwards to descendants, each of the persons signified by these marks is immobilized on one spot, their entire life compressed into a single position within the genealogical grid, from which there is no escape.

The genealogical model

The logic that transforms the string or thread-line of the pedigree into the genealogical point-to-point connector – that is, the logic of the dotted line – had already become an established part of scientific thinking long before Rivers penned his essay of 1910. Nevertheless the two kinds of line continued to enjoy an uneasy coexistence, as was apparent, for example, in the debates surrounding the evolution of life that raged throughout the late nineteenth and early twentieth centuries. Already at the turn of the nineteenth century the founder of biology, Jean-Baptiste Lamarck, had seen in the evolution – or what he called the 'transformism' – of organic forms the clearest evidence that creatures of every kind were working their ways up the scale of nature, with each generation taking up the cumulative achievements of its predecessors and passing them on enhanced by its own (Ingold 1986: 130). Thus the life of every being is the gradual growing beyond, or supersession, of its ancestor in the process of becoming its descendant. It was largely thanks to Charles Darwin that the image of the single scale was replaced by that of a branching tree – an image for which, as we have already seen, there was ample precedent in the illustration of biblical themes. Darwin himself, in *The Origin of Species*, was not averse to using metaphors of arboreal growth, comparing the evolution of life to the burgeoning of a tree, thick with branches, twigs and buds (Darwin 1950: 112–13). Nor did he rule out the possibility that characteristics developed by an organism during its lifetime might be transmitted to offspring.

Yet Darwin had also to acknowledge that according to his theory of variation under natural selection, by which he claimed to account for the modification of organisms along lines of descent, each organism on a line exists solely to be itself, to fulfil a project coterminous with the bounds of its own existence. It neither carries forward the life-course of its antecedents nor anticipates that of its descendants, for what it passes on to the future, by

own reproduction, is not its life but a suite of hereditary character-
t may be recombined or reassembled in the formation of other
or other lives. In this Darwinian conception, evolution is absolutely
process. Whereas evolution takes place across generations, life is
expended within each generation – in the task of passing on the heritable
components, nowadays known as genes, needed to get it restarted in the next.
As historian of science Charles Gillespie has rightly observed, the logic of
this argument drives a wedge between Lamarckian and Darwinian under-
standings of the evolutionary process, for what Darwin did 'was to treat the
whole range of nature which had been relegated to becoming, as a problem in
being, an infinite set of objective situations reaching back through time'
(Gillespie 1959: 291). It follows that the continuity of evolution is not a *real*
continuity of becoming but a *reconstituted* continuity of discrete individuals
in genealogical sequence, each of which differs minutely from predecessors
and successors. As I put it in an earlier work, 'the life of every individual is
condensed into a single point; it is we who draw the connecting lines between
them, seeing each as a moment of a continuous process' (Ingold 1986: 8).

Figure 4.4 reproduces Darwin's original diagram from *The Origin of Species* – the only diagram, in fact, in the book. In the diagram, each horizontal
band is supposed to represent an interval of a thousand generations, such
that any line of descent spanning this interval could be traced through a

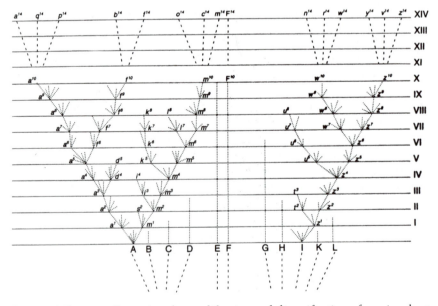

Figure 4.4 Diagram illustrating the modification and diversification of species along
lines of descent, through variation under natural selection. Lower-case
letters depict distinct varieties, and each 'little fan of diverging dotted
lines' (Darwin 1950: 102) represents varying offspring. Reproduced from
Darwin (1950: 90–1).

thousand organisms, each differing ever so slightly from the one preceding. But notice how the lines in Darwin's diagram are made up of dots! He was quite right to draw them so – indeed his theory required it. Far from depicting the tree of life, however, about which Darwin had waxed so eloquent in his text, the diagram presents its ghostly spectre. Where once grew a trunk and branches, sprouting 'green and budding twigs' (the phrase is Darwin's, 1950: 112), there now stands a lifeless, artificially reconstructed skeleton of points and connectors. The original growth-lines of the tree appear shattered into many thousands of generational segments, each compacted into a dot. To draw a diagram of evolutionary phylogeny is, then, a matter of joining the dots.

Despite the vastly greater number of generations than would ever be found on an anthropological chart of genealogical descent, the underlying principle involved in the construction of the Darwinian phyletic line is precisely the same. It is the core principle of what I call the *genealogical model* (Ingold 2000: 134–9), and lies in the assumption that organisms and persons are endowed with the essential specifications for carrying on a particular form of life, independently and in advance of their growth and development in an environment, through the bestowal of attributes – whether of make-up, character or identity – received from predecessors. With non-human organisms these specifications are generally taken to be genetic, and to make up what is technically called the *genotype*; with humans it is often supposed that they are complemented by elements of culture, making up an analogous 'culture-type' (Richerson and Boyd 1978: 128). Either way, the lines connecting ancestors and descendants, according to the genealogical model, are *lines of transmission*, down which are supposed to pass not the impulse of life but information, genetic or cultural, for living it. And since the model stipulates that the inheritance of genotypic or culture-typic attributes be separated from their subsequent *phenotypic* expression, these lines of transmission have to be strictly distinguished from the *lines of action* mapped out in individual life-cycles. Whereas the cycle of life is confined within each generation, inheritance crosses from one generation to the next in a step-by-step sequence.

Now in so far as they connect points, the lines of action resemble those of the transport network described in Chapter 3. Such lines, as I have shown, ideally lack duration: they thus map out the totality of an individual's moves on the plane of the present. Lines of transmission, by contrast, connect the sources and recipients of information in diachronic sequence. It follows that transport and transmission are arrayed upon the separate axes of synchrony and diachrony, as indicated schematically in Figure 4.5. Whereas on the plane of synchrony an individual may be depicted like a piece on a gaming-board, as though making a sequence of strategic point-to-point moves across a surface, looked at diachronically its entire trajectory – the sum of its moves – appears condensed into a single point. But if, as we saw in the last chapter, pure transport is a practical impossibility, then so too must be pure

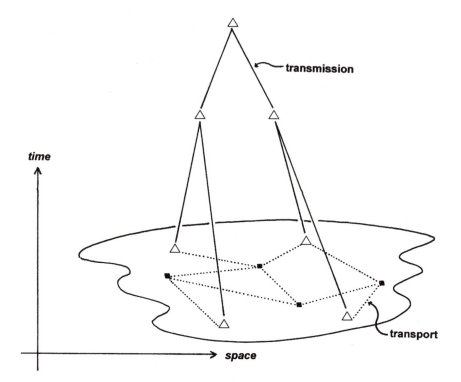

Figure 4.5 Lines of transmission and transport. Lines of transport connect points marked out in space upon some arbitrarily delimited territory. Lines of transmission connect individuals in a diachronic, ancestor–descendant sequence, irrespective of their spatial locations.

transmission. Individuals can no more be everywhere at once than they can receive the specifications for life in advance of living it. I have argued that, as inhabitants of the world, creatures of all kinds, human and non-human, are *wayfarers*, and that wayfaring is a movement of self-renewal or becoming rather than the transport of already constituted beings from one location to another. Making their ways through the tangle of the world, wayfarers grow into its fabric and contribute through their movements to its ever-evolving weave. This is to think of evolution, however, in a way that contrasts radically with the genealogical conception implied by conventional models of biological and cultural transmission. And it takes us back to the fundamental idea that life is lived not at points but along lines.

The braid of life

For a definitive statement of this idea, we can look away from Darwin to the very different view of evolution that was being propounded around the turn of the twentieth century, and across the Channel, by the philosopher

Henri Bergson. In his *Creative Evolution* of 1911, Bergson argued that every organism is like an eddy cast in a flow. So well however does it feign immobility that we are readily deceived into treating each 'as a *thing* rather than as a *progress*, forgetting that the very permanence of its form is only the outline of a movement'. In truth, Bergson declared, 'the living being is, above all, a thoroughfare' (1911: 135). Along this thoroughfare flows the current of life, 'passing from germ to germ through the medium of a developed organism' (ibid.: 28). It would therefore be wrong, Bergson thought, to compare the organism to an object. As with eddies in the stream, and as we have already noted of the topics of a story and of the named personages of a pedigree, organisms do not so much *exist* as *occur*.

By the middle of the twentieth century, Bergson's vision of evolution, as a meshwork of intertwined thoroughfares along which organisms follow their respective ways of life, had been comprehensively discredited. A resurgent Darwinism had dismissed the key idea of the vital force, *élan vital*, as a metaphysical delusion that could in no way account, as Bergson had claimed, for the creation of novel forms. In its place it substituted an equally metaphysical idea of the gene, conceived as a particle of information allegedly capable of magically inserting itself into the organism-to-be before its life in the world has even begun. With that, science legitimized the triumph of the genealogical model. The flowing, growing line of the pedigree had finally been expelled by the point-to-point connector. It has not however been extinguished altogether. Perhaps, taking a leaf out of Bergson's book rather than Darwin's, it can be rekindled once again.

Let us suppose, with Bergson, that every being is instantiated in the world not as a bounded entity but as a thoroughfare, along the line of its own movement and activity. This is not a lateral movement 'point to point', as in transport, but a continual 'moving around' or coming and going, as in wayfaring. How then would we depict the passage of generations, where each, far from following the previous ones in a connected sequence of synchronic 'slices', leans over, as Bergson put it (1911: 135), and touches the next? Figure 4.6 depicts a descent line of five generations, on the left, according to the conventions of the genealogical model and, on the right, according to our alternative view, as a series of interlaced trails. As generation B matures it follows a path increasingly divergent from that of the parental generation A; likewise C diverges from B. Yet it is from the grandparental generation A that C learns the stories that it, in turn, will carry forward in life, above all through its offspring D (who may, in fact, take the grandparental name and be regarded as a continuation of the ancestral namesake). Similarly D's offspring E follow in the footsteps of generation B. The result is a braid of lines that continually extends as lives proceed.

Of course this depiction is highly schematic, and any real history is bound to be very much more complex. But it should suffice to illustrate the possibility of an open-ended way of thinking about the history of life, as a trans-generational flow in which people and their knowledge undergo

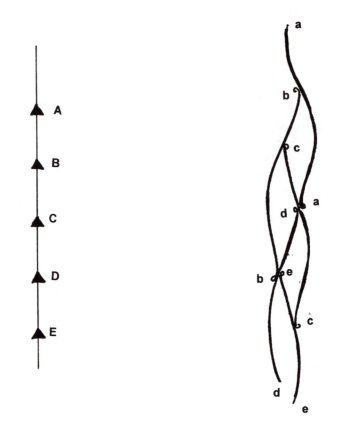

Figure 4.6 A sequence of five generations depicted, on the one hand, according to the conventions of the genealogical model and, on the other, as a series of interlaced and overlapping trails.

perpetual formation. It also gives us a way of describing ancestry and descent which, I believe, more faithfully reflects the way people generally talk about such matters – in terms of the narrative interweaving of present and past lives rather than the plotting of connections between unique and self-contained individuals. And finally, it recasts the way we think about the relation between past and present and, as a corollary, about the form of time. For although the time of life is linear, its linearity is of a particular kind. It is not the kind of line that goes from point to point, connecting up a succession of present instants arrayed diachronically as locations in space might be arrayed synchronically. It is rather a line that grows, issuing forth from its advancing tip rather like a root or creeper probes the earth. 'Our duration', Bergson wrote,

> is not merely one instant replacing another; if it were, there would never be anything but present – no prolonging of the past in the actual . . .

Duration is the continuous progress of the past which gnaws into the future and which swells as it advances.

(1911: 4–5)

The past, in short, does not tail off like a succession of dots left ever further behind. Such a tail is but the ghost of history, retrospectively reconstructed as a sequence of unique events. In reality, the past is *with* us as we press into the future. In this pressure lies the work of memory, the guiding hand of a consciousness that, as it goes along, also remembers the way. Retracing the lines of past lives is the way we proceed along our own.

5 Drawing, writing and calligraphy

My concern in this chapter is with drawing and writing. We draw lines as well as write them, and in each case the line is the trace of a manual gesture. But what is the difference between these gestures? Where does drawing end and writing begin? If, in the history of the line, writing was progressively differentiated from drawing, then how is this reflected in the changing capacities and performances of the human hand? To make a start in answering these questions, I want to review four different ways in which writing and drawing might be distinguished. Here they are, boldly stated. First, writing is in a *notation*; drawing is not. Secondly, drawing is an *art*; writing is not. Thirdly, writing is a *technology*; drawing is not. Fourthly, writing is *linear*; drawing is not. None of these distinctions, as it turns out, is entirely trustworthy. But it pays to pursue them, since a number of important issues can be clarified along the way.

Drawing letters

I begin with a question that I touched upon in the very first chapter, but deliberately set aside. Recall how Nelson Goodman, in his *Languages of Art*, attempts to distinguish between the script and the score. The script, he argues, is a work, whereas in the case of the score the work comprises the set of performances compliant with it. Likewise the drawing is a work, but in etching the work comprises the set of impressions compliant with the plate. Yet both the drawing and the etching, according to Goodman, differ from both the script and the score, in that the latter are rendered in a notation whereas the former are not (Goodman 1969: 210; see also Figure 1.2). I shall not dwell further on the distinction between script and score. Nor will I consider further the case of etching, which raises a number of rather technical issues that lie beyond the scope of the present study. I am concerned, however, with the question of what it takes for a drawn line to be part of a notation. For on this criterion, in Goodman's scheme, hinges the difference between drawing and writing.

Consider the classic picture from *The House at Pooh Corner*, drawn by Ernest H. Shepard for the book by A. A. Milne, and reproduced in Figure 5.1.

Figure 5.1 Eeyore's A. Reproduced from Milne (1928: 84). © The Estate of E. H. Shepard, reproduced with permission of Curtis Brown Limited, London.

Eeyore, the old grey donkey, has arranged three sticks on the ground. Two of the sticks were almost touching at one end but splayed apart at the other, while the third was laid across them. Up comes Piglet. 'Do you know what that is?', Eeyore asks Piglet. Piglet has no idea. 'It's an A', intones Eeyore proudly. By recognizing the figure as an A, however, would we be justified in crediting Eeyore with having produced an artefact of writing? Surely not. All he has done is to copy a figure he has seen somewhere else. He knows it is an A because that is what Christopher Robin called it. And he is convinced that to recognize an A when you see one is of the essence of Learning and Education. But Christopher Robin, who is starting school, knows better. He realizes that A is a letter, and that as such it is just one of a set of letters, called the alphabet, each of which has a name, and that he has learned to recite in a given order. He is also learning to draw these letters. But at what stage does he cease to draw letters and begin instead to write?

The great Russian psychologist Lev Vygotsky, in his studies of early child development, worried a good deal about this question. He realized that the child's first drawings are merely the traces of deictic gestures, made by a hand that happens to be holding an inscribing tool. 'Children', Vygotsky observed, 'do not draw, they indicate, and the pencil merely fixes the indicatory gesture' (Vygotsky 1978: 108). There is a critical moment, however, at which the child discovers that the mark he has made on paper is a depiction of something, and moreover that this thing bears a name. Thenceforth the naming of the object can precede rather than follow the act of drawing it, so that the child can set out, for example, to 'draw an A'. But he is still not writing it. Writing calls for one further shift, prompted by the discovery that letters can be arranged in meaningful combinations to form words. This discovery marks the birth of the child's capacity to read. A child who cannot yet read is bound to practise letter-forming exercises. Only when he can read can he also be truly said to write (ibid.: 110–15).

All of this suggests, as the linguist Roy Harris has forcefully argued, that we ought to make a clear distinction between a *notation* and a *script*. Drawing the letters of the alphabet, recognizing their shapes and learning to tell them apart are exercises in notation. Spelling, however, is an exercise in script. It is a matter of being able to combine the elements of a notation in ways that make sense in the terms of a specific system (and clearly the same elements may be put to use in any number of different systems). *Within the texts of that system*, elements such as letters can then take on a value as written signs (Harris 2000: 91). As such, they belong to a script. Thus Figure 5.2, which illustrates how the letter A is derived from the Egyptian hieroglyph depicting the head of an ox, tells us something about the history of a notational form, but nothing specifically about *writing* at all. Or consider one further example. We often say that a picture is worth a thousand words. But it is for the words that the picture is exchanged, not for the letters in which it is written. To confuse the two is, once again, to confuse the script with the notation. It is akin to supposing that we pay for goods not with coins but with the figures – of the Queen's head, Britannia, numerals and so on – that are inscribed on them. These figures form a notation for coinage, which enables those of us familiar with the system of British currency to recognize small discs of metal as tokens bearing certain values. Likewise, we could argue, letter-shapes form a notation that enables anyone who can spell with a reasonable degree of proficiency to recognize inscriptions on the page as words having particular meanings. But if you are completely unfamiliar with the currency, or if you cannot spell at all, then the notational elements – even though you may recognize them for what they are (letters, figures, etc.) – will mean nothing. They would not be part of any script known to you.

Though it seems logical to distinguish the notation and the script in this way, it has an odd consequence. Suppose you were asked to copy out a passage of text in an alphabetic script you did not understand. You would be compelled to proceed letter by letter, reproducing as faithfully as possible the model before you without having any idea of what it all meant. Would you then be writing, or would you have reverted to drawing letters? This is not such an unrealistic scenario as it might seem. The historian Michael Clanchy reminds us that, although they were esteemed specialists in their craft, medieval scribes often 'scarcely understood the exemplars before them' (Clanchy 1979: 126). They could however recognize the letters, and it was these that they copied onto the page. Do we have to conclude that they were not really writing after all, but drawing? Such a conclusion would go against the grain of the entire approach that I have tried to develop in this book, which is to regard writing, in the first place, as a species of line-making rather than of verbal composition. Moreover it would force us to introduce a division into the work of the scribes when in their experience there was none. The act of writing, so far as they were concerned, was quite indifferent to whether they could actually decipher what was written.

For this reason I am reluctant to regard writing as a practice that supplants drawing. Writing is still drawing. But it is the special case of drawing in which *what is drawn comprises the elements of a notation*. Thus the drawing

Figure 5.2 Variations on the letter A. Reproduced from Kapr (1983: 273, Fig. 427).

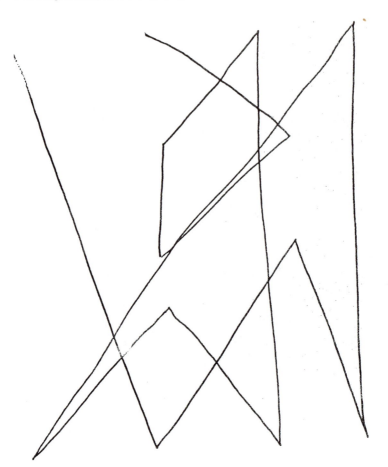

Figure 5.3 'Point to Point: In an imagined H', a drawing by the Canadian writer and poet bp Nichol. If drawing an H as a notational element differed from drawing it as part of a word as much as pronouncing the letter does from its pronunciation in speech, then this is what we might come up with. Reproduced from Nichol (1993: 40).

reproduced in Figure 5.3, entitled 'In an imagined H', may or may not be described as writing, depending on whether we are prepared to accept that it bears any relation whatever to the letter called by this name in any recognized script or typeface (in this instance the drawing reflects on the bizarre incongruity between the vocal pronunciations of this letter as a separate notational element, *aitch*, and as a component of the spoken word, *h*). The notation in question need not consist of letters. It could just as well consist of numerals, or of the notes of the stave score. Or it could consist of characters, as in Chinese script. My main point is this, however: the hand that writes does not cease to draw. It can therefore move quite freely, and without interruption, in and out of writing. Perhaps a parallel might be found in the manual gestures involved in the course of eating a meal. At one moment they govern our handling of the knife and fork; at another they form signs in the air to accompany our conversation. But the gesturing hand, in this example, runs as seamlessly into signing as the drawing hand runs into writing.

In some cases, the elements of a notation are clearly also depictions. That the ox-head hieroglyph, the precursor of our letter A, is a depiction becomes obvious if we compare it with the way oxen themselves were drawn in Ancient Egypt (Figure 5.4). We would not hesitate to say that the glyph is a drawing of something other than itself, even though it is also incorporated into a script. Another well-known example may be taken from recent ethnography. I refer to Nancy Munn's (1973b) celebrated study of the Walbiri, an Aboriginal people of the Central Australian Desert whom we have already encountered, in passing, in Chapter 3. Both men and women among the Walbiri routinely draw designs in the sand with their fingers, as they talk and tell stories. This drawing is as normal and as integral a part of conversation as are speech and gesture. The markings themselves are standardized to the extent that they add up to a kind of vocabulary of graphic elements whose precise meanings, however, are heavily dependent on the conversational or storytelling contexts in which they appear. Thus a simple straight line can be (among other things) a spear, a fighting or digging stick, or a person or animal lying stretched out; a circle can be a nest, water hole, tree, hill, billy can or egg. As the story proceeds, marks are assembled into little scenes, each of which is then wiped out to make way for the next (Munn 1973b: 64–73).

Since the repertoire of marks forms a closed set, and since they can be combined in any number of ways to describe different scenes, it seems perfectly reasonable to suppose that they add up to a notation. But it is also clear that the meanings assigned to each element, though context-dependent, are far from arbitrary. There is an obvious iconic resemblance, for example, between the spear and the straight line. For just this reason Munn describes the Walbiri notation as an *iconography* (ibid.: 87–8). In a case such as this it makes no sense to ask whether graphic elements are written or only drawn. They are at once both written *and* not written, depending on whether the line in the sand is taken to depict a notational element (in the same sense as I might, for example, set out to draw an A) or the object that this element is supposed, in the specific context of the story, to represent. Because of the iconic resemblance between the two, the matter can be interpreted either way. The same might be said of the Queen's head on, say, a two-pence coin. On the one hand the head profile is clearly modelled on that of the reigning monarch, and could be likened to a portrait. But on the other hand it is as much an element of the notation for coinage as is the figure 2, stamped on the opposite side, which depicts nothing but itself.

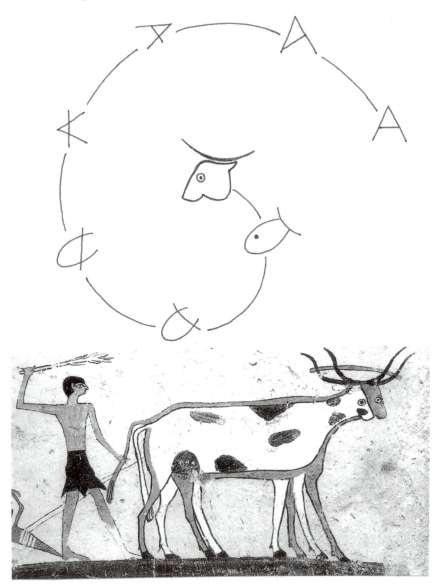

Figure 5.4 The evolution of the letter A, from ox-head hieroglyph to Roman capital. A detail (below) from an agricultural scene in the chapel of Djar, Thebes, shows the clear iconic resemblance between the hieroglyph and the way the head was conventionally depicted in Ancient Egyptian representations of the ox. The crossbar of the Roman A is derived, after several rotations, from the line of the ox's horns.

Writing as drawing

Let me turn now to the second of my four propositions concerning the distinction between drawing and writing. It is often alleged that drawing is an *art*, whereas writing is not. This proposition, along with the third which I shall consider in a moment – namely, that, unlike drawing, writing is a *technology* – hinges upon a dichotomy between technology and art that has become deeply entrenched within the modern constitution. The dichotomy, however, dates back no more than three hundred years. Until well into the seventeenth century, artists were thought no different from artisans, and their methods of working were equally described as 'technical'. In the early seventeenth century the word 'technology' was coined to denote the systematic treatment of these methods (Williams 1976: 33–4; Ingold 2000: 349; Ross 2005: 342). The word was formed on the stem of the classical Greek *tekhne*, whose original connotation was human skill or craftsmanship. 'Art', derived from the Latin *artem* or *ars*, meant much the same thing, applying 'quite broadly to all skilled craftsmanship, work, expert techniques, technologies, and professions' (Mitchell 2005: 6).

However, the subsequent growth of industrial capitalism, coupled with concomitant changes in the division of labour, led in a whole range of fields to the decomposition of skill into the components of creative intelligence and imagination on the one hand, and routine or habitual bodily techniques on the other. The more the concept of art came to be reserved for the former, the more the latter were reduced to what were now regarded as 'merely' technological operations. Once bodily practice had been thus 'factored out' from the creative impulse, the way was open to construct machines to execute, faster and more efficiently, what bodies had done before. With that, the very concept of technology shifted from mind to machine, from principles for the systematic study of processes of production to principles incorporated into the machinery of production itself. Thenceforth an object or performance would be deemed a work of art to the extent that it escapes the determinations of the technological system, and expresses the genius of its creator. Conversely, operating a technology meant being bound to the mechanical implementation of an objective and impersonal system of productive forces. Art creates; technology can only replicate. Thus was the artist distinguished from the artisan, and the work of art from the artefact.

I have already drawn attention, in Chapter 1, to an example of this division of labour, namely that between the author engaged in verbal composition, and the printer whose job it is to run off innumerable copies of the author's work. If the author is a literary artist, the printer is a typographic artisan. It was in the England of the late eighteenth century, according to Raymond Williams, that the notion of the artisan as a manual labourer without intellectual, imaginative or creative purpose really took root. Significantly, as we shall see, the issue revolved around the status of engraving. From the late seventeenth century, the arts had been taken to include painting, drawing, engraving and sculpture. But a hundred years later, the gentlemen of the Royal Academy determined that there should be no place in it for engravers. They were considered to be not artists but artisans, whose natural affiliations lay with the printing trade (Williams 1976: 33). It was around this time, too, that the writer began to be seen, by profession, as a composer of texts rather than a maker of lines, that is, as an author rather than a scribe. It was in such a capacity – along with his counterpart, the composer of musical works – that he joined the ranks of practitioners of 'the arts'. Thenceforth, from around the middle of the nineteenth century, the kind of line-making involved in textual production was relegated to the domain of technology. Drawing, on the other hand, retained its original affiliation with painting and sculpture, within the overall field of what came to be known as the 'fine arts'. And here it has remained. Thus we have arrived at the peculiar contrast between the graphic artist and the writer that is so firmly institutionalized today. The former draws lines in the practice of his art; the latter does not. He is not a line-maker but a wordsmith.

This is what makes it possible for a contemporary anthropologist such as Clifford Geertz to say of the ethnographer that he ' "inscribes" social discourse, he *writes it down*' (Geertz 1973: 19), even though the last thing he does is actually to draw any lines on the page. Still more recently, James Clifford has characterized *inscription* as a 'turn to writing' in the midst of the practical engagements of ethnographic fieldwork, as in the mundane business of note-taking. As such, he argues, it is to be distinguished from *description*, which entails the production of an account, based on reflection, analysis and interpretation, usually in a place well separated from the field (Clifford 1990: 51–2). But in these terms, neither inscription nor description has anything to do with line-making. In both cases it is a matter of *finding the right words* to record or convey what has been observed. Although Clifford calls his analysis 'graphocentric' (ibid.: 53), the inscriptions and descriptions he is talking about are of a kind that you can set down just as well with a typewriter as with a pen. It makes no difference to his argument whether the ethnographer is working with the one or the other (ibid.: 63–4).[1] But in our terms the difference is fundamental. You can write with a pen but you cannot draw with a typewriter.

I believe that in retrojecting our contemporary understanding of writing as verbal composition on to the scribal practices of earlier times (even as we adopt terms such as 'inscription' and 'manuscript' from the latter in order to characterize the former) we fail to recognize the extent to which the very art of writing, at least until it was ousted by typography, lay in the drawing of lines. For writers of the past a feeling or observation would be *described* in the movement of a gesture and *inscribed* in the trace it yields. What mattered was not the choice and semantic content of the words themselves – these could be wholly conventional, as in a liturgical text – but the quality, tone and dynamic of the line itself. Rosemary Sassoon, who trained as a scribe around the end of the Second World War, finding employment for her skills in writing the books of remembrance that were in demand at the time, notes that, despite the rigid discipline of the craft, any scribe can feel how a letter was written just by looking at it (Sassoon 2000: 12). 'The form and line of a letter', she concludes, 'is as sensitive and expressive as the line quality in a drawing, and as individual as the interpretation of colour and light and shade are to a painter' (ibid.: 179).

Among artists of modern times, Paul Klee stands out as having recognized the original identity of drawing and writing. In notes he prepared for his Bauhaus lectures in autumn 1921, Klee remarks of the line that, 'at the dawn of civilisation, when writing and drawing were the same thing, it was the basic element' (Klee 1961: 103; see also Aichele 2002: 164). He went on to explore the resonances between the graphic line and the line of song which again, even as it pronounces words, is sensitive and expressive in itself. However, with the possible exception of graphologists (Jacoby 1939), only in rare instances have Western scholars looked at writing as a kind of drawing. One of the few to have done so is Nicollette Gray. Introducing her remarkable book *Lettering as Drawing* (1971), Gray acknowledges that her approach in linking the fields of writing and drawing is novel, not because of any lack of scholarly research in both, but because the belief that they deal with quite distinct kinds of activity, each calling for separate study, has stifled attempts at synthesis. Yet between writing and drawing, she insists, there can be no hard-and-fast boundary, for the medium of both is the line. And as she justly observes, 'the same sort of line which writes also draws' (Gray 1971: 1). Gray's focus is on the Western tradition of calligraphy, which in modern times has had to struggle for recognition as a legitimate form of art. By and large, students of graphic art have been trained in typography instead. But the lines of typography, like the engraved lines from which they are derived, are quite unlike the drawn lines of a freely flowing, cursive script. A line that is drawn, in Gray's view, is one that *moves* (ibid.: 9).

Indeed the apprehension of movement, and its gestural re-enactment, is fundamental to the practice of drawing. 'At its most essential', writes artist Andy Goldsworthy, drawing describes 'an exploring line alert to changes of rhythm and feelings of surface and space' (Goldsworthy 1994: 82). I showed in Chapter 2 how the two senses of drawing – as pulling threads and scribing traces – are intimately related. Goldsworthy's drawn lines include both traces and threads: the former scratched with stick on sand, or stone on stone; the latter consisting of grass stalks pushed end to end and pinned with thorns to a support such as the ground or a tree trunk. But whatever the medium, drawing 'is related to life, like drawing breath or a tree drawing nourishment through its roots to draw with its branches the space in which it grows. A river draws the valley and the salmon the river' (ibid.).

Long before, in his treatise of 1857 on *The Elements of Drawing*, John Ruskin had advised his novice readers in very similar terms. They were to seize upon what he called *leading lines*, that is, the lines that embody in their very formation the past history, present action and future potential of a thing. The lines of the mountain show how it has been built up and worn away, those of the tree show how it has contended with the trials of life in the forest and with the winds that have tormented it, those of the wave or cloud show how it has been shaped by currents of air and water. In life as in art, Ruskin declared, wisdom lies in '*knowing the way things are going*'.

> Your dunce thinks they are standing still, and draws them all fixed; your wise man sees the change or changing in them, and draws them so, – the animal in its motion, the tree in its growth, the cloud in its course, the mountain in its wearing away. Try always, whenever you look at a form, to see the lines in it which have had power over its past fate and will have power over its futurity. Those are its *awful* lines; see that you seize on those, whatever else you miss.
>
> (Ruskin 1904: 91)

Ruskin illustrates his point with a drawing, reproduced in Figure 5.5, which

Figure 5.5 John Ruskin's drawing of the leafage around the root of a stone pine, on the brow of a crag at Sestri near Genoa. Reproduced from Ruskin (1904: 88). By permission of Historic Collections, King's College, University of Aberdeen.

depicts the foliage growing around the root of a pine, with sapling sprays initially thrust outwards from the root as water splashes from the impact of a stone, before recovering their upwards orientation towards the sky (ibid.: 88, 91–2). However, Ruskin's advice, as we shall see, might just as well have been given to an apprentice Chinese calligrapher.

An art of movement

It is conventional to say of the calligrapher that he writes. Yet as Yuehping Yen has shown, Chinese calligraphy is, in essence, 'an art of rhythmic movement', wherein the constituent lines of each character have a power and dynamic of their own (see Figure 5.6). 'Through the observation of nature', Yen explains, calligraphers 'observe the principles of every type of movement and rhythm and try to convey them through the calligraphic brush' (Yen 2005: 84–5). In an influential treatise one of the most celebrated calligraphers of the Tang Dynasty, Sun Guoting (AD 648–703), wrote as follows:

> Consider the difference between the 'suspended needle (*xuanzhen*)' and 'hanging-dewdrop (*chuilu*)' brush strokes, and then consider the marvels of rolling thunder and toppling rocks, the postures of wild geese in flight and beasts in fright, the attitudes of phoenixes dancing and snakes startled, the power of sheer cliffs and crumbling peaks, the shapes of facing danger and holding on to rotten wood, which are sometimes heavy like threatening clouds and sometimes light like cicada wings; consider that when the brush moves, water flows from a spring, and when the brush stops, a mountain stands firm; consider what is very, very light, as if the new moon were rising at the sky's edge, and what is very, very clear like the multitude of stars arrayed in the Milky Way – these are the same as the subtle mysteries of nature: they cannot be forced.
>
> (cited in Yen 2005: 84)

Preserving these subtle inflections of the brush on absorbent paper, the lines of calligraphy are indeed 'awful' in Ruskin's sense. Every line is the trace of a delicate gesture of the hand that holds the brush, a gesture inspired by the calligrapher's close observations of movements in the world around him.

Throughout history, Chinese calligraphers have sought inspiration from such observations. One thirteenth-century master vividly compares the attack – that critical moment at which the tip of the brush makes contact with the paper at the commencement of a stroke – to 'the hare leaping and the hawk swooping down on its prey' (Billeter 1990: 163). Another tells of how, to capture the distinctive movements of the characters *tzu* and *pu*, he attempted to imitate with the hand the movement of a flying bird. For the characters *wei* and *ju* he tried to motion in the air the somersaulting of rats at play (ibid.: 185–6). Two centuries earlier, in the period of the Sung

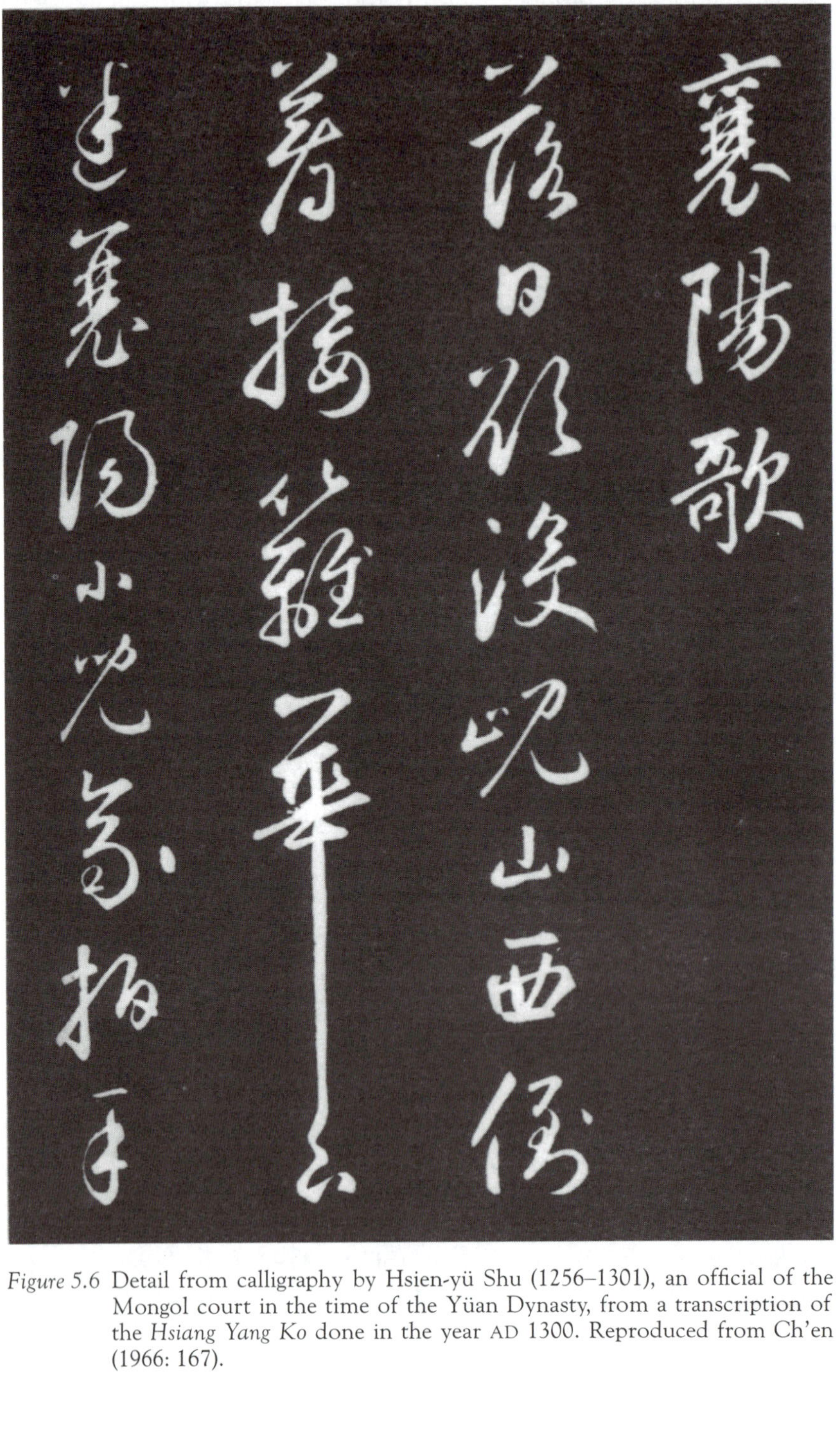

Figure 5.6 Detail from calligraphy by Hsien-yü Shu (1256–1301), an official of the Mongol court in the time of the Yüan Dynasty, from a transcription of the *Hsiang Yang Ko* done in the year AD 1300. Reproduced from Ch'en (1966: 167).

Dynasty, the calligrapher Lei Chien-fu described how he heard a waterfall, and imagined the water swirling, rushing and tumbling into the abyss. 'I got up to write', he recalled, 'and all that I had imagined appeared beneath my brush' (ibid.: 183). A treatise on painting from the same period explains why Wang Hsi-chih, who lived from AD 321 to 379, was fond of geese. 'It was', the author tells us, 'because to form the characters, he took inspiration from the resemblance between the undulations of the neck and those of the wrist as it twirls the brush' (ibid.: 184, 200, fn. 65). Another calligrapher of the Sung Dynasty, Huang T'ing-chien, describes how, after years of frustration in his attempts to master a particular gesture, he found the secret late in life while crossing the gorge of the Yangtze River on a ferry boat. Observing the boatmen working with their oars, how they angled them as they entered the water, pulled through in the development of the stroke, and lifted them out at the end, and how they put their whole body into the work, he immediately grasped how his brush should be manoeuvred (ibid.: 183).

From these examples, all taken from Jean-François Billeter's remarkable work on *The Chinese Art of Writing*, it seems indisputable that these master calligraphers, while ostensibly writing, were also drawing what they observed. But it was not the shapes or outlines of things that they sought to render; the aim was rather to reproduce in their gestures the rhythms and movements of the world. As Yuehping Yen explains, one would not expect calligraphic lines inspired by the attack and counter-attack of battling snakes to actually *look like* snakes; the important thing is that the lines should move like them (Yen 2005: 85). It could be questioned, however, whether Chinese writing consists of lines at all. Of course it is technically feasible to produce lines with a fine brush, just as it is with a pen. In the style of Chinese painting known as *kung-pi*, the artist would begin by drawing such lines, before colouring them in. These lines are called *hsien*, which literally means 'thread'. This term, however, is never used in calligraphy. Instead, the vocabulary of calligraphy – including the terms for brush (*pi*) and stroke (*hua*) – is shared with a quite different style of painting known as *hsieh-i*, which is produced by applying ink washes to silk or paper with no preliminary drawing at all.

It would seem, from this evidence, that the one form calligraphers do *not* produce is the line. To get around the problem of nomenclature, Billeter uses the neutral term 'element' for each constituent mark of a written character (Billeter 1990: 50–1). I see no cause to be so circumspect, however. As the trace left on a surface by a continuous movement, the calligrapher's brush stroke, or *pi-hua*, fully qualifies as a line in terms of the taxonomy set out in Chapter 2, and I shall continue to refer to it as such. It is nevertheless important to acknowledge that the pen of the Western letter-writer and the brush of the Chinese calligrapher produce lines of very different kinds. Not only does the brush produce a trace of continually varying width, but it can also be moved with equal facility in all directions. Thus the calligrapher is able to 'play' with the flexible tip of the brush in a way that would be quite impossible with the nib of a pen that is rigidly fixed to its shaft (Billeter 1990: 11–12, 54). It is rather more possible with a pencil, however. As the predominant instrument of drawing in the Western tradition, the pencil affords a considerably greater degree of flexibility than the pen, and is not unlike the brush in this respect. Indeed the word 'pencil', derived from the Latin *penicillum* (meaning a little tail, as of the ermine or sable), originally referred to the fine painter's brush, and as such was quite distinct from 'pen' (from the Latin *penna*, feather). Whereas the resemblance between the two words is accidental, the difference between the instruments they denote is fundamental.

The penman draws on a comparatively small repertoire of repeated move-ments to describe a continuous letter-line whose oscillations, loops and trails create a texture, the patterns of which emerge as the writing proceeds. As we saw in Chapter 2, the analogy here is with weaving, epitomized in the metaphor of the text. Along the line, each letter seems to lean over and touch the next, rather as in a line of people standing in single file where each person has raised an arm and placed their hand on the shoulder of the person in front. Thus the reader has the impression of viewing the letters from the side, as one would view the figures of such a file as they go by. In Chinese calligraphy, by contrast, characters are observed face on. As Paul Claudel writes, 'the Chinese letter faces you, the Latin letter shows its profile' (cited in Billeter 1990: 28). Relative to the position of the viewer, it is as though characters were stacked up behind one another rather than side by side. One has therefore to 'see through' each character for the next to be revealed. For this reason there is nothing comparable to the letter-line of the Western cursive script. Chinese writing is in no sense akin to the art of weaving. The analogy is rather with dancing (Billeter 1990: 163, 178, 220; Yen 2005: 100).

In calligraphy as in the dance, the performer concentrates all his energies and sensibilities into a sequence of highly controlled gestures. Both call for the same preparation and attack, but, once begun, are executed swiftly and without any break. In both, too, the entire body is caught up in the action. Though we might think that the calligrapher works with the hand alone, in fact his manual movements have their source in the muscles of the back and torso, braced by his seating position on the ground, whence they extend through the shoulder and the elbow to the wrist (Billeter 1990: 64). Perhaps there is a difference in that, whereas dance tends to be centrifugal, animated by an outburst of pent-up energy from an active centre in the dancer's body, calligraphy is centripetal, as all the energy is focused down through a succes-sion of 'checkpoints' – shoulder, elbow, wrist, knuckles – to the ever-moving tip of the brush whose hundreds of hairs meet the paper (Yen 2005: 86). And of course, the gestures of the calligrapher usually (but not always) leave a trace, whereas those of the dancer generally do not (although they sometimes do). In their enactment, however, calligraphic gestures unfold in much the same way as do choreographic ones, as a series of miniature scenes, each dissolving as soon as it is formed to make way for the next.

A parallel could just as well be drawn, however, with manual gestures such as those that routinely accompany ordinary speech or in more specialized usages such as the signed language of the deaf or even orchestral conducting. As I showed in Chapter 1, to focus on the hand and its work is at once to dispel the illusion that what we see are necessarily quiescent things. The silent words of signed language, for example, can be as lively as the sounded words of speech, and their apprehension calls for a visual attention that is as dynamic and participatory – just as much a matter of joining *with* the practitioner in his or her performance – as is listening. If, as we have seen, medieval European readers could hear written words as though they were being spoken or sung, then could not readers accustomed to a language of manual gesture see written words as though they were being signed, or even as a kind of manual dance? Indeed they could, as the example of Chinese calligraphy once more proves. Nothing better illustrates the fact that the characters of Chinese writing were apprehended, in the first place, as the traces of gestures than the curious practice – curious, that is, to Western readers – of 'writing in the air'.

This is how children in China have traditionally learned to write (Yen 2005: 109). They begin by motioning the characters with sweeping gestures of the arm and hand, naming each element of the character as it is formed, and then pronounce the character at the end. Only when the gesture has been learned is it then written down and, with practice, gradually reduced in amplitude and increased in speed of execution (Billeter 1990: 85). The words, then, are remembered as gestures, not as images: indeed it is precisely for that reason – because they are incorporated through practice and training into the *modus operandi* of the body – that it is possible for one person to remember so many characters (DeFrancis 1984: 163). The hand knows how to form each character even if the eye has forgotten its design. But this also means that it is as easy for a person to 'read' a gesture traced in the air as it is to read the same gesture traced on paper. Indeed the physical trace is almost an incidental by-product, since it is the movement of forming it that counts.[2] The converse of this, however, is that too much emphasis on the design can paralyse one's capacity to write. Chinese readers commonly report that staring at a character for a long time can lead to the disconcerting sensation that it is falling apart into randomly disposed elements. Before you can write it again you have to practise a few times in order to recover the movement, whereupon – as Yen puts it – 'the character re-emerges like a submarine resurfacing from the depths of the sea' (2005: 110).

Staring, in this example, is a special kind of vision that immobilizes its object – that does indeed nail it down. But far from being formed under the impress of such visual surveillance, the written character is undone by it. For in Chinese writing the coherence of the character lies in the movement by which it is drawn. Arrest the movement, and the character disintegrates. In

Western societies, to the contrary, movement is tantamount to 'noise' that interferes with the perception of literate form. True, children in both East and West may share the same point of departure. More or less universally, as Vygotsky recognized, children taking their first steps towards writing perceive gestures as 'writing in the air' and written signs simply as 'gestures that have been fixed' (Vygotsky 1978: 107). But in Western societies, education in literacy has taken a radically different course. In their early exercises in drawing letters Western children are drilled in the manual gestures required to form them. The goal of such exercises, however, is not to reproduce the gestures but to copy the forms of the letters as neatly as possible on the page. And in learning to read, children are likewise taught to recognize the letterforms, not the gestures entailed in making them. Thus by the time they are proficient in reading and writing on paper, they are no longer able to write, or to read what is written, in the air.

Printing and engraving

Starting with the freely drawn traces of gestural air-writing and ending with the reproduction of pre-determined letter-forms bearing no relation to the gestures that deliver them, every child of modern Western society recapitulates in his or her education in literacy a much longer history of graphic production. It is however above all a history not of drawing alone but of the shifting balance between drawing and engraving. We may recall from Chapter 2 that the origins of the word 'writing' lie in the incision of hard surfaces. Roy Harris likewise reminds us that, in Greek Antiquity, the verb for 'to write', *graphein*, from which is derived the plethora of words in English that include the morpheme *graph*, originally meant 'engrave, scratch, scrape' (Harris 1986: 29). Whatever the specific nomenclature of line-making and its etymological derivation, it could well be that the distinction, in practice and experience, between making reductive traces with a sharply pointed implement in a resistant material like stone, and making additive traces in flowing ink on papyrus, parchment or paper, using a pen or brush, was a harbinger of things to come, finding a distant echo, millennia later, in the modern idea of writing as an art of composition separate from drawing.

In China, this distinction was already well established from an early date, through the coexistence of brush calligraphy with the practice of engraving stone seals (Billeter 1990: 165, 286–9). For this the engraver uses a chisel of tempered steel. He holds the chisel in the right hand rather as we would hold a pencil, at about 45 degrees to the surface, while the seal is held in the left hand. Applying considerable force, he cuts each line from beginning to end in one go, then turns the seal around and cuts in the other direction, continuing to cut back and forth until he has obtained a satisfactory groove. To make a curve he gradually turns the seal in his left hand while cutting with his right. The result is a character whose lines erase rather than reveal the gestures that gave rise to them. For quite unlike the calligraphic brush stroke, which registers the fleeting moment of its production and can on no account be repaired or retouched (Yen 2005: 89), in cutting back and forth with the chisel each successive cut eliminates the trace of the preceding gesture. Moreover the curved line testifies to the movement of the hand that is holding the stone, not of the hand manoeuvring the tool. And the engraver cannot alter the width of the line at will, as can the calligrapher. Sometimes the engraver will begin with a character drawn with a brush on thin rice paper, which is inverted on the moistened surface of the seal. He can then cut using the brush-drawn trace as a template. The resulting character, however, attests to the gestures involved in the original brush drawing, not of the engraving. On the completed seal the character stands alone, as a finished artefact, immobile and complete in itself (Figure 5.7). It is in this static form that it is transferred, through the simple act of impression, to any document destined to bear its imprimatur.

By the fourth century AD, the Chinese had all the ingredients necessary for printing: namely, engraved surfaces, paper, and ink of the right consistency. By the eighth century they had transferred their engraving techniques to wooden blocks, and by the eleventh century they were experimenting with movable type. Meanwhile in Europe, the Romans had been developing the majuscule script – the precursor of our modern capital letters – specifically for the purpose of engraving inscriptions in stone. Minuscule letters, derived from the majuscule, began to appear in Roman manuscripts from the third century AD, and under the Carolingian reforms of the eighth century the two alphabets were eventually combined into a single system. Although techniques of paper-making had already arrived in Europe by the eleventh century, imported from China by way of the Arab world, it would be another three hundred years before printing with movable type was invented in Europe, apparently independently of the Chinese precedent, on the basis of metal-processing techniques – of engraving, casting and punching – that had been used since antiquity for minting coins.[3] It would take too long to describe the subsequent history of printing, and its relation to handwriting, in any detail. Suffice it to say that it is as printed letters – that is, as the familiar upper and lower cases of modern typography – that the Roman majuscule and minuscule have come down to us today.

It is significant that the forms of printed letters or characters have their origins in the engraving of stone, wood and metal rather than in hand-writing. For in the engraved inscription the gestures of the artisan are not so much preserved as cancelled out. We have already seen how this is so in the case of Chinese seals, but the same could also be said of Roman inscriptions. Based on the square, triangle and circle, the forms of the Roman *capitales quadratae*, or square capitals, are exceedingly awkward to write with the pen. They simply do not answer to any free-flowing movement of the hand. They do, however, come relatively easily to the chisel (Gray 1971: 95). This is not to deny that chiselling stone is hard work. But in the engraved inscriptions, no trace remains of the energetic movement of the

Figure 5.7 Seals carved by famous Chinese calligraphers. The three seals on the right are by the Ch'ing calligrapher Têng Shih-ju (1743–1805), the four in the middle column are by the Ch'ing calligrapher Chao Chih-ch'ien (1829–84), the seal in the upper left is by the Ch'ing calligrapher-painter Wu Chün-ch'ing (1844–1927), and the remaining seals on the left are by the contemporary painter Ch'i Huang. Reproduced from Ch'en (1966: 249).

hands that made them. Like the characters on Chinese seals, Roman capitals are strikingly static. Though read in sequence, each letter is simply being itself; it is not ceasing to be the one before or transforming into the one after. So called because of their placement on the surfaces of monuments – though not necessarily at the tops of columns or pillars as the name suggests (Avrin 1991: 177) – capitals were assembled into compositions whose construction was integral to the architecture of the monuments themselves. Staring impassively at the spectator, face on, they convey an overwhelming impression, doubtless intended, of monumental permanence and immobility (Figure 5.8).

Thus it was the technique of engraving that broke the link between the gesture and its trace, immobilized the letter or character and, in so doing, laid the foundations for the modern perception of words as things composed and arranged by art, but not inscribed by it. With this we return to our conclusion in Chapter 1, responding to the thesis put forward by Walter Ong, that it was not writing as such that reified the word but rather the disconnection of the gestural movement from its graphic inscription brought about by the transition from handwriting to print. We are now in a position to project this conclusion much further back in time, finding precursors for the reified and immobile word in the letters and characters of ancient monuments and seals, inscribed in stone, hardwood or metal. Considering such artefacts, how then should we judge Ong's (1982) claim that writing entailed 'the technologizing of the word'? This question brings me to the third of the four propositions with which I began, namely that writing – unlike drawing – is essentially a technology of language.

According to Ong, writing 'was and is the most momentous of all human technological inventions', and has utterly transformed the world in which we live (Ong 1982: 85). Statements to this effect abound in the literature, and are rarely thought to call for any justification. Thus in a recently published textbook on writing systems one leading authority in the field, Florian Coulmas, asserts that writing is a 'technology that has evolved over thousands of years' (Coulmas 2003: 2). What is it then, in the eyes of these and other scholars, that makes writing a technology? Why should it be considered to be any more technological than drawing? There appear to be three possible answers. The first is because writing had to be invented, the second is because writing involves the use of tools, and the third is because writing is artificial. Let me take a look at each of these answers in turn.

The invention of writing

If writing was an invention, then in what exactly did the novelty consist? What did it introduce to the world that was not there before? Inventions, moreover, require inventors. Who were these people, the alleged architects of writing systems, and what did they think they were doing? In only a very few cases do we know who they were: for example the celebrated Cherokee

Figure 5.8 Classical Roman capital on a tombstone from the first century AD. Reproduced from Kapr (1983: 28, Fig. 34).

Indian Sequoyah, who in the early decades of the nineteenth century devised a complete syllabary of 85 signs for his native language (Rogers 2005: 247–8), and the Korean King Sejong, who in the year 1443 promulgated a 28-letter alphabet of his own design, in a document entitled 'The correct sounds for the instruction of the people' (Coulmas 2003: 156–66). These were individuals who were already familiar with literate traditions, which is of course why we have records attesting to their achievements. We should naturally resist the temptation to assume that there were no inventors in prehistory just because – in the absence of documentation – they cannot be identified. The linguist John DeFrancis claims to have come close to identifying the individual inventor of what is widely held to be the earliest known writing system in the world, the Sumerian (DeFrancis 1989: 75). He was an anonymous inhabitant of the town of Jemdet Nasr, in Mesopotamia, living around 3000 BC. What, then, did he invent?

The answer, according to DeFrancis (1989: 74), is the *rebus principle* – that is, the principle whereby a pictographic sign is used to represent not the thing it depicts but the sound of the spoken word for that thing. For example, by combining a picture of a bee with a picture of a leaf one could construct a phonetic representation of the word 'belief' (ibid.: 50). In an early tablet from Jemdet Nasr, the picture of the reed in the upper left corner represents the sound of the word for 'reed', which happened to be homophonous with the word for 'reimburse' (Figure 5.9). The scribe evidently intended the latter meaning. Like so many tablets from the period, this one was part of a record for the local temple, detailing income and outgoings.

Now the precise significance of the rebus principle is a matter of some debate among historians of writing, and I am certainly not qualified to pronounce on the issue. There seems to be little doubt that the principle was crucial to the process of phonetization, whereby graphic icons came to stand

Figure 5.9 Inscription on a tablet from Jemdet Nasr, Sumeria, around 3000 BC. Reproduced from Vaiman (1974: 18).

for the sounds of speech. But it is quite another matter to claim, as DeFrancis does, that this step amounted to 'one of the greatest inventions of human history' (1989: 50), for that is to cast a retrospective judgement in the light of a subsequent history that its originators can have known nothing about. We misconstrue the problem of origin, as Roy Harris has observed, by posing it from the point of view of a civilization that has already assimilated writing and its consequences (Harris 1986: 29). It is all too easy for us, trained as we are in the tradition of academic literacy, to imagine that the first people to represent speech sounds by means of graphic elements, whoever they may have been, were motivated by a futuristic vision of a fully literate society. It is this teleological conception of the history of writing that lies behind the popular idea of an inevitable, unilinear progression from pictography through syllabic scripts to the alphabet.

Of one thing, I think, we can be relatively sure. Those nameless individuals credited by modern scholars with having invented the earliest scripts – and there seem to have been several, who hit on the same idea quite independently – did not first conceive in the abstract, and then proceed to construct, full-blown, purpose-built writing systems. They did not even imagine the possibility of writing as we would think of it now. All they did was to find expedient solutions to the very specific, local difficulties involved in such tasks as keeping accounts, recording proper names, registering ownership or divining fortunes. In each case, the solution lay in pressing well-known and readily identifiable icons into service for the new purpose of standing for speech sounds. What modern historians rather grandly call 'writing systems' undoubtedly developed as accumulations of expediences of this kind. DeFrancis is right to call them 'jerry-built structures' that 'bear less resemblance to carefully constructed schemes for representing spoken languages than they do to a hodgepodge of mnemonic clues that adept readers can use to arrive at coherent messages' (DeFrancis 1989: 262). They were, in short, more like Rube Goldberg devices than the exemplary instances of engineering design that the notion of writing as a technology would lead us to expect.[4]

The tools of the trade

Let me turn now to the second possible answer to the question of what makes writing technological: namely because it involves the use of tools and other equipment. For Ong this is the first thing that comes to mind in thinking of writing as a technology (Ong 1982: 81–2). Likewise in his study of the work of scribes in eleventh- to thirteenth-century England, Michael Clanchy gives the title 'The technology of writing' to a chapter devoted to the instruments and materials of the trade (Clanchy 1979: 114–44). These were numerous and diverse. The principal materials were wood, wax and parchment. The text would be written in draft with a stylus on coloured wax, overlaid upon wooden tablets, and only then would it be copied on to parchment. The tools of the scribe included a knife or razor for scraping the parchment, a pumice for smoothing it, a boar's tooth for polishing the surface, then the stylus, pencil, ruler, plumb-line and awl for ruling the lines and, for the writing itself, quill-pens and penknife, inkhorn and inks of various colours. This is not to mention furniture, lamp lighting and all the other paraphernalia of the study (ibid.: 116). But that is just one example. Clearly, where writing consists of marks impressed on wet clay, as in Sumerian cuneiform, or where it is engraved in stone, stamped on metal, laid in mosaic, or embroidered or brocaded in tapestry, the equipment and techniques involved would have been quite different and in many cases of a kind that we would not specifically associate with writing at all. We have already come across some of these techniques, in connection with the practices of weaving and engraving. I do not now intend to elaborate on them in further detail. The question at hand is rather whether the mere use of tools is enough to constitute writing as a technology.

Ong thinks so. Writing, he suggests, is like playing the violin or the organ. In either case the musical instrument may be understood as a 'mechanical contrivance' that enables the player to 'express something poignantly human' that could not be expressed without it. But to succeed in this the musician has to incorporate – through rigorous training and regular practice – the principles of the instrument's acoustic functioning so as to make them second nature. He or she, as Ong puts it, has to have 'interiorized the technology'. And if this is a prerequisite for the performance of instrumental music, it is even more so, Ong claims, for the practice of writing (Ong 1982: 83). Now of course, some musical instruments *are* like machines, embodying in their very construction the principles of their operation. An organ is a machine in this sense. When you press a key on the organ a pre-determined sound comes out. Similarly, when you press a key on a typewriter, a predetermined letter-form appears on the page. There is thus a certain parallel between playing the organ and typing. The violin, however, is *not* a machine. Like singing, which involves no extra-somatic instrument at all, violin playing is an art. The player is no more an operator of her instrument than is the singer an operator of her voice. And just as violin playing differs in this regard from playing the organ, so handwriting differs from typing. The difference lies not in the degree to which a technology has been interiorized, but in the extent to which musical or graphic forms issue directly from the energetic and experiencing human subject – that is, from the player or writer – rather than being related, by operational principles embedded in the instrument, as output to input.

Of violin playing, Kandinsky observed that 'the pressure of the hand upon the bow corresponds perfectly to the pressure of the hand upon the pencil' (1982: 612). Only the pencil, however, leaves a trace. In the lines left upon its surface the handwritten page bears witness to gestures that, in their qualities of attentiveness and feeling, embody an intentionality intrinsic to the movement of their production. The typewriter, however, neither attends nor feels, and the marks that are made by its means bear no trace of human sensibility. Of course I do not deny that typing is a manual operation: indeed more than that – and like organ playing, which can even involve the feet as well – it is actually *bi*manual. Nor is it unskilled. Moreover the original typewriter, powered by nothing else than muscular fingers, might even be better compared to the piano than the organ, in so far as the force of the impact on the keys is reflected in the blackness and heaviness of the graphic marks on the page. But modern electronic keyboards have removed even this possibility of expression. Interrupted by the mechanism of the apparatus, the *ductus* of the hand never finds its way on to the page. The hands of skilled typists dance on the space of the keyboard, not on that of the page, and on the hard keys their soft fingers leave no trace at all.

We have already seen in the case of Chinese writing how the calligrapher is absorbed in the action with the whole of his being, indissolubly body and mind. In Chinese understanding, Yen observes, 'the person and the hand-writing are mutually generative' (Yen 2005: 66). But the same could have been said of handwriting in the Western tradition, at least until the nineteenth century when the quill – after a heyday that lasted for over a millennium – was eventually replaced by the metallic nib. We are used today to allowing the hand that holds the pen to rest on the page while most of the work of manipulation is done by the fingers. Thus our only arm movements consist of periodic adjustments of the hand's resting position as the writing proceeds across the page, while the remainder of the body is relatively passive and immobile. Perhaps this contributes to an illusion of disembodiment, to a sense that, in writing, the hand, along with the tool it holds, obeys the dictates of a mind that inhabits a world of its own, aloof from the action it initiates. In the Western discipline of graphology, as Yen points out, this illusion is sustained by the idea that the role of the body in handwriting is to act as 'a conduit between the mind and the surface of the paper', authentically passing messages and content from one to the other (Yen 2005: 66).

But if you are writing with a quill-pen, the illusion is virtually impossible to sustain. Since the pen is most effective when angled almost orthogonally to the surface, it is held quite differently from its metal-tipped counterpart. The writing hand scarcely touches the page, while all the movement comes from the arm (Hamel 1992: 37). Writing on parchment, moreover, was a two-handed operation. As the right hand held the pen, the left held a knife against the springy surface of the page in order to keep it steady. Intermittently, the knife was also used for sharpening the quill and erasing errors. Medieval scribes would sit bolt upright, often on a tall-backed chair, with the manuscript laid before them on a steeply sloping desk or on a board attached to arms projecting at an incline from the chair itself (Figure 5.10). Theirs was not light work. On the contrary, writing was perceived as an act of endurance in which, as one scribe lamented, 'the whole body labours' (Clanchy 1979: 116). But of course the scribe was referring to himself. In his experience, he does not *put* his body to work in writing; rather he *is* his body at work.

Figure 5.10 Laurence, Prior of Durham 1149–54, depicted as a scribe in a contemporary manuscript of his own works. While writing with the pen held in his right hand, he is holding back the springy surface of the parchment with a knife held in his left. MS Cosin V.III.1, f.22v. Reproduced by permission of Durham University Library.

Accustomed as they are to their creature comforts, modern scholars tend to emphasize the intellectual effort of verbal composition at the expense of the sheer physical exertion that, in past times, was entailed in the act of inscription itself. No one has put this more plainly than Mary Carruthers, in her account of writing on parchment in medieval Europe:

> We should keep in mind the vigorous, if not violent, activity involved in making a mark upon such a physical surface as an animal's skin. One must break it, rough it up, 'wound' it in some way with a sharply pointed instrument. Erasure involved roughing up the physical surface even more: medieval scribes, trying to erase parchment, had to use pumice stones and other scrapers. In other words, writing was always hard physical labour, very hard as well on the surface on which it was being done . . .
>
> (Carruthers 1998: 102)

Even today, however, handwriting places demands on the practitioner that are as much physical as mental, if indeed the two can be distinguished. Although modern paper, compared with medieval parchment, may not have to be treated so brutally, the body with its writing implement still will not, simply and mechanically, answer to the imperatives of the mind.

In her studies of the condition known as 'writer's cramp', Rosemary Sassoon shows how twisted postures and awkward penholds, often induced by injunctions – for example in the school classroom – to sit and write in a prescribed manner that makes no allowance for variability in body proportions or handedness, can lead not just to pain but to a progressive inability to write at all. Patients, Sassoon reports, 'explain how frightening it is when some part of their body ceases to obey their commands' (2000: 103). A hand that will no longer write may fail in other operations as well. Seeing in their increasingly unsatisfactory efforts a mirror of their own personal failure, patients lose the confidence to write, and find themselves locked in a vicious circle. Writing, as Sassoon shows, is not merely a means for the communication of messages or ideas: 'it is oneself on paper. If you are successful, your writing reassures you; if it fails you, the constant visual reminder of your failure is there to remind you' (ibid.). When writing fails, it is experienced not as a failure of technology or a mechanical breakdown, but as a crisis of the whole person.

Finally, Ong's claim that writing is a technology because it involves the use of tools appears even less credible when we take into account the possibility that writing requires no instrument beyond what the body provides, nor even any artificial materials. Try it next time you are on holiday on the beach – all you need to do is to run your finger through the sand. If this seems a trivial example, then consider Munn's account of Walbiri iconography, which I mentioned earlier in this chapter. The gestures of the Walbiri storyteller are traced in the sand, using the hand and fingers. No other accessories are needed. As I have already shown, the issue of whether or not these traces amount to writing cannot be settled unequivocally. I need only add that the issue is hardly resolved, one way or the other, by the presence or absence of an inscribing tool. If Walbiri people scratched in the sand with a stick rather than with their fingers, it would not make the result any more like writing, or any less like drawing, nor would it convert their inscriptive practice into the operation of a technology. And of course the converse also holds. If you can write without a tool, you can also draw with one. Indeed almost all drawing is tool-assisted, just as almost all writing is. The draughtsman's workshop is liable to contain a toolkit that not only is as broad and diverse as that of the writer's study, but also includes many of the same items.

Nature and artifice

Of course, Ong was comparing writing not with drawing but with speech, and speech does not normally require the use of any implement. Yet he seems to think that drawing comes as 'naturally' to humans as speech does. Noting that the first 'true' writing, the Sumerian script, did not make its appearance until some five millennia ago, Ong admits that 'human beings had been drawing pictures for countless millennia before this' (Ong 1982: 84). The massive discrepancy between the alleged dates of origin for drawing and writing brings me to the third reason why writing is often considered a technology of language. Drawing, it is supposed, is an expressive art that human beings have practised from earliest prehistory, from the moment when they began to make inscriptions of one kind or another on wood, bone or stone. As such, it is said to manifest a capacity for art that is universal and distinctive to our species – as distinctive as the capacity for speech. Writing, on the other hand, is widely regarded as a much later innovation that, in some societies and regions of the world but not all, marked the transition from prehistory to history and set in train the processes of civilization. Thus drawing is said to have emerged in the course of human evolution, while writing is a product of human history. Drawing is natural; writing is artificial or man-made.

But drawing is not natural. It is not a trait or capacity that is somehow installed in all human individuals in advance of their entry into the world. Nor is writing a capacity subsequently 'added on' to a body pre-programmed to draw. Learning to write is a matter not of interiorizing a technology but of acquiring a skill. Precisely the same is true of learning to draw. Indeed since writing is itself a modality of drawing, the two processes of enskilment are strictly inseparable. Recalling the analogy with playing a musical instrument, we could compare the acquisition of line-making skills to the process of learning to play the violin. The novice violinist has to practise regularly, under expert guidance, ideally from a young age when her body is still undergoing rapid growth. In the course of this training certain patterns of posture and gesture, and of attentiveness and response, are incorporated into her body as it develops. Novices are of course expected to follow certain rules as they take their first steps. But these are in the nature of rules of thumb: they scaffold the learning process, but form no part of what is learned. As the novice advances in proficiency, and has no further need of their support, they can be simply discarded (Ingold 2000: 415–16).

In just the same way, the young apprentice draughtsman, scribe or calligrapher learns the craft of line-making. At first he is taught to follow basic rules of execution, possibly following a guide or template for each figure or letter. But these are gradually set aside as, through frequent practice, he gains fluency in his manual movements and precision in handling the inscribing implement. At the same time he learns to bring the implement into the right angular relation with the surface, and this, as we have seen, can call for further adjustments not only to the movements of his arm but in his entire bodily comportment. Yen describes how the traditional procedure for learning Chinese calligraphy, still adopted in elementary schools, comprises three stages. Novices first learn to copy a model work by placing the paper over the model so that it shows through, and tracing the shadows. Next, paper and model are placed side by side, forcing them to reproduce the necessary movements for themselves, rather than being guided by the shadows of the master (Yen 2005: 116–18). Then in the final stage of learning, apprentices are encouraged to shake themselves loose from the clutching 'hands' of the masters that have already shaped their bodily conformation. In this final 'de-shaping', at the culmination of the learning process, 'all the learned rules are banished into oblivion and the heart becomes the only guide of the hand' (ibid.: 123).

In the West, too, children have traditionally been taught to write by first copying models, though with the cursive script there has been a particular concern with how to join letters up. In writing the word *the*, for example, children are taught to go back and cross the *t* before picking up the loop at the foot of the letter and carrying it towards the following *h*. But as writers become fluent, most find themselves leaving the lower loop disconnected and carrying the crossbar directly on into the *h* (Sassoon 2000: 40–50). Figure 5.11 shows an example of this development in the handwriting of a curate in the early decades of the nineteenth century, from his first copy book, through school exercise books, to a mature hand used in writing a diary. As this example shows, the capacity to write is not acquired as a corpus of man-made rules and procedures but emerges in and through the growth and development of the human being in his or her environment. Exactly the same is true of the capacity to draw, which does not come ready-made in the human organism but has also to undergo development. Indeed both capacities, of drawing and writing, emerge literally hand in hand – for the same hands do both.

What then remains of our initial proposition, that writing is a technology? Very little. Was writing invented? No. What was invented was the rebus, a device that has been exploited in some but not all writing systems to facilitate the depiction of speech sounds. Does writing use tools? Usually yes, but not

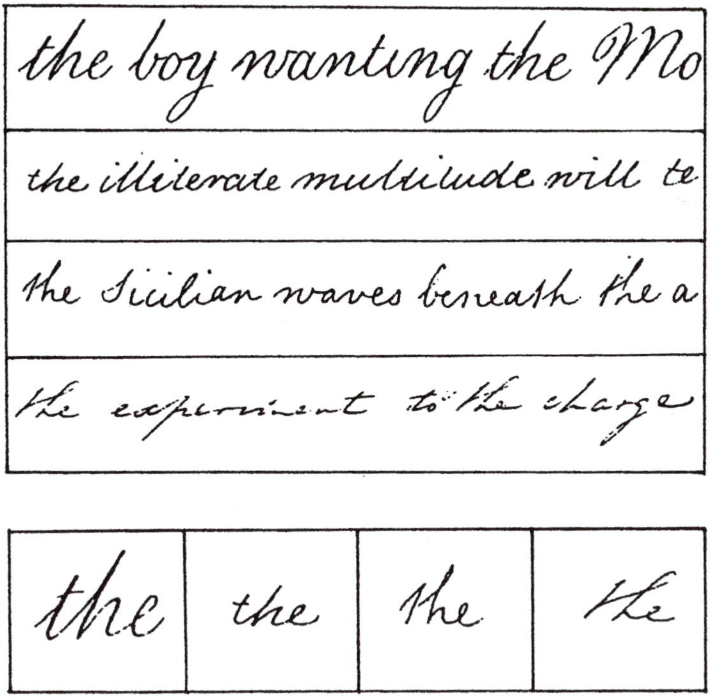

Figure 5.11 The maturation of the handwriting of a curate, between 1799 and 1820. Enlargements of *the*, inset in the boxes below, show the development of the crossbar joins. From original material in the possession of Rosemary Sassoon and reproduced in Sassoon (2000: 49). Reproduced by permission of Rosemary Sassoon.

necessarily. And anyway, the use of tools does not imply the operation of a technology. Is writing artificial? No. Nor is it natural. It is a product of development. If there is one thing, however, of which we can be reasonably sure, it is that line-making of one sort or another is as old as speech. For as long as people have been talking to one another, they have surely also been gesturing with their hands, and of these gestures a proportion will have left traces on surfaces of various kinds. Probably the vast majority of these traces would have been quickly erased, either to make way for new ones, or simply through normal processes of erosion. Thus only a small sample actually survive for any length of time. But if we are interested in the history of the line, these are the ones we have to work with.

The linearization of the line

Now nearly all of these points were made almost forty years ago by one of the doyens of French prehistory, André Leroi-Gourhan, in his extraordinary work on *Gesture and Speech* (1993). In this book, Leroi-Gourhan argues that the defining character of writing as we know it today, by contrast to drawing, is that it is linear. This is the last of the four propositions with which I began, and I would like to conclude this chapter with a few words about it. Leroi-Gourhan is well aware of the distortions that can arise when we look at the past through the lens of concepts and categories shaped by the very history that we seek to explain. Writing and drawing are two such categories. We have already seen, for example, how our modern concept of writing mistakes the skilled craft of the scribe at one moment for the 'purely intellectual' or imaginative art of creating a verbal composition and, at the next, for its 'merely technical' or mechanical replication in typing or print. To avoid these pitfalls, I have had resort to the notion of line-making. The term that Leroi-Gourhan uses, in much the same sense, is *graphism* (ibid.: 187–90).

Every graph, for Leroi-Gourhan, is the trace of a dextrous movement of the hand and as such embodies the rhythmicity characteristic of all movements of this kind. The earliest forms of graphism would have accompanied, and in turn commented upon, performances of storytelling, song and dance. Since these performative contexts are now irretrievably lost, we cannot know what the original significance of the traced lines would have been. However one striking feature that Leroi-Gourhan claims to find in prehistoric graphism is that its basic geometry is radial, 'like the body of the sea urchin or the starfish' (Leroi-Gourhan 1993: 211). Every graph spirals out from a centre, with its rhythmically repeated elements – or ideograms, in Leroi-Gourhan's terminology – arranged in concentric rings. The designs by which Walbiri people describe the movements of their ancestors, introduced in Chapter 3, perfectly exemplify this kind of radial graphism (see Figure 3.9). Only much later do we find the graphs being stretched out into lines running consistently in one direction.

It is by this 'linear graphism', Leroi-Gourhan thinks, that we recognize writing proper, and the more it is linearized the more does writing come to be distinguished from drawing (ibid.: 209–10). Graphism became linear, according to Leroi-Gourhan's account, to the extent that it was released from the contexts of oral narrative, only to be subordinated to the demands of representing the sounds of speech. Admittedly, in not all systems of writing has linearization proceeded to the same degree. In Chinese writing, for example, linear and ideographic components are held in a fine balance. It was with the establishment of alphabetic writing that linearization was taken to its fullest extent. Thenceforth the rounded cosmos of human dwelling with the figure of man at the centre, and from which all lines radiate outwards, was replaced – in Leroi-Gourhan's vivid expression – 'by an intellectual process which letters have strung out in a needle-sharp, but also needle-thin, line' (ibid.: 200).

Whether it was really the alphabet itself that made the difference or – as is more likely – the separation of letters in print need not detain us further here. My concern is rather with a conundrum at the heart of

Leroi-Gourhan's argument. Surely every trace left by a dextrous movement of the hand is itself a line. How, then, can the lines of prehistoric graphism be non-linear? How could it be that the storytellers of old, as they traced their lines, followed a non-linear trail? And how, conversely, can graphism be linear when, as in a sequence of printed letters, it leaves no trail to follow at all? In short, how can the line be non-linear and the non-line linear? In fact we have already encountered this paradox, albeit in another form, in Chapter 3. It is the paradox of the line that is not a line, namely the dotted line. Recall that in the evolution of the dotted line an original trace is broken into segments, each of which is then compressed into a point. It is in precisely this fragmentation and compression – in the reduction of the flowing movement of the *ductus* to a succession of moments – that the process of linearization consists. No wonder that the resulting line, as Leroi-Gourhan put it, is both needle-sharp and needle-thin! It is sharp because it goes to a point. And it is thin since it exists only as a virtual connector rather than a physical trace. Understood in a purely geometrical sense, it has length but no width at all. Fully linearized, the line is no longer the trace of a gesture but a chain of point-to-point connections. In these connections there is neither life nor movement. Linearization, in short, marks not the birth but the death of the line. In the next chapter we shall consider its ghostly spectre: the straight line of plane geometry.

6 How the line became straight

The line of Culture

In algebra, a line is defined by the equation of any two terms, each of which is the product of a constant and the first power of a variable. It might be expressed by the formula $ax + by = 0$, where a and b are constants, and x and y variables. Plotting the possible values of the two variables by means of Cartesian co-ordinates, the result is a line that is perfectly straight. Other, more complex algebraic functions yield figures of the kind mathematicians call curves. For example, the equation $y^2 = 4ax$ generates a parabola. Equations of this kind are called non-linear, even though the curves they specify are composed of lines. It seems as though the quality of straightness has become somehow fundamental to the recognition of lines *as lines*, not just in the specialized field of mathematics but much more widely. Yet there is no reason, intrinsic to the line itself, why it *should* be straight. We have already encountered plenty of instances where it is not. Thus our question becomes a historical one: how and why did the line become straight?

In Western societies, straight lines are ubiquitous. We see them everywhere, even when they do not really exist. Indeed the straight line has emerged as a virtual icon of modernity, an index of the triumph of rational, purposeful design over the vicissitudes of the natural world. The relentlessly dichotomizing dialectic of modern thought has, at one time or another, associated straightness with mind as against matter, with rational thought as against sensory perception, with intellect as against intuition, with science as against traditional knowledge, with male as against female, with civilization as against primitiveness, and – on the most general level – with culture as against nature. It is not difficult to find examples of every one of these associations.

Thus we suppose that protean matter, being the physical stuff it is, has a *texture* revealed to close inspection as a mass of almost chaotically tangled threads. We saw in Chapter 2 that the word 'tissue' – applied to the materials of living things – carries a similar connotation. This is the stuff we feel with our senses. But we imagine that, in the formation of interior mental representations of the material world, the shapes of things are projected onto the surface of the mind – much as in perspective drawing they are projected onto the picture plane – along straight lines modelled on rectilinear rays of light. And if the lines along which light travels are straight, then so are the ways of enlightenment. The man of reason, wrote Le Corbusier, the supreme architect of rectilinearity in modern urban design, 'walks in a straight line because he has a goal and knows where he is going, he has made up his mind to reach some particular place and goes straight to it' (Le Corbusier 1924: 274). As he walks, so he thinks, proceeding without hesitation or deviation from point to point. What Ong calls the 'sparsely linear' logic of the modern analytic intellect has often been compared in this vein with the more circuitous, mytho-poetic intuitions attributed to people in 'traditional' societies, and above all to those without writing of any kind (Ong 1982: 40). Through this comparison, 'thinking straight' comes to be regarded as characteristic of literate science as against oral tradition. Moreover, since the straight line can be specified by numerical values, it becomes an index of quantitative rather than qualitative knowledge. 'Its function', as Billeter notes, 'is to separate, to define, to order, to measure, to express number and proportion' (Billeter 1990: 47).

The sexual associations of the opposition between straight and curved lines are so obvious that they hardly need to be spelled out, and there is probably no society in which they have not been elaborated in one way or another. Rather more peculiar to Western societies is the mapping of the sexual distinction onto an overriding opposition between male and female genders, as though the whole of humanity were divided into two essential classes, membership of which is unalterably given for every individual at the very start of life and subsumes all other aspects of personal and social identity. Under these conditions, straightness becomes an unambiguous index of masculinity, as curvature indexes femininity. The posture of 'standing straight', commonly expected of men but not of women (who should rather fold their bodies into lines symbolic of deference), carries strong connotations of moral uprightness and social dignity. These connotations extend to judgements of the relative stature not only of men and women but also of 'civilized' and 'primitive' people, and even of human beings and their evolutionary antecedents. Textbooks of human evolution regularly depict *Homo sapiens sapiens* – so-called 'modern humans' – standing tall and straight by comparison with the slouching Neanderthals and stooping Australopithecines! An example is reproduced in Figure 6.1 (see also Ingold 2004). Moreover throughout the history of speculation on human origins, savages and proto-humans have been accused of all sorts of fecklessness and debauchery, from incest to cannibalism, and the vocabulary of the English language includes a rich repertoire of circumambulatory metaphors for talking about their errant ways. There is the *twisted* mind of the pervert, the *crooked* mind of the criminal, the *devious* mind of the swindler and the *wandering* mind of the idiot.

Once, however, the straight line comes to connote a moral condition, it sets itself apart from lines of every other sort in very much the same way as,

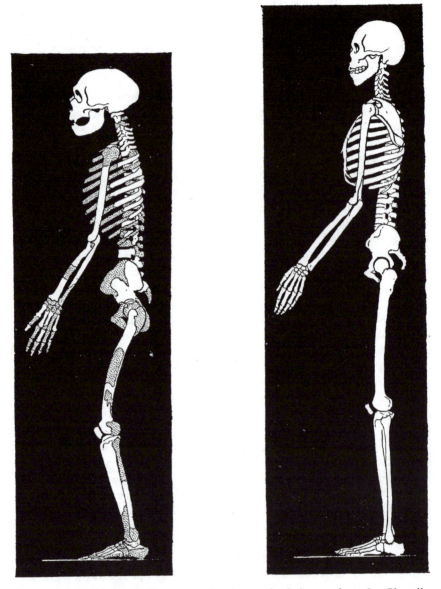

Figure 6.1 Reconstructed skeleton of fossil Neanderthal man from La Chapelle-aux-Saints (left) compared with skeleton of a modern Australian. About one-fifteenth natural size. Reproduced from Boule (1923: 239).

in the history of Western thought and science, humanity came to be distinguished from animality. In place of the infinite variety of lines – and lives – with which we are presented in phenomenal experience, we are left with just two grand classes: lines that are straight and lines that are not. The first are associated with humanity and Culture, the second with animality and Nature. For an absolutely unequivocal statement to this effect, we can turn to one of the doyens of twentieth-century social anthropology, Edmund Leach:

> Visible, wild Nature is a jumble of random curves; it contains no straight lines and few regular geometrical shapes of any kind. But the tamed, man-made world of Culture is full of straight lines, rectangles, triangles, circles and so on.
>
> (Leach 1976: 51)

This statement is, on the face of it, pretty extraordinary. On the one hand, as anyone will know who has perused D'Arcy Wentworth Thompson's masterpiece of 1917 *On Growth and Form*, the world of nature is teeming with regular lines and shapes of all sorts. Many of these, moreover, have been sources of inspiration for human architects (Thompson 1961; see Steadman 1979: 9–22). On the other hand, as we have already seen in the preceding chapters, of all the lines made by human inhabitants as they go about their lives probably only a minority are at all regular. The hegemony of the straight line is a phenomenon of modernity, not of culture in general.

Nevertheless, Leach's statement clearly resonates with a powerful impulse in modern thought to equate the march of progress, whether of culture or civilization, with the increasing domination of an un*ruly* – and therefore non-linear – nature. In the fields of agriculture and landscape planning, modernizers sought to enclose the land within rectilinear bounds and to lay out parks with perfectly straight tree-lined avenues, hedges and garden walls. And this, in turn, sparked off a counter-reaction in the form of a yearning for the circuitous entanglements of nature with ruined, ivy-encrusted walls, rustic fences, twisting garden paths and rampant weeds. It was the eighteenth century architect and landscape designer, William Kent, who coined the mantra of romanticism: 'nature abhors a straight line'. Whether, in truth, she does or not – and there would be plentiful examples, from straight-standing pines and poplars to oriental bamboos, to suggest that she does not – this mantra only goes to confirm the perception that there is something fundamentally *artificial* about straightness. It is apparently a quality of things that are made, rather than of things that grow.

Guidelines and plotlines

In earlier chapters, following de Certeau, I have shown how the modern maker or author envisions himself as though he were confronting a blank surface, like an empty page or a wasteland, upon which he intends to impose an assembly of his own design. The straight line is implicated in this vision in two quite distinct ways: first, in the constitution of the surface itself; secondly, in the construction of the assembly to be laid upon it. For the first, imagine a rigid line that is progressively displaced along its entire length, in a direction orthogonal to it. As it moves, it sweeps or rolls out the surface of a plane (Klee 1961: 112–13). For the second, imagine that the plane is marked with points, and that these points are joined up to form a diagram. This, in a nutshell, is the relation between our two manifestations of the straight line. One is intrinsic to the plane, as its constitutive element; the other is extrinsic, in that its erasure would still leave the plane intact. In what follows, and for reasons that will become evident as we proceed, I shall call lines of the first kind *guidelines*, and those of the second *plotlines*. A few familiar examples will help to clarify the distinction.

In the assembly line of modern manufacture, the surface upon which the assembly takes shape is literally rolled out in the movement of the conveyor belt. On the surface of this belt, components are joined together in the construction, piece by piece, of the final product. Here, the unrolling line of the belt is a guideline; the joints of the construction are plotlines. However, the first assembly line, as Ong has pointed out, 'was not one that produced stoves or shoes or weaponry, but one which produced the printed book' (Ong 1982: 118). In printing it is the job of the compositor to assemble the blocks of type on a composing stick before placing them in the galley. The line of assembled type is a plotline, but the straight, raised edges of the composing stick and the galley, against which the type rests, are guidelines. Of course, on the printed page, neither guidelines nor plotlines are visible as such. On the modern musical score, however, we can see both. Here the five parallel lines of the ruled stave are guidelines that establish a space, arrayed on the dimensions of pitch and tempo, on which the values of individual notes can be plotted. The ligatures connecting successive notes into phrases are then plotlines. 'Musical notation', as Kandinsky observed, 'is nothing other than different combinations of points and lines'; however it should be added that the lines, respectively, forming the stave and joining the notes are of an entirely different character and significance (Kandinsky 1982: 618–19).

Next, imagine a modern scientific graph. The lines of the graph, drawn with a ruler, connect points, each of which has been plotted by means of co-ordinates on the surface of the page. To facilitate this, the page itself is ruled with fine lines in two parallel sets, running respectively horizontally and vertically. These are guidelines that effectively establish the page as a two-dimensional space. And the lines connecting the points of the graph are plotlines. When graphs are reproduced in published texts, the original guidelines usually vanish, such that the plotlines figure against a plain white background. It is as though they had been swallowed up by the very surface they have brought into being. All that remain are the straight lines marking the axes of co-ordinates. Yet they are still followed implicitly when we 'read' the graph, running our eyes or fingers either up or across to reach each point. It is rather the same with a cartographic map. Here the ruled lines of latitude and longitude are guidelines that enable the navigator to plot a course from one location to another.

Of course, guidelines are not always drawn or conceived as lying in parallel, and the conventions of perspective drawing offer the most obvious example of where they are not. In this case, as the fifteenth-century artist and architect Leon Battista Alberti explained in his revolutionary treatise *On Painting*, dating from 1435, a ground plane envisioned as a regular chequerboard or pavement of squares is imaginatively projected as if seen through a vertical window, such that on the picture plane of the window the longitudinal lines of the ground plane, as they recede into the distance, appear to converge at a vanishing point, while the lateral lines become ever closer (Alberti 1972: 54–8). Here it is the convergence of lines that constitutes the plane *as a picture plane*, that is, as a projective surface upon which constructions are not so much assembled – as they would be on a real pavement – as represented (Figure 6.2).

Now both guidelines and plotlines have a long history. In both instances, as I shall show, this history is one in which threads were transformed into traces. But the search for their origins leads us to two quite distinct sources: in the practices, respectively, of weaving and land-measurement. Let me start with guidelines, which offer a perfect illustration of how – following my argument in Chapter 2 – threads turn into traces in the constitution of surfaces.

As the metaphor of the text indicates, the straight lines of the ruled manuscript, which guided the writer's hand in weaving the letter-line, can be traced back to the parallel warp-threads of the loom. The threads were straight because they were *taut*. Leila Avrin describes how Hebrew scribes in the medieval Near East created ruled lines on parchment through the use of a frame, called a *masara*, on which parallel cords were strung tight as on a miniature loom. The frame was placed under the sheet to be ruled. All the scribe had to do was to press down the parchment with his finger on to the cord beneath it, whereupon the thread would show up as a crease on the surface which he could then use to guide his writing (Avrin 1991: 115). A rather similar device, known as a 'ruling board' (*tabula ad rigandum*), is recorded from north-eastern Italy in the fifteenth century. The frame was strung with criss-cross wires that would leave their impression on a blank sheet placed over it and rubbed with the fist. By and large, however, medieval European scribes ruled their parchment with a pointed stylus against a straight edge. For writing music on a stave, they would bind five points together to form a 'rake' (*rastrum*). Using a straight edge, they could rule all five lines at once rather than having to measure up each line separately (Hamel 1992: 25). Whether with a single point or a rake, however, the fact that they scored these guidelines *into* the parchment rather than drawing them *upon* it indicates that the lines were considered integral to the surfaces on which they wrote. They were constitutive of the ground, as distinct from the configurations of the written manuscript.

Turning now to plotlines: they go back to the days when people first began to mark out plots of land by means of strings stretched between pegs or

Figure 6.2 Linear, architectural construction placed upon the chequerboard guidelines of a level pavement, projected on to a picture plane through Albertian perspective. This drawing comes from a work of the Dutch painter and architect Jan Vredeman de Vries, first published in 1568. Reproduced from Vredeman de Vries (1968).

stakes struck in the ground. In Ancient Egypt such practices of land surveying and measurement were of particular importance, since every year the flooding of the Nile would bury or destroy boundary markers which had then to be reset in order to establish rights of ownership as well as to determine the rents and taxes based on them. Surveying operations were overseen by a scribe who had the necessary practical and mathematical knowledge. The basic tool of surveying was a rope of one hundred cubits in length, marked off at intervals with knots. Surveying was known as 'stretching the rope', and the surveyor as a 'rope-stretcher' (Paulson 2005). An inscription from the temple of the king Edfu, where he is placed alongside a priestess impersonating Seshet – goddess of writing and knowledge – reads: 'I take the stake and I hold the handle of the mallet. I hold the (measuring) cord with Seshet' (Edwards 1961: 259).

The term *geometry*, of course, literally means 'earth-measuring', and its origins lie in practices that spread in antiquity from Egypt to Greece. But in Greek mathematics, and above all in the work of Euclid of Alexandria, the discipline of geometry took on a life of its own, laying the foundations – in turn – for the science of optics whose principles rest on the fundamental premise that light travels in straight lines. A straight line, according to Euclid's first postulate, 'may be drawn from any point to any other point' (Coxeter 1961: 4). Clearly, Euclid envisaged the line as a connector – that is as a plotline rather than a guideline – taking no account of the linearity intrinsic to the constitution of the two-dimensional plane upon which all the figures of his geometry were supposed to be arrayed. Euclid believed that rays shone out from the eyes to illuminate the objects on which they fell, and depicted them accordingly – as straight lines connecting the eye and the object. Since however the line was drawn not as a movement but as a static point-to-point connector, it was indifferent to whether rays were emitted from the eyes or intromitted into them, and the eventual triumph of the latter view, after centuries of debate, made no difference to the form of the line itself. As Margaret Hagen states, 'whether the visual rays come to or from the eyes is not critical for determination of appearance even in Euclid's system. The critical factor is the *rectilinearity*, the straightness, of the rays' (Hagen 1986: 303).[1] Using optical instruments to measure the earth, navigators went on to plot sight-lines whose straightness epitomized both the tension of taut strings and the rectilinearity of light rays (Mitchell 2006: 348–9). They became the inscribed plotlines of maps, charts and diagrams.

Though today we are inclined to think of the straight line as a unitary phenomenon, the division between guidelines and plotlines, with their very different origins in weaving and land-measurement, is still with us. Generally it is the plotlines that command our attention. We see them in every kind of construction that is engineered through the assembly of prefabricated components: in struts, stays and girders, braces and buttresses, frames and scaffolds, held together by joints and screws (Kandinsky 1982: 621–4). Guidelines, by contrast, tend to hide from view or to disappear altogether into the backgrounds that they constitute. We often fail to notice them. Yet they remain integral to many of the surfaces on or around which life in the built environment is conducted. Think of lines of paving, of bricklaying, of floorboards, even of wallpaper – the lines where strips adjoin are still there, even though interior decorators do their best to hide them! Or the lines of seating in a railway carriage, aircraft fuselage or auditorium. We use guidelines, too, to convert an existing surface into a field of action, as when they are painted on grass to create a racetrack or a tennis court. Just like the rules and margins that still appear in school exercise books, these lines present no physical barrier to movement, but nevertheless entail consequences – more or less dire – should they be crossed.

Before leaving the subject of guidelines and plotlines, a word should be said about roads, railways and canals, for it seems there are two senses in which such channels of communication can be understood. On the one hand they are plotlines in themselves, joining specific locations by a route that pre-exists the traffic that flows between them. On the other hand, the asphalt of the road, the tracks of the railway and the breadth of the canal form surfaces over which vehicles (cars, trains, barges) move, and these surfaces are themselves constituted by guidelines that can be more or less constraining. Train drivers, fortunately, do not have to steer, but bargemen and motorists do: the former within limits determined by the canal banks, the latter observing lines painted down the centre of the road as well as on each side. The centre line separates oncoming and outgoing traffic, and to drive 'on the wrong side' is to precipitate an accident. But it is still possible – if dangerous – for the motorist to cross over, such as when overtaking. In every case, however, whether we see a channel of communication as a plotline or as a set of guidelines depends on whether we focus on its communicative aspect, of 'going from A to B', or its channelling aspect, of guiding movement over a surface.

Using a ruler

A ruler is a sovereign who controls and governs a territory. It is also an instrument for drawing straight lines. These two usages, as we have already hinted, are closely connected. In establishing the territory as his to control, the ruler lays down guidelines for its inhabitants to follow. And in his political judgements and strategic decisions – his rulings – he plots the course of action they should take. As in the territory so also on the page, the ruler has been employed in drawing lines of both kinds.

For centuries, scribes used rulers for scoring guidelines on parchment or paper, while surveyors and navigators used them for drawing plotlines on diagrams and charts. With the development of printing the former use has been rendered more or less obsolete, since notepaper, graph paper and manuscript paper now all come ready ruled. Every schoolchild, however, must include a ruler in his or her 'geometry set', for use in constructing figures, tables and graphs. Moreover the ruler remains an essential part of the toolkit for the navigator or surveyor. And ever since architects and engineers ceased to be masters among builders and mechanics, moving off-site to become 'gentlemanly' designers of structures for artisans of lower status to assemble or put up, the ruler has become essential to their toolkit too.[2] The sociologist of science David Turnbull, in a now classic article, has shown how, throughout the Middle Ages, the designs for major monuments such as cathedrals were not drawn up in advance but improvised on-site. Lines were drawn in the earth itself or stretched with string, at full scale, or incised directly on to materials by means of templates (Turnbull 1993). Only when the architect ceased to be a master-builder and retreated to the drawing-board were templates replaced by the ruler, and taut threads by the ruled traces of the diagram. From that time on, builders were no longer ruled by the architect in person but by the straightness of his lines, on plans and specifications nowadays backed by force of law and contractual obligation.

The act of drawing a line with a ruler is ostensibly quite different from that of drawing it freehand. As John Ruskin noted, no free hand – not even the best trained – can ever draw a line that is without any curvature or variety of direction. 'A great draughtsman can', he observed, 'draw every line *but* a straight one.' For this reason Ruskin thought it futile for novices to practise drawing straight lines. What is the point, when this is the one thing that no draughtsman can or should ever be able to do? In order to train novices to an accurate perception of the relations between straight lines and curves, for example in the forms of Roman capitals, Ruskin accordingly recommended that they be allowed to use a rule (Ruskin 1904: 38). In his book *The Nature and Art of Workmanship*, theorist of design David Pye arrives at a rather similar conclusion, by way of a distinction between what he calls the 'workmanship of risk' and the 'workmanship of certainty'. In the workmanship of risk, the result is not pre-determined but 'depends on the judgement, dexterity and care which the maker exercises as he works' (Pye 1968: 4). Thus the quality of the outcome is never assured until the work is actually finished. In the workmanship of certainty, by contrast, the result is exactly pre-determined before the task is even begun. This determination is given in the settings and specifications of the apparatus of production, which in turn controls the movements of the working point. The workmanship of risk, Pye suggests, is exemplified by writing with a pen, and the workmanship of certainty by modern printing.

In the workmanship of risk, however, practitioners are continually devising ways to limit risk through the use of jigs and templates, which introduce a degree of certainty into the proceedings. Thus 'if you want to draw a straight line with your pen', Pye advises, 'you do not go at it freehand, but use a ruler, that is to say, a jig' (1968: 5). The difference between drawing a line freehand and with a ruler precisely parallels that between wayfaring and transport, as explained in Chapter 3. In the first case, only when the traveller has arrived at a place can he truly be said to have found his way there. All along the trail he has to attend to his path in relation to the ever-changing vistas and horizons as he proceeds. So too with your pen or pencil: you have all the while to keep an eye on where you are going and make adjustments accordingly. That is why some degree of twisting or bending is inevitable. In the second case, by contrast, the traveller has already plotted the route prior to setting out. To travel, then, is simply to execute the plot. It is just the same when you draw a line with a ruler to connect two points. By lining up the ruler so that the straight edge is in contact with both points, the trajectory of the pen nib or pencil tip is already fully determined even before it has begun to draw. It is for this reason that we typically think of the point-to-point connector as a straight line drawn with a ruler. It seems as though, as soon as the ruler is taken into use, the workmanship of risk intrinsic to the wayfaring pen gives way to a workmanship of certainty that goes straight to the point.

Yet in reality, things are not that simple. Just as transport can never be perfect but always entails an element of wayfaring, so no line that is ever drawn – even with a ruler – can ever be *perfectly* straight. An element of risk is always involved. For one thing, there is the constant danger that the ruler will slip. For another, the precise distance of the line from the edge of the rule will depend on the angle at which the pen is held, which is inclined to vary in following through the manual gesture. It is difficult, too, to keep the pressure on the tip exactly constant, so that the width and density of the line may be inconstant. Nor can one be sure that the edge of the ruler is perfectly straight, as it is likely to have been warped or nicked by previous wear and tear. Moreover, drawing the line *takes time*. It cannot be reduced to a single instant. Reflecting on his own architectural practice of producing axonometric projections on a drawing-board with a rule and set-square, Ray Lucas observes that, however many times certain actions are repeated, 'it remains essential to the process that I go through the motions each time' (Lucas 2006: 174–5).

Most contemporary architects love to draw but hate to write. They always carry pencils with them, and are constantly doodling and sketching (Medway 1996: 34–5). They draw as they think, and think as they draw, leaving a trace or trail both in memory and on paper. Nor is their drawing necessarily a solitary activity. Often enough it may take the form of a conversation in which two or more interlocutors take turns to add lines, or to modify them, as an idea takes shape and is collaboratively developed (see Figure 6.3). Of course they often have to write as well, but most often this is 'writing on drawing', where the words point to particular features of the drawn sketch. Writing, in architecture, is left for what cannot be drawn. This turns upside down the convention that drawing is a practice of illustration. Architects do not draw to illustrate their works, except for publicity purposes or to impress clients. Such illustrative drawings, often done in perspective, are known disparagingly as 'pretty pictures' and are considered entirely superfluous to the architectural design process itself (Henderson 1999:

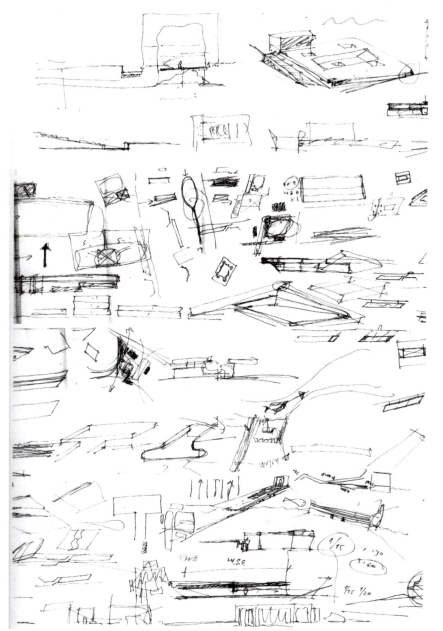

Figure 6.3 Extract from a collaborative sketch drawing made by from three to six architects working together over a four-hour period. Reproduced from Gunn (2002: 324). Reproduced by permission of Wendy Gunn.

32–3). *Real* drawings are works in themselves, not illustrations of works. Writing is subservient to drawing, and not the other way around.

One consequence, however, of the separation of architectural design from the construction industry is that architects are required to produce drawings not only to help them in working out their ideas but also to convey precise instructions, to the builder, of what is to be done. Architectural drawings thus come in two broad kinds: sketches, made in the course of developing an idea, and specification drawings – usually done in plan, section and elevation (but *not* in perspective) – that direct the builder. Whereas sketches are done freehand, specification drawings are precisely measured and ruled. A rather similar situation obtains in music, as a consequence of the parallel separation of composition from performance. Composers sketch freehand as they work out their ideas, but for the purposes of performance it is necessary to produce a score on which the composer's requirements are exactly specified in terms of the rules of the stave. In Figures 6.4 and 6.5 I have juxtaposed an example of an architectural sketch and one of a musical sketch: the first from the Portuguese architect Alvaro Siza, the second from the Czech composer Leoš Janáček. Although in both cases the drawings follow notational conventions – of plan and elevation in the one case, of the stave score in the

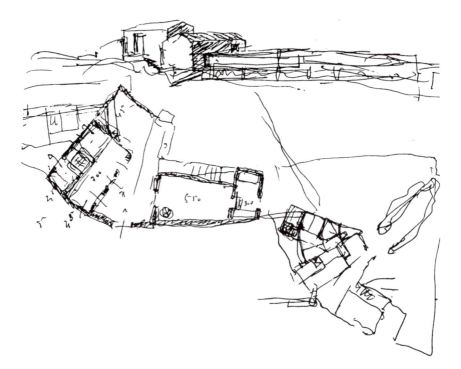

Figure 6.4 Sketch for the adaptation and reconstruction of two small agricultural buildings, Moledo de Minha, Portugal, 1971, by Alvaro Siza. Reproduced from Siza (1997: 158).

Figure 6.5 Sketch from Janáček's last compositon, *I await thee*. Reproduced from Janáček (1989: 68), by permission of Marion Boyars Publishers.

other – they would be of little use to the builder or performer. Yet compared with the formally ruled, straight lines of the specification drawing or the printed score, these sketches convey a powerful sense of movement. The building in the one case and the music in the other seem to be *alive* on the page. These lines are active, in Paul Klee's sense. They go out for a walk.

Why should meandering lines drawn freehand look so much more life-like and realistic than lines drawn with a rule, even when they depict what should be straight edges in an environment? One answer is that, whereas the abstract geometrical line, in the depiction of an edge, represents the junction of two *planes*, an actual edge in the built environment is formed by the junction of two *surfaces*. As James Gibson pointed out in his work on the psychology of visual perception, surface and plane are very different things. The geometric plane – 'a very thin sheet in space' – is but the insubstantial ghost of the real surface – 'an interface between a medium and a substance' (1979: 35). The medium is usually air, but the substance can be any solid material from which buildings are made, or that of the ground itself. In the environment we perceive edges as edges, not as lines, and however sharp they may be (no real edge can be perfectly sharp, just as no real line can be perfectly straight), this perception is always inflected by the characteristic textures of adjoining surfaces. A freehand line can convey something of this texture, whereas a ruled line cannot. But a second answer may be still more significant. It is that in real life, as I have already shown in Chapter 3, we perceive the environment not from a stationary point, nor from a succession of such points, but in the course of our movement along what Gibson calls 'a *path* of observation' (ibid.: 197). In the freehand sketch, the movement of the observer relative to a stationary feature is translated into the movement of the line depicting that feature relative to a viewer who is now stationary.

I have not dwelt upon the impacts of the computer in such fields as engineering design, musical composition and architecture, and am happy to leave speculation on these matters to others more competent than myself. Suffice it to say that one of the consequences of computer-assisted design (CAD), as Wendy Gunn has shown in a study of the effects of introducing CAD into the design processes of a number of architectural practices in Norway, may be to eliminate the hand-drawn sketch (Gunn 2002). The computer enables the designer to generate near-perfect orthogonal or perspectival projections – even more perfect than traditional hand-drafted specification drawings – which can be as precise and detailed as you like. The lines of these projections are neither drawn nor ruled; indeed they embody no movement or gesture of any kind. Each is rather the geometrically configured output of an instantaneous computation. These lines can be modified at will, at any stage in the design process. Unlike sketching, however, CAD leaves no trace of these modifications or of the many hands that contributed to them. Printed out, a computer-generated diagram is complete in itself. Of course you can change the design and print it again, but each print-out is a new drawing, not a moment in the evolution of a still-growing one. Whereas the sketch embodies its history on a single sheet, you can only reconstruct the history of a CAD process by stacking a whole pile of sheets in genealogical sequence (ibid.: 324–7).

Breaking up

I began with the observation that the straight line has become an icon of modernity. It offers reason, certainty, authority, a sense of direction. Too often in the twentieth century, however, reason has been shown to work in profoundly irrational ways, certainties have bred fractious conflict, authority has been revealed as the mask of intolerance and oppression, and directions have been confounded in a maze of dead ends. The line, it seems, has been broken into fragments. If the straight line was an icon of modernity, then the fragmented line seems to be emerging as an equally powerful icon of postmodernity. This is anything but a reversion to the meandering line of wayfaring. Where the latter goes along, from place to place, the fragmented, postmodern line goes across: not however stage by stage, from one destination to the next, but from one point of rupture to another. These points are not locations but *dislocations*, segments out of joint. To put it in terms suggested by Kenneth Olwig, the line of wayfaring, accomplished through the practices of dwelling and the circuitous movements they entail, is *topian*; the straight line of modernity, driven by a grand narrative of progressive advance, is *utopian*; the fragmented line of postmodernity is *dystopian*. 'Perhaps it is time', Olwig writes, 'we moved beyond modernism's *utopianism* and postmodernism's *dystopianism* to a *topianism* that recognizes that human beings, as creatures of history, consciously and unconsciously create places' (Olwig 2002: 52–3).

In Figures 6.6 and 6.7 I reproduce two examples of the fragmented line, taken respectively from architecture and music. They may perhaps be compared with the two sketches reproduced in Figures 6.4 and 6.5. The first example shows the ground-floor plan of the Jewish Museum in Berlin, designed by architect Daniel Libeskind. The second is from a piece for twelve male voices entitled *Siciliano* by the Italian composer Sylvano Bussotti. In fact a musical analogy lies at the heart of Libeskind's work, and his original competition entry, entitled *Between the Lines*, was submitted on manuscript paper with the text literally between the lines of the five-line stave. Libeskind explains that his choice of title for the project was based on the idea that it is about 'two lines of thinking, organization, and relationship. One is a straight line, but broken into many fragments; the other is a tortuous line, but continuing indefinitely' (Libeskind 2001: 23). This explanation can be taken as a paradigmatic summation of both the calamities of modern history and the irrepressible potential of life to find a way through, and to keep on going, even under the most trying of circumstances. Indeed fragmentation can be read positively in so far as it opens up passages – albeit unconventional

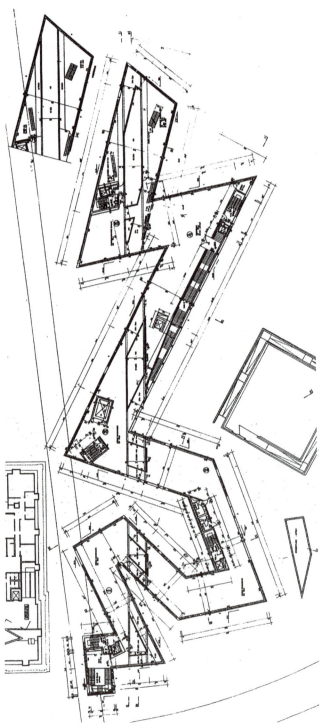

Figure 6.6 Ground-floor plan for the Jewish Museum in Berlin, designed by Daniel Libeskind. Reproduced from Libeskind (2001: 27). © Studio Daniel Libeskind. Reproduced by permission.

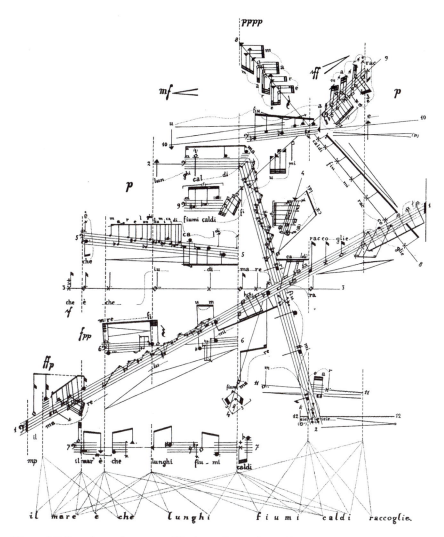

Figure 6.7 Page from the score of *Siciliano* for twelve male voices by Sylvano Bussotti (1962).

ones – that might previously have been closed off, allowing inhabitants to find their own 'ways through', and thereby to make places for themselves, amidst the ruptures of dislocation.

It is traditional, on reaching the conclusion of a work, for the author to announce that it is now time to draw the threads of the argument together. What I have shown through this book, however, is not only that such drawing together is a way of establishing a place in the world but also that drawn threads invariably leave trailing ends that will, in their turn, be drawn into other knots with other threads. Lines are open-ended, and it is this open-endedness – of lives, relationships, histories and processes of thought – that I have wanted to celebrate. I hope that, in doing so, I have left plentiful loose ends for others to follow and to take in any ways they wish. Far from seeking closure, my aim has been to prise an opening. We may have come to the end of this book, but that does not mean we have reached the end of the line. Indeed the line, like life, has no end. As in life, what matters is not the final destination, but all the interesting things that occur along the way. For *wherever you are, there is somewhere further you can go.*

Notes

1 Language, music and notation

1 Cited in Strunk (1950: 4). Plato's insistence on this rule, may, however 'indicate the frequency with which it was broken by modern [i.e. contemporary] composers' (Barker 1984: 130, fn. 19).

2 Jeremiah (36: 15, 18), from the King James Bible. For further commentary and analysis of the mode of reading evinced here, as 'oral declamation', see Boyarin (1992: 12–16).

3 David Levin, for example, insists that vision is 'the most reifying of all our perceptual modalities' (Levin 1988: 65).

2 Traces, threads and surfaces

1 In a recent paper, ethologists Chris Herzfeld and Dominique Lestel (2005) point out that our closest primate cousins, the great apes, are predominantly fibre-users rather than tool-users. Apes are even known to tie knots, using their hands, feet and mouth. 'The primate that makes knots', however, 'is always a primate that lives in close association with humans' (ibid.: 647).

2 I am most grateful to Elizabeth Hallam for bringing this wonderful passage to my attention.

3 I first found this statement of Liu Hsieh in a recent text by Florian Coulmas (2003: 4), where it is rendered as follows: 'Writing originated when drawing of bird trace replaced string knitting.' I thought it more prudent, however, to remain with the wording of the original translation to which he refers (Liu Hsieh 1983: 17).

3 Up, across and along

1 This observation is confirmed by Beatrice Collignon (1996: 98), who points out that Inuinnait people perceive their territory as an ensemble of itineraries, and 'as organized by a network of lines through which people and game move' (cited in Aporta 2004: 12).

2 In his *Dictionary*, Johnson reproduced only the last two lines of this verse, and slightly misquoted them: 'We as by *line* upon the ocean go / Whose paths shall be as familiar as the land.'

4 The genealogical line

1 My interpretation differs in this respect from that of Mary Bouquet (1996) who, in an otherwise admirable article, argues that, in transforming pedigree into genealogy, Rivers appealed to the imagery of the family tree.

2 I owe a special debt of gratitude to John Barnes, who would go on to supervise my doctoral studies.

5 Drawing, writing and calligraphy

1 Clifford also distinguishes both inscription and description from *transcription*, which implies taking things down – as in dictation. It is once again immaterial, in Clifford's argument, whether this is done by hand or with a typewriter.

2 Another illustration of this point comes from the practice of what Yen calls 'evanescent calligraphy'. She reports that, in the central square of the city of Luoyang, people 'bring huge calligraphic brushes and bottles of water to write on the concrete surface of the square at dusk every day'. The characters evaporate and vanish within minutes; evidently what counts is the bodily invigoration and mental relaxation that the practice affords (Yen 2005: 112).

3 Leila Avrin (1991: 327–39) provides a wonderfully detailed account of the history of block printing and movable type in the Far East, Near East and Europe, up to the development of the printing press. I have also drawn on her authoritative account of the emergence of majuscule and minuscule scripts (ibid.: 177–91), and of the history of paper-making (ibid.: 283–9). On the history of printing in Europe, see Lechêne (1992: 73).

4 This paragraph partially reproduces material from an earlier essay on 'The dynamics of technical change' (in Ingold 2000: 371).

6 How the line became straight

1 The straight lines indicating rays of light in modern optical depictions are interestingly ambiguous. On the one hand, as incident sunlight, rays are depicted in the form of bands of parallel lines constitutive of the visual field. On the other hand, as reflected beams, they are shown in the form of lines connecting objects seen with the eye of the viewer. They look like guidelines in the one case and plotlines in the other.

2 This is an instance of the same division, between intellectual and manual labour that – as we saw in Chapter 5 – also divided the author from the printer. It is worth recalling that, in medieval times, the *machina* (machine) was essentially a kind of hoist, an instrument for lifting the heavy material for the higher walls and roof of a building under construction. The machine was operated by *masiones* (masons) under the direction of *architecti* (master-builders). See Carruthers (1998: 22).

References

Adams, J. L. (1997) 'The place where you go to listen', *Terra Nova: Nature and Culture*, 2(3): 15–16.

Aichele, K. P. (2002) *Paul Klee's Pictorial Writing*, Cambridge: Cambridge University Press.

Alberti, L. B. (1972) *On Painting*, trans. C. Grayson, ed. M. Kemp, Harmondsworth: Penguin.

Aporta, C. (2004) 'Routes, trails and tracks: trail breaking among the Inuit of Igloolik', *Études/Inuit/Studies*, 28(2): 9–38.

Augustine, Saint (1991) *Confessions*, trans. H. Chadwick, Oxford: Oxford University Press.

Avrin, L. (1991) *Scribes, Script and Books: The Book Arts from Antiquity to the Renaissance*, Chicago: American Library Association.

Barber, E. (1994) *Women's Work: The First 20,000 Years*, New York: W. W. Norton.

Barker, A. (1984) *Greek Musical Writings*, Vol. I: *The Musician and his Art*, Cambridge: Cambridge University Press.

Barker, A. (1989) *Greek Musical Writings*, Vol. II: *Harmonic and Acoustic Theory*, Cambridge: Cambridge University Press.

Barnes, J. A. (1967) 'Genealogies', in A. L. Epstein (ed.), *The Craft of Social Anthropology*, London: Tavistock.

Belyea, B. (1996) 'Inland journeys, native maps', *Cartographica*, 33: 1–16.

Berger, J. (1982) 'Stories', in J. Berger and J. Mohr, *Another Way of Telling*, New York: Vintage Books.

Bergson, H. (1911) *Creative Evolution*, trans. A. Mitchell, London: Macmillan.

Bergson, H. (1991) *Matter and Memory*, trans. N. M. Paul and W. S. Palmer, New York: Zone Books.

Billeter, J. F. (1990) *The Chinese Art of Writing*, trans. J.-M. Clarke and M. Taylor, New York: Rizzoli International.

Bogoras, W. G. (1904–09) *The Chukchee*, Jesup North Pacific Expedition Vol. VII (3 parts), American Museum of Natural History Memoir 11, Leiden: E. J. Brill.

Boule, M. (1923) *Fossil Men: Elements of Human Palaeontology*, trans. J. E. Ritchie and J. Ritchie, Edinburgh: Oliver and Boyd.

Bouquet, M. (1993) *Reclaiming English Kinship: Portuguese Refractions of British Kinship Theory*, Manchester: Manchester University Press.

Bouquet, M. (1996) 'Family trees and their affinities: the visual imperative of the genealogical diagram', *Journal of the Royal Anthropological Institute*, 2(1): 43–66.

Bourdieu, P. (1977) *Outline of a Theory of Practice*, trans. R. Nice, Cambridge: Cambridge University Press.

Boyarin, J. (1992) 'Placing reading: Ancient Israel and Medieval Europe', in J. Boyarin (ed.), *The Ethnography of Reading*, Berkeley, CA: University of California Press.

Brown, T. (1978) *The Tracker: The Story of Tom Brown, Jr. as Told by William Jon Watkins*, New York: Prentice Hall.

Brown, T. J. (1992) 'Punctuation', in *The New Encyclopædia Britannica*, 15th edn, Vol. 29, pp. 1050–2.

Carruthers, M. (1990) *The Book of Memory: A Study of Memory in Medieval Culture*, Cambridge: Cambridge University Press.

Carruthers, M. (1998) *The Craft of Thought: Meditation, Rhetoric and the Making of Images, 400–1200*, Cambridge: Cambridge University Press.

Certeau, M. de (1984) *The Practice of Everyday Life*, trans. S. Rendall, Berkeley, CA: University of California Press.

Chatwin, B. (1987) *The Songlines*, London: Jonathan Cape.

Ch'en Chih-Mai (1966) *Chinese Calligraphers and their Art*, London: Melbourne University Press.

Clanchy, M. T. (1979) *From Memory to the Written Record*, Oxford: Blackwell.

Clifford, J. (1990) 'Notes on (field)notes', in R. Sanjek (ed.), *Fieldnotes: The Makings of Anthropology*, Ithaca, NY: Cornell University Press.

Colgrave, B. and Mynors, R. A. B. (eds) (1969) *Bede's Ecclesiastical History of the English People*, London: Oxford University Press.

Collignon, B. (1996) *Les Inuit: Ce qu'ils savent du territoire*, Paris: L'Harmattan.

Cotton, L. (1896) *Palmistry and its Practical Uses*, London: Kegan Paul, Trench, Trubner.

Coulmas, F. (2003) *Writing Systems: An Introduction to their Linguistic Analysis*, Cambridge: Cambridge University Press.

Coxeter, H. S. M. (1961) *Geometry*, New York: John Wiley.

Darwin, C. (1950) *The Origin of Species by Means of Natural Selection, or the Preservation of Favoured Races in the Struggle for Life* (reprint of first edition of 1859), London: Watts.

Dearmer, P., Vaughan Williams, R. and Shaw, M. (eds) (1964) *The Oxford Book of Carols*, London: Oxford University Press.

DeFrancis, J. (1984) *The Chinese Language: Fact and Fantasy*, Honolulu, HI: University of Hawai'i Press.

DeFrancis, J. (1989) *Visible Speech: The Diverse Oneness of Writing Systems*, Honolulu, HI: University of Hawai'i Press.

Deleuze, G. and Guattari, F. (1983) *On the Line*, trans. J. Johnston, New York: Semiotext(e).

Domat, J. (1777) *Les Loix Civiles dans leur ordre naturel: Le Droit Public, et Legum Delectus*, nouvelle édition, Paris: Knapen.

Donovan, M. (2003) 'Line', *Poetry*, 181(5): 333.

Dryden, J. (1958) *The Poems and Fables of John Dryden*, ed. J. Kinsley, Oxford: Oxford University Press.

Edwards, I. E. S. (1961) *The Pyramids of Egypt*, Harmondsworth: Penguin.

Feld, S. (1996) 'Waterfalls of song: an acoustemology of place resounding in Bosavi, Papua New Guinea', in S. Feld and K. Basso (eds), *Senses of Place*, Santa Fe, NM: School of American Research Press.

Fuchs, R. H. (1986) *Richard Long*, London: Methuen.

Gebhart-Sayer, A. (1985) 'The geometric designs of the Shipibo–Conibo in ritual context', *Journal of Latin American Lore*, 11(2): 143–75.

Geertz, C. (1973) *The Interpretation of Cultures*, New York: Basic Books.

Gell, A. (1998) *Art and Agency: An Anthropological Theory*, Oxford: Clarendon Press.

Gibson, J. J. (1979) *The Ecological Approach to Visual Perception*, Boston, MA: Houghton Mifflin.

Gillespie, C. S. (1959) 'Lamarck and Darwin in the history of science', in B. Glass, O. Temkin and W. L. Straus, Jr (eds), *Forerunners of Darwin: 1745–1859*, Baltimore, MD: Johns Hopkins University Press.

Goehr, L. (1992) *The Imaginary Museum of Musical Works: An Essay in the Philosophy of Music*, Oxford: Clarendon Press.

Goldsworthy, A. (1994) *Stone*, London: Penguin (Viking).

Goodman, N. (1969) *Languages of Art: An Approach to a Theory of Symbols*, London: Oxford University Press.

Goodwin, C. (1994) 'Professional vision', *American Anthropologist*, 96: 606–33.

Gow, P. (1990) 'Could Sangama read? The origin of writing among the Piro of eastern Peru', *History and Anthropology*, 5: 87–103.

Gray, N. (1971) *Lettering as Drawing*, London: Oxford University Press.

Guaman Poma de Ayala, F. (1987) *Nueva Cronica y Buen Gobierno, Tomo A*, ed. J. V. Murra, R. Adorno and J. L. Urioste, Mexico City: Siglo XXI.

Gunn, W. (1996) 'Walking, movement and perception', Unpublished Master's thesis, University of Manchester.

Gunn, W. (2002) 'The social and environmental impact of incorporating computer aided design technologies into an architectural design process', Unpublished doctoral dissertation, University of Manchester.

Hagen, M. A. (1986) *Varieties of Realism: Geometries of Representational Art*, Cambridge: Cambridge University Press.

Hallam, E. (2002) 'The eye and the hand: memory, identity and clairvoyants' narratives in England', in J. Campbell and J. Harbord (eds), *Temporalities, Autobiography and Everyday Life*, Manchester: Manchester University Press.

Hamel, C. (1992) *Scribes and Illuminators*, London: British Museum Press.

Harris, R. (1986) *The Origin of Writing*, London: Duckworth.

Harris, R. (2000) *Rethinking Writing*, London: Continuum.

Hauser-Schäublin, B. (1996) 'The thrill of the line, the string, and the frond, or why the Abelam are a non-cloth culture', *Oceania*, 67(2): 81–106.

Havelock, E. A. (1982) *The Literate Revolution in Greece and its Cultural Consequences*, Princeton, NJ: Princeton University Press.

Henderson, K. (1999) *On Line and on Paper: Visual Representations, Visual Culture, and Computer Graphics in Design Engineering*, Cambridge: Cambridge University Press.

Herzfeld, C. and Lestel, D. (2005) 'Knot tying in great apes: etho-ethnology of an unusual tool behavior', *Social Science Information*, 44(4): 621–53.

Howe, N. (1992) 'The cultural construction of reading in Anglo-Saxon England', in J. Boyarin (ed.), *The Ethnography of Reading*, Berkeley, CA: University of California Press.

Iguchi, K. (1999) 'How to play the flute in Kyoto: learning, practice and musical knowledge', Unpublished doctoral dissertation, University of Manchester.

Ingber, D. E. (1998) 'The architecture of life', *Scientific American*, 278(1): 30–9.

Ingold, T. (1986) *Evolution and Social Life*, Cambridge: Cambridge University Press.

Ingold, T. (2000) *The Perception of the Environment: Essays on Livelihood, Dwelling and Skill*, London: Routledge.

Ingold, T. (2001) 'From the transmission of representations to the education of attention', in H. Whitehouse (ed.), *The Debated Mind: Evolutionary Psychology versus Ethnography*, Oxford: Berg.

Ingold, T. (2004) 'Culture on the ground: the world perceived through the feet', *Journal of Material Culture*, 9(3): 315–40.

Jacoby, H. J. (1939) *Analysis of Handwriting*, London: Allen & Unwin.

Janáček, L. (1989) *Janáček's Uncollected Essays on Music*, trans. and ed. M. Zemanová, London: Marion Boyars.

Jarvis, R. (1997) *Romantic Writing and Pedestrian Travel*, London: Macmillan.

Kandinsky, V. (1982) 'Point and line to plane', in K. C. Lindsay and P. Vergo (eds), *Kandinsky: Complete Writings on Art*, Vol. 2 (1922–1943), London: Faber & Faber.

Kapr, A. (1983) *The Art of Lettering: The History, Anatomy and Aesthetics of the Roman Letter Forms*, trans. I. Kimber, München: K. G. Saur Verlag.

Kelley, K. and Francis, H. (2005) 'Traditional Navajo maps and wayfinding', *American Indian Culture and Research Journal*, 29(2): 85–111.

Klapisch-Zuber, C. (1991) 'The genesis of the family tree', *I Tatti Studies, Essays in the Renaissance*, 4(1): 105–29.

Klee, P. (1961) *Notebooks*, Vol. 1: *The Thinking Eye*, ed. J. Spiller, trans. R. Manheim, London: Lund Humphries.

Küchler, S. (2001) 'Why knot? A theory of art and mathematics', in C. Pinney and N. Thomas (eds), *Beyond Aesthetics: Essays in Memory of Alfred Gell*, Oxford: Berg.

Kurttila, T. and Ingold, T. (2001) 'Perceiving the environment in Finnish Lapland', in P. Macnaghten and J. Urry (eds), *Bodies of Nature*, London: Sage.

Kwon, H. (1998) 'The saddle and the sledge: hunting as comparative narrative in Siberia and beyond', *Journal of the Royal Anthropological Institute* (N.S.), 4: 115–27.

Langer, S. K. (1953) *Feeling and Form: A Theory of Art*, London: Routledge & Kegan Paul.

Leach, E. R. (1961) *Pul Eliya: A Village in Ceylon. A Study of Land Tenure and Kinship*, Cambridge: Cambridge University Press.

Leach, E. R. (1976) *Culture and Communication: The Logic by which Symbols are Connected*, Cambridge: Cambridge University Press.

Lechêne, R. (1992) 'History of printing', in *The New Encyclopædia Britannica*, 15th edn, Vol. 26, pp. 72–8.

Leclercq, J. (1961) *The Love of Learning and the Desire of God*, trans. C. Mrahi, New York: Fordham University Press.

Le Corbusier (1924) *Urbanisme*, Paris: Editions Cres.

Lefebvre, H. (1991) *The Production of Space*, trans. D. Nicholson-Smith, Oxford: Blackwell.

Leroi-Gourhan, A. (1993) *Gesture and Speech*, trans. A. Bostock Berger, Cambridge, MA: MIT Press.

Levin, D. M. (1988) *The Opening of Vision: Nihilism and the Postmodern Situation*, London: Routledge.

Libeskind, D. (2001) *The Space of Encounter*, New York: Universe Publishing.

Liu Hsieh (1983) *The Literary Mind and the Carving of Dragons*, trans. V. Yu-chung Shih, Hong Kong: Chinese University Press.

Low, C. (2007) 'Khoisan wind: hunting and healing', *Journal of the Royal Anthropological Institute*, 13(1) (in press).

Lucas, R. P. (2006) 'Towards a theory of notation as a thinking tool', Unpublished doctoral dissertation, University of Aberdeen.

Lye, T. P. (1997) 'Knowledge, forest, and hunter-gatherer movement: the Batek of Pahang, Malaysia', Unpublished doctoral dissertation, University of Hawai'i.

Lye, T. P. (2004) *Changing Pathways: Forest Degradation and the Batek of Pahang, Malaysia*, Lanham, MD: Rowman & Littlefield.

Mall, A. (2007) 'Structure, innovation and agency in pattern construction: the kolam of Southern India', in E. Hallam and T. Ingold (eds), *Creativity and Cultural Improvisation*, Oxford: Berg.

Matthews, W. H. (1922) *Mazes and Labyrinths: A General Account of their History and Developments*, London: Longmans, Green.

Mazzullo, N. (2005) 'Perception, memory and environment among Saami people in northeastern Finland', Unpublished doctoral dissertation, University of Manchester.

Medway, P. (1996) 'Writing, speaking, drawing: the distribution of meaning in architects' communication', in M. Sharples and T. van der Geest (eds), *The New Writing Environment: Writers at Work in a World of Technology*, Berlin: Springer.

Meehan, A. (1991) *Celtic Knotwork: The Secret Method of the Scribes*, London: Thames and Hudson.

Milne, A. A. (1928) *The House at Pooh Corner*, London: Methuen.

Mitchell, V. (2006) 'Drawing threads from sight to site', *Textile*, 4(3): 340–61.

Mitchell, W. J. T. (2005) 'Art', in T. Bennett, L. Grossberg and M. Morris (eds), *The New Keywords*, Oxford: Blackwell.

Munn, N. (1973a) 'The spatial presentation of cosmic order in Walbiri iconography', in J. A. W. Forge (ed.), *Primitive Art and Society*, London: Oxford University Press.

Munn, N. D. (1973b) *Walbiri Iconography: Graphic Representation and Cultural Symbolism in a Central Australian Society*, Chicago: University of Chicago Press.

Nichol, bp (1993) *Truth: A Book of Fictions*, Stratford, Ontario: Mercury Press.

Novikova, N. (2002) 'Self government of the indigenous minority peoples of West Siberia', in E. Kasten (ed.), *People and the Land: Pathways to Reform in Post-Soviet Russia*, Berlin: Dietrich Reimer Verlag.

Oatley, K. (1978) *Perceptions and Representations: The Theoretical Bases of Brain Research and Psychology*, London: Methuen.

Olson, D. R. (1994) *The World on Paper: The Conceptual and Cognitive Implications of Writing and Reading*, Cambridge: Cambridge University Press.

Olwig, K. (2002) 'Landscape, place, and the state of progress', in R. D. Stack (ed.), *Progress: Geographical Essays*, Baltimore, MD: Johns Hopkins University Press.

Ong, W. (1982) *Orality and Literacy: The Technologizing of the Word*, London: Methuen.

Orlove, B. (1993) 'The ethnography of maps: the cultural and social contexts of cartographic representation in Peru', *Cartographica*, 30: 29–46.

Orlove, B. (2002) *Lines in the Water: Nature and Culture at Lake Titicaca*, Berkeley, CA: University of California Press.

Paasi, A. (2004) 'Boundaries', in S. Harrison, S. Pile and N. Thrift (eds), *Patterned Ground: Entanglements of Nature and Culture*, London: Reaktion Books.

Parkes, M. B. (1992) *Pause and Effect: An Introduction to the History of Punctuation in the West*, Aldershot: Scolar Press.

Parrish, C. (1957) *The Notation of Medieval Music*, New York: W. W. Norton.

Paulson, J. F. (2005) 'Surveying in Ancient Egypt', in *From Pharaohs to Geoinformatics*,

Proceedings of the FIG Working Week 2005 and the 8th International Conference on the Global Spatial Data Infrastructure (GSDI–8), Cairo, Egypt, 16–21 April 2005, http://www.fig.net/pub/cairo.

Pye, D. (1968) *The Nature and Art of Workmanship*, Cambridge: Cambridge University Press.

Quilter, J. and Urton, G. (eds) (2002) *Narrative Threads: Accounting and Recounting in Andean Khipu*, Austin, TX: University of Texas Press.

Rabasa, J. (1993) *Inventing A-M-E-R-I-C-A: Spanish Historiography and the Formation of Eurocentrism*, Norman, OK: University of Oklahoma Press.

Rée, J. (1999) *I See a Voice: A Philosophical History of Language, Deafness and the Senses*, London: Harper Collins.

Reichard, G. (1936) *Navajo Shepherd and Weaver*, New York: J. J. Augustin.

Richerson, P. J. and Boyd, R. (1978) 'A dual inheritance model of the human evolutionary process, I: Basic postulates and a simple model', *Journal of Social and Biological Structures*, 1: 127–54.

Riegl, A. (1992) *Problems of Style: Foundations for a History of Ornament*, trans. E. Kain, Princeton, NJ: Princeton University Press.

Rivers, W. H. R. (1968) 'The genealogical method of anthropological inquiry', in *Kinship and Social Organization*, London: Athlone Press.

Rogers, H. (2005) *Writing Systems: A Linguistic Approach*, Oxford: Blackwell.

Rosaldo, R. (1993) 'Ilongot visiting: social grace and the rhythms of everyday life', in S. Lavie, K. Narayan and R. Rosaldo (eds), *Creativity/Anthropology*, Ithaca, NY: Cornell University Press.

Rose, D. B. (2000) *Dingo Makes Us Human: Life and Land in an Australian Aboriginal Culture*, Cambridge: Cambridge University Press.

Ross, A. (2005) 'Technology', in T. Bennett, L. Grossberg and M. Morris (eds), *The New Keywords*, Oxford: Blackwell.

Ruskin, J. (1904) 'The elements of drawing', in E. T. Cook and A. Wedderburn (eds), *The Works of John Ruskin*, Vol. 15, London: George Allen.

Sassoon, R. (2000) *The Art and Science of Handwriting*, Bristol: Intellect.

Saussure, F. de (1959) *Course in General Linguistics*, ed. C. Bally and A. Sechehaye, trans. W. Baskin, New York: Philosophical Library.

Sciama, L. D. (2003) *A Venetian Island: Environment, History and Change in Burano*, Oxford: Berghahn.

Semper, G. (1989) 'Style in the technical and techtonic arts or practical aesthetics (1860)', in *The Four Elements of Architecture and Other Writings*, trans. H. F. Mallgrave and W. Herrman, Cambridge: Cambridge University Press.

Silverman, E. K. (1998) 'Traditional cartography in Papua New Guinea', in D. Woodward and G. M. Lewis (eds), *The History of Cartography: Cartography in the Traditional African, American, Arctic, Australian, and Pacific Societies*, Chicago: University of Chicago Press.

Siza, A. (1997) *Alvaro Siza: Writings on Architecture*, Milan: Skira Editore.

Solnit, R. (2001) *Wanderlust: A History of Walking*, London: Verso.

Steadman, P. (1979) *The Evolution of Designs: Biological Analogy in Architecture and the Applied Arts*, Cambridge: Cambridge University Press.

Sterne, L. (1978) *The Life and Opinions of Tristram Shandy, Gentleman*, Vol. VI, ed. M. and J. New, Gainesville: University Press of Florida [original 1762].

Strunk, O. (ed.) (1950) *Source Readings in Music History: From Classical Antiquity through the Romantic Era*, New York: W. W. Norton.

Takemitsu, T. (1997) 'Nature and music', *Terra Nova: Nature and Culture*, 2(3): 5–13.

Tedlock, B. and Tedlock, D. (1985) 'Text and textile: language and technology in the arts of the Quiché Maya', *Journal of Anthropological Research*, 41(2): 121–46.

Tessmann, G. (1928) *Menschen ohne Gott: Ein Besuch bei den Indianern des Ucayali*, Stuttgart: Verlag Strecker und Schröder.

Thompson, D. W. (1961) *On Growth and Form*, abridged edn, ed. J. T. Bonner, Cambridge: Cambridge University Press.

Thomson, J. A. (1911) *Introduction to Science*, London: Williams and Norgate.

Turnbull, D. (1991) *Mapping the World in the Mind: An Investigation of the Unwritten Knowledge of Micronesian Navigators*, Geelong, Victoria: Deakin University Press.

Turnbull, D. (1993) 'The ad hoc collective work of building Gothic cathedrals with templates, string and geometry', *Science, Technology and Human Values*, 18: 315–40.

Vaiman, A. A. (1974) 'Über die Protosumerische Schrift', *Acta Antiqua Academiae Scientiarum Hungaricae*, 22: 15–27.

Vredeman de Vries, J. (1968) *Perspective*, New York: Dover.

Vygotsky, L. (1978) *Mind in Society: The Development of Higher Psychological Processes*, ed. M. Cole, V. John-Steiner, S. Scribner and E. Souberman, Cambridge, MA: Harvard University Press.

Wagner, R. (1986) *Symbols that Stand for Themselves*, Chicago: University of Chicago Press.

Wallace, A. D. (1993) *Walking, Literature and English Culture*, Oxford: Clarendon Press.

Wassmann, J. (1991) *The Song of the Flying Fox: The Public and Esoteric Knowledge of the Important Men of Kandingei about Totemic Songs, Names and Knotted Cords (Middle Sepik, Papua New Guinea)*, trans. D. Q. Stephenson, Boroko, Papua New Guinea: National Research Institute (Cultural Studies Divison).

Weiner, J. F. (1991) *The Empty Place: Poetry, Space and Being among the Foi of Papua New Guinea*, Bloomington, IN: Indiana University Press.

West, M. L. (1992) *Ancient Greek Music*, Oxford: Clarendon Press.

Wiebe, R. (1989) *Playing Dead: A Contemplation Concerning the Arctic*, Edmonton, Canada: NeWest.

Williams, R. (1976) *Keywords*, London: Fontana.

Wilson, P. J. (1988) *The Domestication of the Human Species*, New Haven, CT: Yale University Press.

Wood, D. (1993) 'What makes a map a map?', *Cartographica*, 30: 81–6.

Yen, Y. (2005) *Calligraphy and Power in Contemporary Chinese Society*, London: RoutledgeCurzon.

Young, D. (2001) 'The life and death of cars: private vehicles on the Pitjantjatjara lands, South Australia', in D. Miller (ed.), *Car Cultures*, Oxford: Berg.

Index

Related titles from Routledge

The Perception of the Environment
Essays on livelihood, dwelling and skill
Tim Ingold

'*The Perception of the Environment* is a formidable work in terms of its intellectual breadth ... its sheer volume ... and methodical consistency and clarity.' – *The Journal of the Royal Anthropological Institute*

' ... this is an extremely significant book and quite possibly lives up to its promise "to revolutionize the way we think". The book's power lies in its ability to push readers to places previously unimagined ... it is imperative that this book be read by as many people from as broad an audience as possible.' – *Anthropological Forum*

In this work Tim Ingold offers a persuasive approach to understanding how human beings perceive their surroundings. He argues that what we are used to calling cultural variation consists, in the first place, of variations in skill. Neither innate nor acquired, skills are grown, incorporated into the human organism through practice and training in an environment. They are thus as much biological as cultural.

The twenty-three essays comprising this book focus in turn on the procurement of livelihood, on what it means to 'dwell', and on the nature of skill, weaving together approaches from social anthropology, ecological psychology, developmental biology and phenomenology in a way that has never been attempted before. The book is set to revolutionise the way we think about what is 'biological' and 'cultural' in humans, about evolution and history, and indeed about what it means for human beings – at once organisms and persons – to inhabit an environment.

The Perception of the Environment will be essential reading not only for anthropologists but also for biologists, psychologists, archaeologists, geographers and philosophers.

ISBN13: 978–0–415–22831–2 (hbk)
ISBN13: 978–0–415–22832–9 (pbk)

Available at all good bookshops
For ordering and further information please visit:
www.routledge.com